D1238339

WITHDRAWN

Reconstructing Beckett

Language for Being in Samuel Beckett's Fiction

In a major, revolutionary contribution to Beckett studies, P.J. Murphy offers the first truly comprehensive treatment of the overall development of Beckett's prose fiction. Challenging conventional interpretations, Murphy argues for the affirmative dimensions of Beckett's efforts in his later prose to accommodate the formal and ontological dimensions of language.

In a provocative introduction he discusses Beckett's prose from 'Assumption' to *The Unnamable*. He argues that Beckett's primary concern in the later works is not the frequently evoked 'art of failure' but the reconciliation of language and being.

Beginning with a definition of the *Avant-Garde* (in the sense advanced by Peter Bürger that aims at a reintegration of art and life), Murphy proceeds to a detailed analysis of the post-trilogy works. He examines Beckett as a realist of a new type whose works are passionately engaged with the issues of referentiality, of existence in time.

He concludes that Beckett is indeed a moral artist whose chief endeavour, rather than integrating art with life, is to bring life to art, to 'let being into literature.' Both an inheritor of and commentator on Shakespeare and the Romantics, Beckett reveals in his prose fiction the struggle for an art of living that would reconstitute the human being within the fictional world of the text.

P.J. MURPHY, who was Coordinator of the Simon Fraser University Prison Education Program at Kent Institution, Agassiz, British Columbia, teaches modern British literature at Cariboo University College.

P.J. MURPHY

RECONSTRUCTING BECKETT

Language for Being in
Samuel Beckett's Fiction

UNIVERSITY OF TORONTO PRESS
Toronto   Buffalo   London

© University of Toronto Press 1990
Toronto   Buffalo   London
Printed in Canada
ISBN 0-8020-5868-X

University of Toronto Romance Series 62

Printed on acid-free paper

Canadian Cataloguing in Publication Data

Murphy, P.J. (Peter John), 1946
  Reconstructing Beckett : language for being in Samuel Beckett's fiction

(University of Toronto romance series ; 62)
Includes bibliographical references.
ISBN 0-8020-5868-X

1. Beckett, Samuel, 1906–   – Language.
2. Beckett, Samuel, 1906–   – Fictional works.
3. Beckett, Samuel, 1906–   – Criticism and interpretation.
I. Title.   II. Series.

PR6003.E282Z75   1990   843'.914   C90-094711-X

This book has been published with the help of a grant from the Canadian
Federation for the Humanities, using funds provided by the Social Sciences
and Humanities Research Council of Canada.

For Jennifer

Contents

Acknowledgments

My greatest debt is to Dr John Pilling, Department of English, the University of Reading, firstly for showing me by the example of his own work that a close reading of Samuel Beckett's prose is not only absolutely necessary, but possible; secondly for his sympathetic understanding of my own difficulties in coming to terms with Beckett's prose; thirdly for his many astute comments on the organization of my argument; finally (and firstly) for his friendship.

I should also like to express my grateful thanks to Professor James Knowlson of the Department of French, the University of Reading, for reading several of the first drafts of chapters in this study; to Professor Ian Ross of the Department of English, the University of British Columbia, for encouraging me to pursue my interest in Beckett; to Mr J.A. Edwards and Mr Michael Bott, Department of Archives and Manuscripts, the University of Reading Library, for facilitating my access to the Samuel Beckett Collection; to Willis Siemens and Leo Compain for the processing of a difficult manuscript which at times must have also seemed to them to be an endless work in progress; to Ron Schoeffel of University of Toronto Press for his steadfast support; to Heather Martin for her careful copy-editing; finally, to my students in the Simon Fraser University Prison Education Program at Kent and Mountain Institutions for their persistent questioning about the value, relevance, and significance of studying Beckett.

Several of the chapters in this study have appeared in somewhat different form in the *Journal of Beckett Studies, English Studies in Canada,* and *The International Fiction Review,* and I wish to thank the editors of these publications for permission to reprint this material.

He who speaks, he who writes is above all one who speaks on behalf of all those who have no voice.

Victor Serge

Foreword / Manifesto:
The Other Beckett

In this study I propose a series of alternative readings which aim at nothing less than a radical reassessment of Samuel Beckett's prose fiction. No apologies, only explanations will be forthcoming for my rejection of the dominant rhetoric of Beckett criticism which has, at best, dealt with only fragments of one aspect of Beckett's literary enterprise and has – almost totally – either missed or misread what might be termed 'the other Beckett,' whose major achievements lie outside of the guiding principles entrenched in the tradition of Beckett scholarship and, more generally, in Anglo-American criticism of the last three decades. The phenomenal growth of Beckett criticism over the last quarter century or so has buried under several distinct strata of critical commentary what I regard as the vital questions which were raised in the first period of Beckett studies, even if they were misunderstood and left unresolved because the very nature of the questions was largely misconstrued. Hence the deconstructive turn of the first part of these prefatory remarks in which I attempt to return to and reconsider in new, more productive ways these basic issues by means of briefly tracing how and why the corpus of Beckett criticism has lost sight of them.

In his hilariously astute *The Pooh Perplex*, Frederick C. Crews manages to anticipate what we might today, with particular reference to the Anglo-American tradition, call the Beckett perplex. Murphy A. Sweat, a popular Yale lecturer circa 1963, identifies Beckett with the then fashionable labels of 'absurdist' and 'existentialist' in his freshman lecture 'Winnie and the Cultural Stream.'[1] The hesitation about whether Beckett should be discussed in formalist (read 'New Criticism') or existentialist terms still haunts Beckett studies which are every bit as daunting as those directed to the ill-fated Winnie. Beckett's major critics of the early sixties, Martin Esslin, Hugh Kenner, Ruby Cohn, and John Fletcher, oscillate between these two categories in varying degrees and would claim both as highly relevant to a description of Beckett's art, without, however, being able to show theoretically how the two can be reconciled.[2] Critical gyrations around the crucial question of the art-life nexus in Beckett's works are at the core of the Beckett perplex. In the period from 1961 to 1965, a number of highly problematical judgments about the nature of Beckett's art assume to a surprising extent a virtually axiomatic status that has largely determined the various strata of the later criticism. The *locus classicus* of these principles is Martin Esslin's Introduction to *Samuel Beckett: A Collection of Critical Essays* (1965), undoubtedly the most influential fifteen pages in the history of Beckett criticism in English. This collection holds such a prominent position because its first entry is 'Three Dialogues,' thereby ostensibly lending Beckett's own authority to Esslin's speculations about the artist trying to shape an existentialist nothingness.[3] The emphasis upon 'Three Dialogues' as a type of key to Beckett's thinking on art is made, however, at the expense and exclusion of other aspects of Beckett's complex critical and creative practice.

Esslin's Introduction summarizes and makes programmatic the basic assumptions underlying the first full-length studies in English which, in various permutations, still pervade Beckett criticism. That these are riddled with contradictions and do not so much constitute a coherent program as a 'perplex' is glaringly evident in the condensed version of Esslin's Introduction, which serves as the basis of his *Encyclopaedia Britannica* entry on Beckett. Beckett is praised for the 'purity of his approach to literature' and for 'seeking ultimate truths' which make 'his writings invaluable documents of human experience'; his works are termed 'important contributions to existential philosophical thought,' even though Esslin quickly adds that Beckett only 'concentrates on the essential aspects of human experience' that have nothing to do with 'mere external trappings of existence.' The whole question of the possible reference of Beckett's literary investigations to our world, that is, the vexed issue of realism, is scanted by Esslin, who consigns such issues to the realm of the trivial. Beckett deals only with 'human experience at its most specific and concrete,' yet – inexplicably – the action of the novels is deemed to take place 'in a highly abstract, unreal world.' And so on, until we reach the inevitable gloss, a version of which is found in the conclusion of study after study: Beckett's work is essentially poetry; he is a comic writer who recognizes 'the triviality and ultimate pointlessness of most human strivings'; but this recognition for the reader is finally termed 'one of cathartic release.'[4] The result is a bourgeoisification of Beckett which renders innocuous some of his potentially most radical comments about art and its relationship to life. Beckett is depicted as somehow safely self-contained, free of any ideological constraints that would compel us to deal with him beyond the formal restrictions of the texts themselves. In this regard, it is important to note an obvious fact that is, oddly enough, often overlooked: Beckett criticism is a historical phenomenon which reflects the larger contexts of Anglo-American criticism. As Frank Lentricchia in *After the New Criticism* has so effectively argued, postmodernist critical theories are often pervaded by hidden or obscured formalist premises which lead to a view of literature that is detached from history and questions of value and meaning in relationship to a world outside the text; and the Beckett industry (circa 1959–) coincides with the entrenchment of these principles within the controlling rhetoric of Anglo-American criticism.[5]

If there is one dominant theme that characterizes the tremendous outpouring of scholarship on Beckett from the early sixties to the present, it is the ever more explicit emphasis upon essentially formalist readings.[6] Recent criticism increasingly presents us with a Beckett simplex: the perplexity of dealing with art-life relationships is no longer even an issue. This trend is particularly evident with reference to the post-trilogy texts; critic after critic has dealt with these very puzzling and difficult texts as a series of only stylistic and formalistic adjustments Beckett has supposedly made in order to carry on writing after the 'impasse' of *The Unnamable's* final 'I can't go on, I'll go on.' Something is very wrong here. We have in twenty-five years of Beckett criticism 'progressed' from Ruby Cohn's intense commitment, if perplexed response, to the 'suffering artist-human'[7] in Beckett's writing to the linguistic centaurs of Susan Brienza, who concludes that 'what remains for the reader to follow in the recent metafictions are half-human creatures metaphorically struggling through fields of language.'[8] It is difficult to see here, as in previous commentaries, that any case for Beckett exploring being has been made since the analyses of 'micro-worlds' 'half-human creatures,' and 'hermetic languages' sealed from contact with the extra-literary are the order of the day. We obviously lack clearly worked out methodologies for dealing with Beckett's art: we have used the very guiding principles of the old 'New Criticism' and the new 'New Criticism' to describe an art which may be striving to subvert in radically new ways these very principles. During this period of great controversy in Anglo-American literary circles, Beckett is, strangely enough, not at the centre of any methodological debates.[9] Instead the corpus of Beckett criticism shows Beckett, in predictable and rather pedestrian ways, being assimilated to the fashionable terminology of postmodernist critical vocabulary. This has, undeniably, resulted in some major achievements, but nearly all of these studies have dealt with only *one* aspect of Beckett's writing, that which is congruent with the prevalent modes and techniques of postmodernism, all of which share, in varying degrees, an aestheticism that tends to be depoliticized and divorced from referential values.[10] Beckett is praised, often exorbitantly, for his technical innovations which challenge the ossified languages of literature, with scarcely any reference to any larger socio-political implications of his mediations.

There is, however, the 'other Beckett' whose achievements need to be gauged against a very different literary tradition. Underlying my detailed examination of specific texts is the premise that Beckett more properly belongs to the tradition of the *Avant-Garde, not* as the term is defined in Anglo-American circles, where it is virtually synonymous with modernism-postmodernism itself, but in the sense advanced by Peter Bürger in which it is a historically conceived attack on the autonomous status of art and aims instead at a reintegration of art and life. For Bürger the *Avant-Garde* of the twenties and thirties was the first art movement to achieve full self-consciousness of the role of 'art as institution' and, consequently, the first significant historical challenge to the restrictions imposed by the subservient role of art as critic cum apologist of the status quo.[11]

I will argue that a radically new interpretation of Beckett's prose would be possible if we proceeded upon the ultimately more defensible assumption that he is trying to discover new means of integrating self and fiction and word and world, rather than being guided by the need to deny the power of words to express, the so-called art of failure which has so fascinated so many Beckett critics. I will maintain that Beckett is primarily concerned with the problem of devising new languages for being and that his works after *The Unnamable* focus upon innovatory combinations of the formal and ontological dimensions of language in order to reunite word and world by means of what he calls the 'the proper syntax of weakness.'[12] In contrast, postmodernist aesthetics is essentially governed by a pervasive scepticism about language as an expressive medium, and this has, in turn, resulted in such central tenets of current critical practice as 'decentring' the discourse, the disappearance of the author, the absence of an ethical dimension in 'vanishing structures,' language as 'trace' and so on. But while Beckett's characters and texts would seem to be – and indeed have been treated as if they were – perfect embodiments of the deconstructive method, they do not revel in it: they strive instead to escape from it to 'a world of solid foundations, solid signifieds.'[13]

There is, as Bürger argues, an exaggerated rejection of bourgeois realism in the first aggressive formulations of modernism; ironically enough, this results in a 'bourgeoisification' of modernist art as it withdraws from a social engagement in its quest for a purity of form which subsumes content, in short, for that point at which 'art becomes the content of art.'[14] Bürger is very careful to point out that the praxis of *Avant-Garde* art does 'not mean that the contents of works of art should be socially significant. The demand is not raised at the level of the contents of individual works. Rather, it directs itself to the way art functions in society, a process that does as much to determine the effect that works have as does the particular content.'[15] I would also maintain that Beckett is, in fact, a realist, a realist of a new type whose works are passionately engaged with the issues of referentiality, of existence in time. Critic after critic has somewhat naïvely started from the premise that Beckett's prose reveals a progressive withdrawal from conventional social realities and hence from realism itself, that there is a 'deterioration of outer realities'[16] in his fiction. Beckett has rejected in no uncertain terms bourgeois realism and the crudities of naturalism, but he has done so in order to grapple with the genuine perplexities of the creative act whereby we give shape to the world from which art is derived and from which it cannot claim fully autonomous status, however much the self-referential nature of language might be acknowledged and developed. Without an exploration of the complex and vexed issues of realism, the term 'being' is itself bound to be simply a meaningless word, a jargon word tacked on at the end of discussions of Beckett's works.

Bürger's very controversial thesis ends on a pessimistic note with an admission of the failure of the historical *Avant-Garde* to effect an integration of art and life. In addition to comments on how the culture industry has nullified the critique of the *Avant-Garde*, Bürger focuses upon a theoretical impasse within the very program of the *Avant-Garde*: 'the avant-gardistes' attempt to reintegrate art into the life process is itself a profoundly contradictory endeavor. For the (relative) freedom of art vis-à-vis the praxis of life is at the same time the condition that must be fulfilled if there is to be a critical cognition of reality. An art no longer distinct from the praxis of life but wholly absorbed in it will lose the capacity to criticize it, along with its distance.'[17] Here are some of the genuine issues which lie at the heart of the Beckett perplex, those critical questions which the tradition of Beckett criticism has obscured or circumvented. I will argue, contra Bürger, that Beckett as a 'post–avant-gardiste' has pioneered radically new ways of dealing with this 'profoundly contradictory endeavor.' Beckett is more than a great writer who occupies a pivotal point at the juncture of modernism and postmodernism. Beckett has incorporated the very principles of postmodernism *within* an expanded perspective afforded by the *Avant-Garde's* attack on autonomous, self-referential art.

Beckett has done this in a strikingly original way: rather than directly trying to integrate art with life, Beckett's literary explorations, particularly in the post-trilogy period, show him trying to bring life to his art, to 'let being into literature'[18] via the formulation of what he calls the 'proper syntax of weakness.' Beckett's art is an eloquent testimony of a power struggle between the conflicting claims of 'author' and 'other' – that alien being or character discovered in the very act of creation. Beckett is a realist of a new sort, a 'literalist of the imagination,'[19] who has obsessively sought the new forms which would allow the 'other' the power to speak in order to substantiate his own hungering for being, and who has also sought to accommodate this incredible struggle to be human with the author's equally real need to corroborate his being through the creation of a self-sufficient formal literary construct. Beckett affirmed in the early sixties his belief that 'Being *has* a form,'[20] but the situation revealed in his fiction involved a perplex of quite fantastic complexity: how to reconcile the conflicting claims of two distinct entities, with separate needs and radically different relationships to language. What constitutes reality, what is its ontological status, what is its significance – these are the crucial issues which Beckett raises in highly original ways. To clarify the status of the different selves unearthed in the creative act committed Beckett to a lifelong quest for an understanding of the artist's role and its responsibilities, and led in later texts to a conception of authority that could allow for a *modus vivendi* between the need for being of both author and other.

Beckett's prose fiction reveals a struggle for an art of living that would reconstitute the human being within the fictional world of the text. Verifying the ontology of this other is the strangest and most bizarre aspect of Beckett's remarkable art, and yet it is by means of this radical alterity that we can mediate Beckett's work so that it affords at points revolutionary perspectives on our world. Power, authority, the expropriations of language, the silencing of others, and the struggle to find a voice – all, in varying ways, find parallels in the real world. The Beckett perplex needs to be seen as our perplex, to which it brings to bear a potentially liberating praxis. There is a vital reactionary dimension to Beckett's radical efforts to find a language that will 'let being into literature'; his art, contrary to the views of most of his commentators, does admit and develop the writer's traditional moral responsibility to make sense of the relationships between language and being.

RECONSTRUCTING BECKETT

1

The Art of Hunger

'Back is on. Somehow on'[1]: these words from Beckett's *Worstward Ho* (1983) might be taken as a most succinct definition of how the concept of the *Avant-Garde* has functioned in his writings. To go forward involves a concomitant movement backwards in order to ascertain how the present vantage point has been reached. And, in the case of Beckett's prose, this 'progression by regression' has involved a compulsion to reconsider a number of first principles (or, more accurately, first needs) which were the very starting points of his literary explorations. These vexed issues all relate to the problematical nature of the art-life nexus and they are still the central concerns over a half-century later in the strange world of *Worstward Ho* with its truncated minimalist syntax. As we will see, these crucial questions are much more traditional in nature than the rhetoric of Beckett criticism would suggest, preoccupied as it is with style, technique, and form. For Beckett, style is, however, more a question of vision than technique.[2] Beckett's vision has remained consistent in that throughout his writing career the greatest need has been to work out – somehow – the perplexities contingent upon the art-life relationship. At times the inability to determine in any genuinely satisfying way what these relationships could actually be has, admittedly, led to an emphasis upon the inadequacies of language, particularly the language of literature. And it is at these points that Beckett's *oeuvre* is most congruent with the guiding tenets of postmodernist critical theory with its deconstruction of the logocentric universe. But the so-called art of failure and the movement towards an ostensibly austere formalism in some of the later texts should be regarded as the consequence of the failure to achieve these integrations whereby the world of the fiction could be validated, *not* as the primary motivation and final aim of his writing. Beckett's essential aims, regardless of the ironic and often debilitating consequences that result from his inability to implement them, are, as we will see at key junctures in the corpus, more accurately portrayed by 'The Vulture,' the first poem of *Echo's Bones* (1935), where the artist-vulture seeks to satisfy his hunger by 'stooping to the prone who must / soon take up their life and walk.'[3]

Critical commentary has been almost exclusively fixated on those untoward consequences of Beckett's rigorous examination of the potential of language to make real the fictional world and has proceeded on the assumption that no successful resolutions – however tentative – are possible. Even more significantly, it has not considered that Beckett might have actually achieved in certain works answers of sorts to the problems he has wrestled with throughout his career. In the penultimate chapter of this study, I will argue that in fact *Worstward Ho* is just such a successful working out of these problems. Its achievements are ones which lie outside of the expectations of postmodernism and are more properly aligned with the goals of the *Avant-Garde* (as defined by Bürger), even though Beckett has effected a series of innovations which make his accomplishments uniquely his own. In *Worstward Ho*, Beckett has quite literally incorporated the 'holes' characteristic of postmodernism (the voids, blanks, gaps, ruptures, silences et al.) *within* encompassing 'wholes' that accommodate author and other, language and being. Beckett definitely does not focus on the 'isolation of individual consciousness' in a world 'devoid of rational purpose and meaning,' the characteristic rhetoric applied to his works of the post-trilogy period – with the usual rider that his spare language is somehow poetically 'expressive'[4] (of what – except the sterile tautology that Beckett is a great writer – it is never exactly made clear). Beckett's post-trilogy texts have in several instances not only been misread (or ill read), but actually read backwards. The very title of *Worstward Ho* is perhaps Beckett's own wryly comic judgment on the rallying cry his commentators have implicitly used when greeting each of his new works with the same old set of critical evaluations.

If read within the overall development of Beckett's prose, *Worstward Ho* appears as Beckett's most explicit rejection of the impasse of *The Unnamable*'s 'I can't go on, I'll go on,' and the attendant rhetoric of 'Three Dialogues' (1949) with its 'nothing to express' formulaic of the so-called art of failure:

The void. How try say? How try fail?
No try no fail. Say only –

First the bones. On back to them.
Preying since first said on foresaid remains.   (17–18)

This pattern of rejection – in which the void is dismissed as a subject for art, and a physical reality thrusts itself toward as the 'aliment' of artistic hunger for expression – is obvious in *Worstward Ho*, but it is a pattern which exists in more subtle ways throughout Beckett's prose. 'Preying since first said on foresaid remains' is, in addition to a comment on this particular work, Beckett's most confessional statement thus far on the 'somehow' of his prose's development. It is an art of hunger which is a most eloquent testimony to a life-long struggle to curb and somehow accommodate essentially contradictory impulses and needs. From the hunger of 'Assumption' (1929) that seeks to be 'irretrievably engulfed in the light of eternity'[5] to the 'gnawing to be gone' (42) of *Worstward Ho*, there is evident in Beckett's prose the very powerful temptation simply to escape from or avoid the obligations of art. What makes Beckett a great writer is that this hunger for the transcendence or negation of 'going on' is continually drawn back to the realm of art where there is an acknowledgment of the hungering for being and expression which necessarily involves an engagement with the concrete real.

There are several reasons why Beckett's prose, in terms of the direction of its overall development, has been misread. Beckett's emergence as a writer of the first rank occurs with the publication of *Three Novels* and *Waiting for Godot* in the early fifties. Whereas the drama criticism develops along with Beckett's career as dramatist and therefore possesses a certain coherence, this is certainly not the case with the prose which he refers to as 'the important work.'[6] Although most critics have paid lip-service to the homily that it is particularly necessary with Beckett to see his works as a whole and to trace their interconnections, that is precisely what we at present lack. The history of Beckett criticism documents the degree to which we have quite literally read Beckett backwards: the trilogy, especially *The Unnamable*, is often taken as an unofficial starting point and the earlier works are then regarded as preliminary steps on the way to the celebrated impasse. The sociology of critical reception is further complicated by the contingencies of publication, for example the delayed publication of *Watt* and Beckett's decision to hold back *Mercier and Camier* for a quarter of a century. The inaccessibility of Beckett's abandoned first novel, 'Dream of Fair to Middling Women,' has further obscured and distorted matters, as has Beckett's own encouragement to critics to concentrate upon *Murphy* as the starting point for a consideration of his prose, with his added emphasis upon the 'nothings' of Democritus and Geulincx as holding a privileged status in an approach to his work.[7] The inordinate and finally unjustified significance which many critics have accorded 'Three Dialogues' with its litany of 'nothing to express' has resulted in a gross oversimplification of Beckett's literary equations.[8]

My intention in this introductory section is to go back to the beginnings of Beckett's prose career and to reconstruct the poetic logic of the most significant developments which occur in the first twenty years of his life as a writer, the period from the short story 'Assumption' (1929) to *The Unnamable* (1949) which represents the *terminus ad quem* of what might now be called early and middle Beckett. We will see that Beckett overcame this critical juncture by going back and rewriting in highly innovative ways a number of key ideas which he had formulated in his earlier work. The genuinely perplexing post-trilogy works have suffered from a one-sided reading which is dominated by a formalist approach. Critics have often found themselves in a position very similar to that of Belacqua in Beckett's early short story 'Dante and the Lobster' (1932) when faced with the famous teaser from *The Divine Comedy*: 'Still he pored over the enigma, he would not concede himself conquered, he would understand at least the meanings of the words, the order in which they were spoken and the nature of the satisfaction that they conferred on the misinformed poet.'[9] But Belacqua's hunger for understanding is not satisfied by merely academic and technical virtuosity: he becomes 'so bogged that he could move neither backward nor forward.'[10] And this is also the situation of most reader-critics before Beckett's post-trilogy prose which, I believe, will come to be recognized as Beckett's most important and challenging contribution to the literary tradition. Belacqua fails to go on because he cannot relate the literary passage on divine justice to the moral and physical realities of the world he lives in; his impasse is obviously moral as well as aesthetic, just as *The Unnamable*'s 'I can't go on, I'll go on' will be. The obligation to make sense of the world of life as well as the world of art is the abiding continuity of Beckett's career. For the critic to go on with Beckett's demanding works of the post-trilogy period, he must first be able to go back: 'Back *is* on.'

Underlying the incredibly complex development of Beckett's art reside almost embarrassingly simple yet profound assumptions. Beckett is a great writer because he is a great moralist: his works testify to a need to corroborate that 'moral integrity'[11] which is necessary for the artist and which Beckett said he learned from James Joyce. The ethical contingencies which bear on the artist's role are what have kept Beckett 'going on,' not a series of merely stylistic adjustments to the impasses which obstruct the postmodernist writer. However, this commitment to the artist's 'moral integrity' has from the beginning challenged Beckett with a perplex of such complexity that it has threatened the very continuation of his writing. The writer is for Beckett always 'with his selves on behalf of his selves.'[12] The act of creation involves coming to terms with another self who is regarded as somehow connected to his own 'selves' yet also is an acknowledged 'other' whose own needs may differ radically from the more conventional needs of the author's persona. The hunger of the artist is ultimately a hunger for words, for the right words: how then to create the proper language which could accommodate the divergent needs of these different entities? This is the vital question that has kept Beckett 'going on.'

It is also the question with which he began: *The Unnamable*'s 'I can't go on, I'll go on' was foreshadowed twenty years earlier in the very first sentence of Beckett's first published prose work, the short story 'Assumption': 'He could have shouted and could not.' (268) The narrative poses a central question: how can art mediate between two conflicting impulses: the desire for survival of the self and the equally powerful pull towards self-dissolution in the 'cosmic discord' (269). If the 'something' buried within the 'he' is allowed expression, it will result in the very destruction of this 'he.' Beckett's first character is ironically disparaged as only 'partly artist,' and tries desperately and ineffectually to 'whisper the turmoil down' (268). Through the agency of a woman the barriers erected against the tidal flood of sound that seeks to be one with the universe are thrown down and an ecstatic revelation occurs. A dismemberment and reintegration follow her nocturnal visits: 'he died and was God, each night revived and was torn, torn and battered with increasing grievousness, so that he hungered to be irretrievably engulfed in the light of eternity, one with the birdless cloudless colourless skies, in infinite fulfilment' (271). In his comments on Marcel's initiation into the mysterious rites of art in *Proust* (1931), Beckett seems to be offering a veiled critical assessment of 'Assumption':

he is to receive the oracle that had invariably been denied to the most exalted tension of his spirit, which his intelligence had failed to extract from the sismic engima of tree and flower and gesture and art, and suffer a religious experience in the only intelligible sense of that epithet, at once an assumption and an annunciation, so that at last he will understand ... the dolorous and necessary course of his own life and the infinite futility – for the artist – of all that is not art. (51)

'Assumption' also rejects the superficial, the art of gesture associated with the artificialities of social discourse, for a deeper experience, but the alternative is not art as religion – it is religion itself in the form of a mystical transcendence: that 'other' or 'something' within the 'he' is engaged in a 'struggle for divinity ... as real as his own, and as futile' (269). Compare 'in the light of eternity ... in infinite fulfilment' with 'the dolorous and necessary course of his own life and the infinite futility – for the artist – of all that is not art.'

The parenthetical phrase 'for the artist' is crucial to an understanding not only of 'Assumption,' but of Beckett's subsequent work. Beckett is in this first work expressing his own doubts about the creative act and the role of an artist. His reservations lead him to embrace an ambiguous role as a 'prestidigitator' who is only 'partly artist.' He virtually announces his abnegation of the full responsibilities of the creative act in the obscure second sentence which has no obvious connection with the strange story that follows – but which, we will see, is intimately connected with the subsequent developments in Beckett's fiction: 'The buffoon in the loft swung steadily on his stick and the organist sat dreaming with his hands in his pockets.' Both the creature of the imagination ('the buffoon in the loft') and its agent ('the organist') are here disengaged from the creative performance. What follows in 'Assumption' is a dream of the reality that lies beyond the boundaries of art. Whilst the final 'drunken scream' (269) that comes with the central character's death points to a trancendental reality beyond art, this very short story has, nevertheless, set out the essential conflict inherent in artistic genesis for Beckett: a life and death struggle between the self and the other.

Of equal importance for Beckett's future development as an artist is a basic distinction between two aspects of language which the writer must somehow come to terms with. To adopt Gerald L. Bruns' words, the first might be termed 'hermetic' as it leads to an emphasis upon the verbal structure as ideally self-contained; 'the writer's use of language deviates sufficiently from the structure of ordinary discourse to arrest the function of signification.'[13] Or, as Beckett puts it in 'Assumption':

'To avoid the expansion of the commonplace is not enough; the highest art reduces significance in order to obtain that inexplicable bombshell perfection' (269). The second might be termed 'Orphic,' since it stresses poetic speech as the source of all meaning and suggests an 'ideal unity of word and being, ... whose power extends therefore beyond the formation of a work toward the creation of a world.'[14] A variant of this Orphic approach, albeit *in extremis*, is evident in the desire of the 'he' in 'Assumption' to fuse with the 'cosmic discord,' to become one with the universe. This particular 'he' is, however, concerned primarily with the last phase of the Orpheus myth in which an ascension to the heavenly bodies occurs: 'the blue flower, Vega, GOD' (271). (Vega is the brightest star in the constellation of Lyre, the zodiacal sign of Orpheus.) Beckett does not in this instance regard the Orphic as essentially signifying a relationship of word and world, but as a striving for an absolute transcendence of both. The growth of Beckett's art, the search for ways of combining the instinctual forces and the two aspects of language which in 'Assumption' were irreconcilable, is the story of the creation of the artist, an Orpheus-figure, in whose being they might be incorporated.

The manifesto 'Poetry is Vertical' which Beckett signed in 1932 is important as an elaboration of the relationship between the Orphic and hermetic aspects of language. Here the poetic vision, the reality of depth, the transcendental 'I' are all identified with the 'orphic forces.'[15] It is worth noting that the discussion of the hermetic follows these references and hence must be read within the context already established: 'The final disintegration of 'I' in the creative act is made possible by the use of a language which is a mantic instrument, and which does not hesitate to adopt a revolutionary attitude toward word and syntax, going even so far as to invent a hermetic language, if necessary.' The last sentences emphasize the need for a 'collective reality' and 'the construction of a new mythological reality.' The hermetic language is only an agent of the fundamental 'orphic forces,' and hence cannot mean a private language known only to the initiated. (It was Hermes who accompanied Orpheus in his descent to the underworld.) One other element here that will have great significance for Beckett's later thought on language is the concern with the concreteness of the poetic vision: the reality of depth becomes associated with the 'telluric depths.' 'Poetry is Vertical' is worth more than a casual dismissive glance by the critic, if only because it focuses on Orpheus as the poet of the word's relationship to the world, a dimension touched upon briefly in 'Assumption' and then only to be dismissed in favour of a romantic quest for absolutes. The manifesto is also the most explicit identification we have of Beckett with a tributary of the historical *Avant-Garde.* 'Assumption,' like 'Poetry is Vertical,' appeared in Eugene Jolas's *transition: An International Workshop for Orphic Creation*, and Beckett over his career has developed a series of radically innovative aesthetic strategies which have allowed for an affirmation, in various ways, of his allegiance to the 'orphic forces' which demand of the writer a commitment to an art that has obligations and connections to the world outside itself. The achievement is all the more impressive since Beckett, perhaps more so than any other contemporary writer, has confronted those opposing forces which would negate the Orphic ones.

The works of the early period show Beckett determining what are for him as an artist-in-training the realities he would express and trying to find the language to convey them. In 'Dante ... Bruno . Vico .. Joyce' (1929), Beckett clearly sides with the empirical nature of Vico's description of languages and their evolution. The only criticism he, in fact, makes of Vico concerns his tendency to equate absolutely the abstraction and the concrete example.[16] For Beckett, hunger for the ideal must somehow accommodate the real in order to bring about a relationship that will not distort either's essential nature. In a series of gastronomical images, Beckett repudiates substances which merely titillate the artist's appetite: 'the carefully folded ham-sandwich of the neatness of identifications,' the decadent conception of figurative language as 'sophisticated confectionery,' the 'distillation of disparate poetic ingredients into a synthetical syrup.' All these corrupt views he refuses to 'swallow without protest.' The artist's hunger involves him in a search for the proper word-food that will enable him to transform reality. The poetic spirit is not 'an exact science within reach of everyone in possession of the recipe.'[17]

Hunger for the real as a historical fact is emphasized and endorsed by Beckett throughout his discussion of Vico: 'Hieroglyphics, or sacred language, as he calls it, were not the invention of philosophers nor the mysterious expression of profound thought, but the common necessity of primitive peoples' (11–12). The 'terribly real' nature of these original confrontations of word and world is an implicit critique of the whole literary tradition, from Plato onwards, of language as a medium that can only hint at vaguely apprehended essences. Orpheus is central to Beckett's critique here, for, as Elizabeth Sewell points out, Vico 'draws his descent direct from Orpheus, who is mentioned several times in his works as the founder of what Vico calls "poetic theology." '[18] Through his championing of Vico's down-to-earth interpretations of the evolution of language, Beckett is supporting his rejection of the Renaissance tradition of literary theorizing typified by Ficino, who 'regarded all Neoplatonic mysteries as derived from Orpheus.'[19] Beckett obviously rejects the allegorizing impulse of the hermetic tradition in which the divine ray cannot reach us unless it is covered with poetic veils.

Edgar Wind's commentary in *Pagan Mysteries in the Renaissance* helps us to see just how radical a departure Beckett's Orphic realism is from the Orphism of Renaissance literary theorists and how it affords him a critical vantage point for tough-minded assessments of the proposed solutions to these problems offered by modernists such as Joyce and Proust:

... all mystical images, because they retain a certain articulation by which they are distinguished as 'hedges' or *umbraculae*, belong to an intermediate state, which invites further 'complication' above, and further 'explication' below. They are never final in the sense of a literal statement, which would fix the mind to a given point; nor are they final in the sense of the mystical Absolute in which all images would vanish. Rather they keep the mind in continued suspense by presenting the paradox of an 'inherent transcendence'; they persistently hint at more than they say. It is a mistake, therefore, to overlook a certain ambiguity in the praise of hieroglyphs which Ficino, and after him Giordano Bruno, adopted from an incidental remark by Plotinus ... it is legitimate to suspect that the Renaissance speculations on 'implicit signs' were not concerned with a positive theory of optical intuition, but with that far less attractive subject called steganography, the cryptic recording of sacred knowledge ... Thus, contrary to the divine intelligence which the reading of hieroglyphs is supposed to foreshadow, the intuitive grasp of them depends on discursive knowledge. Unless one knows what a hieroglyph means, one cannot *see* what it says. But once one has acquired the relevant knowledge, 'unfolded' by more or less exotic instruction, one can take pleasure in finding it 'infolded' in an esoteric image or sign.

Thus the rules of 'explication' and 'complication,' by which we found the Orphic images to be governed, apply to Renaissance hieroglyphs as well. They are, all of them, 'hedges' or *umbraculae* infested with the paradox of self transcendence ...[20]

Beckett's discussion of Vico's originality implicitly raises many of the criticisms made by Wind. Beckett is well aware that Vico's theory of language 'must have appeared nothing less than an impertinent outrage against tradition' (5), and the tradition referred to is quite clearly that of the Renaissance theorists whose views Wind so trenchantly investigates. Beckett emphasizes Vico's rationality in order to forestall any possibility of identifying Vico's views on language with those of the tradition, which oscillates uneasily between the literal and divine significance of the image. For Beckett, Vico's realistic attitude towards the word is of prime importance. Whereas the hieroglyphics of the tradition pointed to 'the cryptic recording of sacred knowledge' (which could only be deciphered if one 'has acquired the relevant knowledge'), Vico's hieroglyphics embody direct poetic contact with a very literal reality.

The discussion of what constitutes reality is much more complex in *Proust*, and much less satisfactorily resolved. The statement that 'the only reality is provided by the hieroglyphics traced by inspired perception (identification of subject and object)' (64) is imposed on a discussion which has failed to satisfy Beckett's own queries about how such a union could be legitimately effected. An obvious reason for the more confused and hesitant response to the problem of the writer's determination and depiction of the real is simply that Proust's narrator is a sophisticated modern (however anti-intellectual), not one of Vico's barbarians. Summarizing Vico's ages of man, Beckett states: 'In the beginning was the thunder: the thunder set free Religion in its most objective and unphilosophical form – idolatrous animism' (5). In dramatic contrast, Beckett characterizes the 'sacred actions' of Proust's universe (such as 'the noise of a spoon against a plate') as an 'intellectualized animism,' even though the 'elements of communion' (23) are still provided by the physical world. Beckett's reading stresses the mythological dimensions of Proust's universe; however, it must be admitted that there is no longer a simple and direct contact with the forces of myth.[21]

Note, for example, the problematical status of the real in Beckett's description of the Proustian artist's efforts to convey an essential reality: 'the spiritual assimilation of the immaterial as provided by the artist, as extracted by him from life' (48). Beckett's reservations about Proust's method relate directly to the increased emphasis upon animism as a spiritual, immaterial reality rather than upon the more primitive sense of animism as life (anima) itself, which Beckett underlined in his readings of both Joyce and Vico. Beckett's only major reservation about Vico, his 'hoisting the real unjustifiably clear of its dimensional limits, temporalizing that which is extratemporal,' also applies, with an important qualification, to Proust. Beckett uses virtually the same words in his discussion of the implications of the art Proust has 'hoisted' from 'this deep source' of 'involuntary memory': 'but if this mystical experience communicates an extratemporal essence, it follows that the communicant is for the moment an extratemporal being' (56). Proust can only escape what Wind calls 'the paradox of an "inherent transcendence"' by making his communicant one with 'the mystical Absolute,' 'an extratemporal being.' Beckett's rigorously logical 'but if' indicates his reservations about this departure from reality. Moreover, if this were indeed the case, then there would not exist a reality for the artist to express – nor any vehicles for its communication.[22]

In terms of literary method, Beckett's reservations about Proust can be most clearly seen in his handling of the term symbol. In *Proust*, Beckett is perplexed by the writer's dilemma of having to integrate abstractions with the living reality from which they originated. Beckett argues that Proust rejects 'the intellectual symbolism of a Baudelaire, abstract and discursive' and prefers instead 'symbolism ... handled as a reality, special, literal, and concrete.' Beckett adds that for Proust 'the object may be a living symbol, but a symbol of itself' (60). 'Symbol of itself' and 'living symbol' are, however, awkward and embarrassing phrases which are inherently, as Wind would say, 'infested with the paradox of self-transcendence.' For although symbol and substance are united in Proust's famous 'reduplication,' the identification finally leads, according to Beckett, to an extratemporal reality where no terms apply, least of all symbol, which appears then to have been used in an allegorical fashion to point to a reality beyond itself – 'an extratemporal being.' Beckett, the would-be realist, had to face in *Proust* the great complexities surrounding the question of the real when he was not willing to confine himself to either conventional, so-called realism (the pseudo-'copiable' of the naturalists) or to an allegorical split between a material and a spiritual meaning. The mention of hieroglyphics at the conclusion of the vexed discussion of reality in *Proust* implies that Beckett is still, however, committed, Vichian-fashion, to an 'ideal real'[23] grounded firmly in the concrete real.

If the theoretical dilemmas facing Beckett were not already imposing enough, they were compounded when he came to apply them in his first novel, the aborted 'Dream of Fair to Middling Women' (1932). What can the already perplexing terms 'concrete real' and 'ideal real' mean when applied to a self-consciously fabricated world of fiction in which an author (referred to as 'Mr Beckett') has to deal with a number of others or characters, foremost of whom is the 'principal boy,' Belacqua, whose own wilful actions cause the author a great deal of trouble? 'The buffoon in the loft swung steadily on his stick and the organist sat dreaming with his hands in his pockets,' Beckett wrote in 'Assumption.' In 'Dream of Fair to Middling Women,' Beckett the 'organist' quite literally pulls out all the stops: the artist and his creations are galvanized into life. It is the problem of the relationship between the two that is vital; the reader is always aware of the clash between the narrator's ideal of art and the disappointing realities of his actual production. The narrator's self-conscious commentary on his art most often employs musical imagery to convey his inability to control his characters and to shape them into the accepted forms of the well-written novel. Once the buffoons are freed from the loft they possess a life of their own. They are no longer 'pure, permanent liŭs' or 'pings' but 'the most regrettable simultaneity of notes.'[24] The novel is out of control because the characters cannot be assimilated to any other system than their own: 'But they will let us down, they will insist on being themselves as soon as they are called upon for a little strenuous collaboration. The music comes to pieces. The notes fly about all over the place, a cyclone of electrons' (100). Beckett mockingly calls attention to the 'unProustian procedure' of his narrator who is periodically forced to suspend belief in the illusions of his art: 'pause in our treacherous theme, ponder what has taken place and what threatens to renew, with the help of Apollo, the reduced circumstances of our naïveté' (100). The Proustian equation is reversed; Marsyas now flays Apollo.

The Orpheus myth, never explicitly elaborated in any of Beckett's works, but by far the most important mythical presence in his prose *oeuvre*, again suggests itself as a means of reconciling apparently antithetical elements. The narrator talks rhapsodically of the poetic labours of the 'ecstatic mind' which would give expression to the 'demented perforation of the colander' of the 'night firmament' (14–15). The narrator is torn between the desire to express this vision in its natural form, that is, incoherently, and an equally strong urge towards 'architechtonics.' This aesthetic statement by the narrator is framed by descriptions of Belacqua also gazing at the starfield: in the passage that precedes he is 'looking for Vega'; in the one which follows he is 'peeping up like a fool at his dear little sweet Fünkelein, green bright and in the Lyre.' The narrator's own Dionysian musings on the genesis of art are absolutely dissociated from Belacqua's: 'Nothing whatever of the kind occupied his fetid head.' The fact that Belacqua is scornfully identified with the Orpheus-figure reveals Beckett's doubts at the time that any reconciliation of the Dionysian and Apollonian could be brought about. A later use of the same Orphic imagery further underlines the parodic elements.

Belacqua is separated from the Smeraldina-Rima, 'his sweet Vega' (63), and the poem that describes their mystical union is in part a burlesque of 'Assumption,' repeating in a quite ridiculous context the 'sublime' words of the short story, 'One with the birdless cloudless colourless skies.'[25] Mocking references to the myth of Orpheus draw the lovers together: Vega is known as 'the falling vulture,' the brightest star in Orpheus' constellation of Lyre, and Belacqua is endearingly called 'my dirty little hungry bony vulture' (64). Since they are both linked with 'the falling vulture,' there is at least a very tenuous justification for the truly dreadful lines:

> Like two merged stars intolerably bright
> conjoined in One and in the Infinite!

Faced with this debased romanticized version of the Orpheus myth, it is no wonder that the narrator despairs of mediating the Apollonian/ Dionysian duality.

'First the bones. On back to them. Preying since first said on foresaid remains,' Beckett elliptically stated in *Worstward Ho*. The 'remains' of Beckett's first literary and critical efforts which we have been examining would not warrant such a detailed exhumation unless it were for the fact that from them Beckett created a remarkable poetic whole, 'The Vulture,' the first poem of *Echo's Bones* (1935), a work which has played a crucial role in the overall development of his prose. This is not, of course, to declare simplistically and naïvely that this very short poem is *the* key to Beckett. It is rather an 'objective' critical judgment based on the evidence that Beckett has at key junctures returned to this work and, as it were, rewritten it in a host of complex ways in order to deal with the seminal issues it incorporates. Beckett's early work exhibits a number of salient concerns: a commitment to a realist aesthetic that must take into account the 'orphic forces,' and an acknowledgment of the author's need to accommodate an 'other,' which proved to be impossible with the 'something' of 'Assumption,' as it was, for different reasons, with that fraudulent alter ego, Belacqua, stolen from Dante and transplanted in Dublin. Unable to bring these elements creatively together, Beckett's only recourse was to parody himself and his views. 'The Vulture' was Beckett's first working model for how these divergent elements might form new wholes.

'The Vulture' is an Orphic poem.[26] In the remarkably short space of six lines, it successfully evokes basic elements of the Orphic creation myth that involves the integration of subject and object, heaven and earth, art and life:

> dragging his hunger through the sky
> of my skull shell of sky and earth
>
> stooping to the prone who must
> soon take up their life and walk
>
> mocked by a tissue that may not serve
> till hunger earth and sky be offal

The artist-vulture is depicted in the first lines as weighed down by the material reality of hunger and the rhythm of the poem conveys a descent into the world ('stooping to the prone'), thus associating the artist in an affirmative way that Belacqua never envisaged with Vega, 'the falling vulture.' The interchange of possessive adjectives in the first lines ('his hunger' / 'my skull') also indicates that it is in the act of poetic creation that an authentic fusion of subject and object may take place, what Beckett referred to in *Proust* as a 'hieroglyph' of 'inspired perception.'

The major achievement of the poem is that for the first time Beckett has effected the coincidence of form and content in an ontologically significant way: 'the one is a concretion of the other, the revelation of a world' (67) to adopt Beckett's words from *Proust* where, as critic, he could only vicariously praise his author's achievement. While the skull of the artist-vulture is hermetically sealed, the correspondence of the outer with the inner realm precludes any solipsistic interpretation. The process of transfer is not simply mentalistic: the physical world is not suitable material for the artist until it becomes 'offal' – this is not the superficial art of the naturalists or pseudo-realists whom Beckett scornfully dismissed as 'worshipping the offal of experience.'[27] The vulture-artist cannot feed upon his creatures until living 'tissue' is metamorphosed by the organic cycle of decay which would strip away the conventional surface and reveal the underlying reality of 'telluric depths.' But, as the second stanza relates, he can, however, still stir them into being ('the prone who must / soon take up their life and walk'). The very enigmatic and highly ambiguous last line suggests that the 'tissue' will not be of use for the artist until 'hunger earth and sky be offal.' This need not imply a total annihilation, an extinction of the poetic microcosm: the cyclical structure of this poem and the subsumption of 'hunger earth and sky' by the 'skull' suggest that the final identification of the artistic quest with its appropriate subject-matter occurs in the endless rhythm of life, decay and regeneration. The artist in time must continuously refashion his creation. In this regard, 'The Vulture' is truly an Orphic poem, as characterized by W.K.C. Guthrie: 'The Orphic poems are pervaded with a sense of the mystery and paradox of life, from their preoccupation with the eternal question – how shall all be one yet each thing apart? – to their culmination in the revealing of our own half-divine, half-earthly nature, with the complete change of outlook, the new obligations and the undreamed of yearnings which that revelation imposes'.[28] This should by no means be construed as an idealistic and sentimentalizing gloss of Beckett's vision; the key words, after all, are 'paradox of life' and 'new obligations.' Nor should it by any means be construed as an attempt to mystify Beckett's works. John Fletcher was, of course, quite right to state a long time ago that 'it is quite absurd to suppose that these works [Beckett's novels] are hidden behind a veil of Orphic esotericism.'[29] This is not to deny, however, the importance of the Orpheus figure or the Orpheus myth itself. W.K.C. Guthrie also makes the eminently judicious decision to use the name Orpheus 'as a reaction against the tendency to regard the term Orphic as vaguely synonymous with the whole mystical element.'[30] In depicting the artist, Beckett has always emphasized 'the need that is the absolute predicament of particular human identity.'[31] And this is the situation of the vulture-artist in Beckett's poem; any pinchbeck mystical element is thoroughly debunked by the focus on decay and the calvary of existence, of inescapable and unavoidable realities which may – somehow – be made significant in the complex interrelationships between life and art.

Read in context, 'The Vulture' is therefore a remarkable achievement that supplies an at least paradigmatic solution – however abbreviated – to central literary questions Beckett had been struggling with. Read in conjunction with and as a matrix for his later prose, 'The Vulture''s significance for Beckett has been quite incredible and its importance can hardly be exaggerated. This poem, whose seminal influence on Beckett's prose has not yet been fully recognized, embodies an 'organic' concept of the creative act, an ostensibly traditional approach to aesthetics which, because of Beckett's highly original and unorthodox development of it, has had a much more important role to play in his writing than the better-publicized quests for a 'literature of the un-word'[32] or the art of failure. A rich perplex of unanswered questions, the remains of this skeletal *mise-en-scène* have provided Beckett with the directions in which he could seek to satisfy the artist's hunger. Beckett, as a realist, will investigate just what is the relationship between 'his hunger' / 'my skull' / 'their life.' How are they all one, yet things apart? How can this tripartite division of 'the absolute predicament of particular human identity' be accommodated within a literary whole? Indeed, how might a fictional creation even be legitimately deemed to have 'a particular human identity'? Where does authority for the creative act ultimately reside: with 'his,' or 'my' or 'their'? An even more fundamental question is what type of stories could these three potentially divisive voices tell which might satisfy their different needs. What words, what type of language would each need in order to corroborate its claims of a being or a life of its own? And, finally and foremost, what must happen before the artist can truly satisfy his hunger?

The vulture-artist was 'mocked by a tissue that may not serve / till hunger earth and sky be offal.' Not until the artist dies will he be able truly to beget fictions from his own flesh, stories which will satisfy his own word-hunger. 'Echo's Bones,' the title poem and the last in the collection, envisages an even more dramatic descent than that of 'The Vulture' – a journey 'below' to the 'asylum under my tread' where real 'carrion' is to be found, where 'the flesh falls.'[33] The subsequent investigation of the death necessary for artistic creation reveals, however, that to gain access to this carrion, the true 'precipitate' upon which art feeds, the clear-cut conventional distinction between reality and fiction must be abandoned. The transition to the world below undermines the encompassing unity and security of the words 'my skull' in 'The Vulture' and leads to the incredible confusion that surrounds the first person pronoun by the time of *The Unnamable*.

Beckett has made 'The Vulture' a major work in his canon by continually 'rewriting' it in his prose works. But it is not until over ten years later in the first works of Beckett's French period that the prose, as it were, catches up with and fleshes out the artist's role as outlined in *Echo's Bones*. Beckett's last two novels in English, *Murphy* (1938) and *Watt* (1944; published 1954), do not reveal a fundamental realignment of the key issues which are present in his earlier works. And the most obvious reason for this is simply that Murphy is not an artist, and Watt is, at best, only a 'semi-artist,'[34] which is to say that in both these works Beckett adopted a critical attitude towards his central characters and, implicitly, towards himself as would-be artist, for, by Beckett's own very rigorous standards, he is essentially engaged in a series of 'exercices de style' in order to camouflage the fact that he too is only as yet 'partly artist.' What needs to be stressed is that these two novels definitely do *not* indicate any type of straightforward or progressive withdrawal from questions of social reality and the question of realism itself, as the tradition of Beckett criticism would maintain as an obvious and self-evident commonplace. On the contrary, the nature of reality and the question of realism remain abiding and central concerns.

The language of *Murphy* is neither hermetic nor Orphic, but oscillatory, moving uneasily to and fro between these two views. *Murphy* is the story of a series of failed quests not only in terms of its plot, but on the artistic plane: while Beckett does succeed in writing a conventional novel, he fails to answer the residual question of 'Dream of Fair to Middling Women,' a determination of what is real and the creation of vehicles for its communication. The narrator of *Murphy* attempts to mediate the question of the real by means of style, and while the elevated style does avoid what 'Assumption' calls 'the expansion of the commonplace,' it cannot completely mask the tawdry circumlocutions of the characters, Murphy included.

If it fails to obtain that 'inexplicable bombshell perfection,' the style does, nevertheless, manage to redeem itself through what Nietzsche called 'the delightful illusion'[35] of an Apollonian sense of form. Murphy's first period of service at the mental hospital seems to effect a balance between Murphy, 'the man of the world,' and Murphy the would-be solipsist; but the growing attraction for 'little Mr Endon and all the other proxies'[36] necessitates an unwelcome either/or decision: 'He could not have it both ways, not even the illusion of it' (189). Beckett cannot have it both ways either, but through style he does at least in *Murphy* have 'the illusion of it.'

The 'pure forms of commotion' (112) of the third zone of Murphy's mind are ironically counterpointed by the language of the novel: 'forms without parallel' (109) are described in a language that is a model of classical rhetoric (balance, antithesis, parallelism). *Murphy*, Beckett's most Apollonian novel, is curiously suspended between an outer and inner reality that becomes more obscure as it is described in a style that is a model of clarity.[37] This 'illusion' of success was necessary for Beckett before he looked more fully at the realities of existence and the realities of fiction which the style of *Murphy* can only thinly and ironically mask. Murphy is finally the victim of a hunger that draws him towards the 'big world'; similarly, Beckett's word-hunger draws him away from the dream of an art of 'pure forms.'

In *Watt* a major advance over *Murphy* is a growing identification between hunger and the need for words which will at least speak of the failure to fathom Mr Knott. The characters seek to deal with 'the difficult problem of hunger'[38] by any means that will not entangle them with the obligations of an art of hunger. The most intriguing comment on hunger comes unexpectedly as Watt walks away from Mr Knott's towards the station: 'Watt felt them suddenly glow in the dark place, and go out, the words, *The only cure is diet*' (226). Diet: from the Greek for 'way of life.' One cannot dwell solely on the world of Knott where all is only vaguely definable by what it is not: it is necessary to establish a carefully controlled regimen that balances something with nothing – a veritable 'what not.'

The complexity of the issues of hunger and need in *Watt* is due to the indeterminate status of the real and the fictional. The artist's needs cannot be satisfied by life as depicted in the pseudo-realistic frame-tales. Nevertheless, the hunger instinct still needs to be directed towards that which has a basis in the concrete – a set of relationships that defines a recognizable human frame of reference. It cannot be uncritically accepted that the journey to the fictional world of Mr Knott simply means that 'reality is subsumed into fiction' and that the characters are 'no longer subjected to reality and realism.' Nor can the choices open to the being who finds himself in the house of Mr Knott be limited to this either/or: 'whoever comes in contact with the world of illusions must either submit to its deceptive conditions and endure complete dehumanization, or retreat to reality.'[39] There is a third possibility which is implicit in *Watt* as an ironic commentary on the protagonist's development: to become an artist, an artist of the real whose vision can incorporate 'somethings' and 'nothings' without becoming entangled with symbols ('intended' or not)[40] which are 'infested with the paradox of an inherent transcendence.' There are other actualities which are just as real and, for the artist, more necessary and more accessible than the 'nothing' of Mr Knott's. The world of Knott is not totally divorced from the other social (or asocial) realities, as indeed the structure of the novel illustrates by placing it between the realms of Mr Hackett (the so-called ordinary world) and Sam (the asylum). The fundamental problem is to deal with the nothing of being, the limited self-perception of the human sufferer, not with the 'being of nothing', as Arsene mistakenly thinks. Knott is indeed a good master; he compels his servants to leave him and to return to the way of life. The only way to negotiate a successful return is through a confrontation with one's self or selves and through the use of words which can communicate that encounter, the only one realistically (in any sense of the word) available to the artist. *Murphy* showed that the Beckett protagonist was still unable to create a fiction that could validate his initial departure from material reality, which is why, in the second sentence, Beckett undercuts him with the remark, 'as though he were free.' The statement in *Watt* that 'the only way one can speak of nothing is to speak of it as though it were something' (77) need not, however, be read as a sweeping indictment of the way in which we inescapably falsify reality in our rhetorical formulations. The task of the artist is to create viable 'as-if' propositions or fictions that will make his own predicaments more real.[41]

In marked contrast to *Watt*, the very first sentence of *Mercier and Camier* (1946; published 1970) announces who the story teller is, ostensibly a traditional third-person narrator, even if he does insist upon using the first-person pronoun: 'The journey of Mercier and Camier is one I can tell, if I will, for I was with them all the time.'[42] Whose story is this, that of the 'I' of the opening line or that of Mercier and Camier? The question of the relationship of Mercier and Camier is really of scant interest or importance; the decisive issue concerns the relationship between the author and his two dupes. The presence of a Mr Knott obscures the fact that the central relationship to be deciphered is not Watt-Knott, but that of Watt-Sam. By dispensing with an 'Endon-Knott' figure in *Mercier and Camier*, Beckett takes a major step towards focusing attention upon the 'not-within' – Mercier and Camier have no destination because they are their own goals. Or rather they would be their own goals if they were not the puppets of an author who controls and thwarts their plans in order to further his own ends. The true 'pseudocouple'[43] is not Mercier and Camier, but the author linked with his two creations. The most important development in *Mercier and Camier* is the emergence of an authentic 'I' that would disown adherence to fictional creations and conventions. In this novel, which has been unjustly neglected by critics, occurs a dramatic turning point in Beckett's fiction, one which has proven decisive for all the later works: a 'fall into fiction' takes place whereby the narrator becomes his own central character. *Mercier and Camier* and *Stories* (most notably 'The Calmative') show Beckett implementing in his prose strategic moves that were anticipated in 'The Vulture' and 'Echo's Bones.'

The essential transition occurs in Chapter 7 in which the two travellers leave the bourgeois necropolis, journey into the countryside and then into the mountains. Mercier and Camier are here led towards what appears to be an austere Beckettian version of Dante's Earthly Paradise. From the last woods 'before leaving the timber line,' Beckett's pilgrims take walking sticks and 'made good headway for their age' (99). They certainly show more energy than Murphy (who in his 'Belacqua fantasy' believes 'he would have a long time lying there dreaming, watching the dayspring run through its zodiac, before the toil up hill to Paradise' [109]), even though they encounter the same temptation: 'It is here one would lie down, in a hollow bedded with dry heather, and fall asleep, for the last time, on an afternoon, in the sun, head down among the minute life of stems and bells, and fast fall asleep, fast farewell to charming things' (98). But a positive step has already been taken; almost imperceptibly an ascent has occurred: 'All seems flat, or gently undulating, and there at a stone's throw these high crags, all unsuspected by the wayfarer' (97). Beckett's 'last word about the Purgatories' in 'Dante ... Bruno . Vico .. Joyce' helps clarify the relationship between the author and the characters in this novel:

Dante's is conical and consequently implies culmination. Mr. Joyce's is spherical and excludes culmination. In one there is an ascent from real vegetation – Ante-Purgatory, to ideal vegetation – Terrestial Paradise: in the other there is no ascent and no ideal vegetation. In the one, absolute progression and a guaranteed consummation: in the other, flux-progression or retrogression, and an apparent consummation. In the one movement is unidirectional, and a step forward represents a net advance: in the other movement is non-directional – or multi-directional, and a step forward is, by definition, a step back. (21–2)

Beckett's Purgatory in *Mercier and Camier* combines essential characteristics of both the Joycean and Dantean purgatories: for the characters the journey is ultimately multidirectional (they do take the 'step back' to the city), but for the narrator a consummation of sorts does take place. The half-way measures of social alienation and madness are finally irrelevant to the terrifyingly simple equation – art = death. Beckett means this quite literally. Mercier and Camier seem now to be no more than spirits, partially purged agents who are susceptible to hallucinations and illusions. While they have penetrated the zone of creative consciousness, this is itself of little importance for they, after all, are not artists. What is important is that the narrator has used them to transport *himself* to this point. The quirky banalities of the opening sentence of the novel thus take on a new and startling significance: he was with them all the time and therefore must also experience death. But for the artist (who must also necessarily return to the world for his subject matter) a consummation of sorts has taken place. The consummation is also a transubstantiation in that it involves an apparent fusion of contraries: the mental with the physical, the past with the present (compare 'for I was with them all the time' with the narrator's use of the present tense in Chapter 7), the ideal with the real. All these changes are contingent upon one fundamental transformation – the narrator's acceptance of the role of the author as character. He must soon take up his life as a 'true fiction' and explore the paradoxes of language involved in trying to determine the being of a fiction.

It is only in 'The Calmative' (1946) – second in the sequence of three 'nouvelles' or stories first published, but the last to be written – that the 'I' begins to exploit creatively its new situation and is able to tell a story which is somehow an authentic likeness of his life, a story that confronts the various aspects of his new being as an artist in his own right. 'The Calmative' deserves recognition as a central work in the Beckett canon because, like 'The Vulture' (to which it is heavily indebted), it is the cradle of future fictions. While 'The Calmative' brings to the fore the paradoxes of fiction and being that clear the way for the great breakthrough of the trilogy, it also contains an affirmative statement of an accommodation of language and being which Beckett will return to in his post-trilogy works.

The aesthetic of death and transubstantiation implicit in Chapter 7 of *Mercier and Camier* now becomes explicit. Only an understanding of what occurred in the novel prepares the way for the amazing opening sentence, 'I don't know when I died.'[44] By accepting responsibility for the creative process, the author undergoes a change that can be truly regarded as a death because it transports him into a new spatio-temporal zone in which there is no simple objective orientation towards what passes as the socially accepted definition of reality. The death of the conventional pseudo-identity requires the fabrication of another in the story he tells in order to calm himself. The rebirth in the act of storytelling creates a new time ('what I tell this evening is passing this evening') which causes the speaker, thinking back on his old dead identity, to comment that he is now 'older than I'll have ever been' (28). The 'I' unites two locales, a 'here' and a 'there'; he is at once in his 'ruins,' the 'refuge' of disembodied creative consciousness represented (as in *Mercier and Camier*) by the 'outskirts,' and in the 'city' to which the creative consciousness must return to find the concrete forms for its embodiment: 'I wasn't returning empty-handed, not quite, I was taking back with me the virtual certainty that I was still of this world, of that world too, in a way' (34). To describe his novel situation, the perplexed teller finally settles on the word 'reality, too tired to look for the right word' (45).

Fiction-making is revealed here to have an undeniably physical nature. The constant reference to the condition of his legs which are not used to walking echoes the lines from 'The Vulture': 'the prone who must / soon take up their life and walk.' There is a point mid-way in the narration where a union of the physical and mental takes place which suggests that he is indeed gaining his bearings in this strange world: 'I thought I could go no further, but no sooner had the impetus reached my legs than on I went, believe it or not, at a very fair pace' (34).[45] The rest of 'The Vulture' is repeated in this story and thus alerts the reader to the nature of the transubstantiation taking place. The first paragraph recreates the image of the vulture 'dragging his hunger through the sky / of my skull shell of sky and earth.' Alone in his 'icy bed,' he recreates the world in his head. He is 'too frightened this evening to listen to myself rot, waiting ... for the slow killings to finish in my skull' (27). The vulture-artist is here converting 'tissue' into the 'offal' from which fictions are made. The second paragraph begins with 'What possessed me to stir ...?' and proposes the quizzical answer, 'Was I hungry itself?' – a touchstone response, as we will see, for a reading of all of Beckett's later prose works.

The densely wrought verbal texture of 'The Calmative' is indicative of Beckett's new technique of allusion. Not only must every word be gauged with associations within the text, it must also be correlated with references in previous works. A case in point is the narrator's strange experience in the cathedral. The 'unshakable pillars' of the mind mentioned in the first sentences now become a complex metaphor based on church architecture:

Suddenly close to where I was, and without my having heard the long preliminary rumblings, the organ began to boom. I sprang up from the mat on which I lay before the altar and hastened to the far end of the nave as if on my way out. But it was a side aisle and the door I disappeared through was not the exit. For instead of being restored to the night I found myself at the foot of a spiral staircase which I began to climb at top speed, mindless of my heart, like one hotly pursued by a homicidal maniac. (35–6)[46]

We recall here the sentence in 'Assumption': 'The buffoon in the loft swung steadily on his stick and the organist sat dreaming with his hands in his pockets.' 'The Calmative' transports the reader back to the second sentence of 'Assumption' and raises in a very different context the relationship between an author and his other. The most recent 'I' would seem to have stumbled into the organist's loft: a fictional creation, hence a buffoon, he scurries up the stairs with the hope perhaps of confronting the organist, his other self responsible for expelling him into fictional being.

The momentous decision made in *Mercier and Camier* whereby the narrator becomes a character creates a host of new problems even while it does allow the 'I' to fuse imaginatively a series of antinomies. If the narrator is now a character, there must remain somewhere an objective author figure responsible for his explusion into fictional being. Since in *Mercier and Camier* the 'I' was severed from its bourgeois reality and thrown into fiction, it is not surprising that the 'I' in 'The Calmative' should seek his other in the realm of the bourgeois. Hence the paranoiac fascination with what is going on behind the curtained windows of the homes in the nearly deserted town in which at night only fictions roam: 'What would, what could happen to me in this empty place? But I felt the houses packed with people, lurking behind the curtains they looked out into the street or, crouched far back into the depths of the room, head in hands, were sunk in dream. Up aloft my hat, the same as always, I reached no further' (31). The 'I' does not confront the organist in the loft because his author is not really there, but 'sunk in dream' in the comforts of a bourgeois home. The 'I' can only hear 'a kind of massive murmur coming perhaps from the house that was propping me up' (44). The organist is safely immured.

Molloy admits, 'What I need now is stories, it took me a long time to know that and I'm not sure of it.'[47] Certainly his successor Malone is not sure of it and tries to use his stories to effect an escape from all fiction, and, finally, the Unnamable tries to suspend all fiction-making in a desperate attempt to locate his supposedly authentic self. *Molloy*, one of Beckett's great works, achieves a precarious balancing of central issues first embodied by 'The Vulture' and developed in his first works in French. Molloy is one of the 'prone who must / soon take up their life and walk.' But in *Molloy* the vulture aesthetic, though still predominant, is becoming increasingly problematical. This is evident, for example, in a series of images that develop and complicate the line from the poem which draws a parallel between the Passion of Christ and the sufferings of the artist's creations. The search for origins has revealed only that there is no end: 'a passion without form or stations will have devoured me down to the rotting flesh itself' (25), 'a veritable calvary, with no limits to its stations and no hope of crucifixion' (78). Given this sense of a never ending incompleteness, it is inevitable that both Molloy and Moran should be attracted to the silence and the void which promise a radical solution to the whole terribly perplexing business of writing. At the beginning of his 'unreal journey,' Molloy states hopefully: 'But I shall not always be in need' (15). But words are something and they steadfastly prevent the depiction of a self beyond need. If an absolute goal is sought, words represent, of course, an impenetrable barrier to the apprehension of a 'sense of identity ... wrapped in a namelessness' (44).

There is an abandonment of the vulture aesthetic in *Malone Dies*. Malone's fiction-making must be clearly distinguished from that embodied in 'The Vulture' in which the artist gives life to beings who incorporate the inner and outer worlds in their own real journeys. Confined to his room, Malone's skull is no longer a 'shell of sky and earth.' Malone emphatically declares that he is in a head that is not his own and is now able only to gaze at the 'big world' with which he no longer has any direct contact. If physical contact with the world is negated, any willed action can only be of a mental nature, which is why Malone, in an outburst of fury, attempts to liquidate some of the useless fictions in his head. If we recall 'Assumption,' the buffoon in the loft and the organist both now seem to have gone mad: Lemuel, the buffoon, runs amok with his hatchet, whilst Malone, the organist, scribbles frantically with his dwindling stub of a pencil. We are, once again, as in 'Assumption,' at a point where Dionysian rage (the 'riot of images' in Malone's head) threatens to sweep away all artistic restraints in the expression of a will-to-nothingness.

There is, however, a method behind Malone's madness. The concluding ten pages of the novel contain another of Beckett's reinterpretations of Dante's Terrestial Paradise, a revision which is very different from that found in Chapter 7 of *Mercier and Camier*, where the motif was employed in order to enable the author to enter the zone of creativity in which he could become an artist in his own right and not simply a manipulator of various pawns or surrogate figures. The striving for an absolute transcendence in *Malone Dies* transforms the Terrestrial Paradise locale so that it is no longer the point at which the artist might integrate the ideal and the real, but a would-be point of departure for a Paradise beyond. Malone tries to sweep away the terrible confusion surrounding the terms real and ideal, human and fictional, by a daring assault on the Absolute, on the 'Paradise' that lies beyond the Terrestrial

Paradise he has suddenly transported his dupe Macmann to, the House of St John of God, located on the top of a mountain or plateau.

Malone's statement, 'Let us try another way' (277), signals the concentration upon the Terrestrial Paradise theme. The 'pure plateau air' (277) echoes the first Canto of *Purgatory* in which Dante and Virgil experience the exhilarating contrast between the 'dead air' of the *Inferno* and this new 'pure air.' The 'fine view ... of the plain, the sea, the mountains, the smoke of the town' also parallels Dante's reaction to his new view.[48] Malone is definitely not a vulture-artist seeking to integrate various aspects of the real and the ideal; instead he seeks an identification with the ideal by 'hoisting the real unjustifiably clear of its dimensional limits,' to use the words Beckett employed to criticize both Vico and Proust. For Malone the Terrestrial Paradise is only a penultimate step in an 'absolute progression.' His death and the departure of his creatures for the island will, he hopes, lead 'to a Paradise that is not terrestrial,' and a consummation beyond the boundaries of art.

The progression towards this consummation is, however, by no means guaranteed, as Beckett said was the case at the end of Dante's *Purgatory*. Malone does not finally succeed in clarifying the confusion between a 'particular human identity' and a fictional character. In *Proust*, Beckett twice made the point that the only Paradise that is not the dream of a madman belongs to a past that cannot be recovered.[49] Malone's action is, in terms of this definition, definitely that of a madman, for he is seeking a Paradise that is to come. Malone's will-to-nothingness could paradoxically indicate either a need to transcend his fictional status (thus becoming one with the historical author-figure responsible for his present situation) or it could imply an annihilation of the very categories of art and life. Neither course is possible for a fiction who is necessarily made of words (and is hence 'something') and who cannot be totally identified with a historical realm outside his fictional one. The authorial 'I' of 'The Calmative,' for example, had tried to mediate this crucial dilemma by creating a life for his fictional 'I,' seeking through the vulture aesthetic to validate the ontology of fiction. Malone, knowing full well the problems contingent upon such an approach, wants to put an end to the whole horrible process of fiction-making. The 'static lifelessness' finally attained in the last sentence does not, however, mean that Malone has been successful in his attempt to reach a Paradise outside the purgatorial cycle of fiction-making. It is clear that for a fiction to deny his fictional being leads not to a Paradise (or a Hell or Purgatory for that matter) but to a state of non-being, a state which inevitably lacks a proper name because it abrogates the responsibilities of investigating the relationships of art and life.

In *The Unnamable*, the initial decision to 'stay in' involves a much more radical rejection of the vulture aesthetic than was ever conceived of by Malone. The Unnamable's anti-vulture aesthetic is determined by his realistic and literalistic awareness that once he accepts life as a fiction there still must exist another authority, an aspect of 'I' that remained 'above' when the other aspect of 'I' died and went 'below.' The Unnamable is, for example, troubled by 'these notions of forebears, of houses where lamps are lit at night' (294). His desperate opening decision to stay in is a refusal to 'take up [his] life' and is designed to avoid the apparently unresolvable issue of fictional identity as found in *Molloy* and *Malone Dies*. But the Unnamable's abode is not hermetically sealed: even though he disowns language – 'I seem to speak, it is not I' (291) – words, as if by tropism, drag the self irresistibly towards fiction and the world. The decision to stay in, to shut out the world, is – however perverse – a moral choice that still admits the necessity of a relationship between subject and object: 'You think you are simply resting, the better to act when the time comes, or for no reason, and you find yourself powerless ever to do anything again' (291). The decision to stay in involves a great deal more than an attempt by the Unnamable to rid himself of his previous fictions. The aesthetic parable of the artist trapped by his fictions has become in *The Unnamable* only a part of a much larger question about the nature of language and the culturally sanctified fictions it engenders – the individuation of the 'I,' a God figure, the twin ideas of guilt and innocence, the will and its freedom or limitations.

The machinations of the Unnamable must be read with just as sceptical an eye as those of Belacqua and Murphy. Unable or unwilling to accept life in time, unable to create a viable fiction for himself, the Unnamable tries to decide whether to proceed 'by aporia pure and simple? Or by affirmations and negations invalidated as uttered, or sooner or later?' (291). The 'idea of obligation' which the Unnamable 'swallows' is nevertheless 'an obligation to say something' (311), and is a far cry from the hierophantic obscurantism of 'Three Dialogues' with its 'nothing to express ... together with the obligation to express.'[50] The obligation to speak is more than a moral responsibility or an act of the will: it is the recognition of a compulsion – the hunger instinct – and there is a more extensive and complex employment of the hunger metaphor in *The Unnamable* than in any of Beckett's previous works. The Unnamable is no less hungry for a transcendental solution than was the hero of

'Assumption.' Hungering to be engulfed in the silence, he is instead engulfed in words. Twenty years of writing have shown that word-hunger is insatiable in that it cannot lead to an ablation of desire.[51] This would-be pure subject remains starved and yet unable to satisfy its hunger. While 'swallowed' by words, he is endlessly 'spewed forth' because the denial of an existence above denies that sense of community upon which the signification of language must finally base itself.

The Unnamable reveals how a being (whether fictional or human) who does not accept the possibility of his own freedom needs to create fictions of guilt and punishment. While the Unnamable dismisses God, man and nature as lies, he finds it impossible not to invoke a God-figure, a master who is responsible for his suffering: all is sin, and at the same time all is innocence in so far as the Unnamable neither accepts nor rejects worldly existence. This is a crucial point for an understanding of Beckett's vision. The conjunction of opposites (guilt and innocence) does not result in a self-cancelling dialectic: the possibility of something – freedom – is created. The Unnamable does not try to make this fiction real because he does not want to accept being in time and, moreover, does not have a language whereby he could speak of himself without being entangled in a world of deceit and illusion.

The crisis of language in The Unnamable can perhaps best be appreciated if placed in the context of Beckett's previous speculations on grammar and rhetoric. An important early statement is Beckett's letter to Axel Kaun (1937) in which he dismisses 'Grammar and Style' as only a mask and advocates instead a 'literature of the un-word': 'Is there any reason why that terribly arbitrary materiality of the word's surface should not be dissolved, as for example, the tonal surface eaten into by large black pauses, in Beethoven's Seventh Symphony, so that for pages at a time we cannot perceive it other than, let us say, as a vertiginous path of sounds connecting unfathomable abysses of silence?'[52] Is there indeed any reason why such a plan should not succeed? Beckett poses the problem in the form of a rhetorical question: a solution by dissolution was at this point at least considered a possibility. Beckett soon discovered that this proposed course of action does not, however, lead to silence. While the signifier may be divorced from the signified – thereby rendering the word devoid of referential meaning since it is identified now only with its acoustic image ('path of sounds') – there is no final negation. Even if the individual word is emptied of signification, it still possesses a virtually unlimited potential for meaning in the interaction with other words. The assault on the word leaves intact the grammar and syntax of the encompassing unit of the sentence. A would-be 'literature of the un-word' results in practice only in an anagrammatical reshuffling of elements: the original desire 'to erode' language appears in fact as a verification of the ineradicable power of language 'to order.' The dream of a 'vertiginous path of sounds' turns into yet another rhetorical collocation, the 'vertiginous panic' (350) of *The Unnamable*.

In his first major article on the van Veldes, Beckett commented upon how the writer is continually frustrated by the self-reflexive nature of language: 'each time that one wishes to make words do a true work of transference, each time one wishes to make them express something other than words, they align themselves in such a way as to cancel each other out.'[53] Throughout the trilogy, but especially in *The Unnamable*, Beckett tries to turn this limitation into an advantage. If self-cancellation is carried to an extreme, a radical negation may take place that would pierce the veil of words. What could be more rhetorical, however, than the attempt to transcend words by means of words? In the Denis Devlin review (1938), Beckett stated that 'art has always been this – pure interrogation, rhetorical question less the rhetoric.'[54] The Unnamable is typical of Beckett's later narrators in his awareness of the inescapability of rhetoric: 'the discourse must go on. So one invents obscurities. Rhetoric' (294). *The Unnamable*, which attempts more than any of the previous novels to oppose the power of rhetoric, is ironically enough his most rhetorical work. Anti-rhetoric remains within the domain of rhetoric. The witticism of *Murphy* – 'scratch an old man and discover a Quintilian' (17) – takes on meaning in earnest in the trilogy. Beckett, the would-be poet of silence, has become a master rhetorician: 'Now it's the orator, the beleaguerers have departed, I am a master on board ...' (392).

The endless permutations of various grammatical forms in the vain hope of making a complete statement indicate that the problem lies deeper than the surface structure and is to be located in the basic structure of subject and predicate. The Unnamable finds it difficult, and at times impossible, to write a sentence that fulfills conventional expectations of an ending. The enormous sentences composed of small syntactical units introduce so many variations on the original subject that it is impossible to determine what, if anything, is the predicate. As he somewhat humorously comments, the apodosis, or concluding clause of the sentence, tends to get lost: 'your thoughts wander, your words too, far apart' (374). These futile gyrations still ineluctably acknowledge the primacy of the sentence unit. The 'I' imprisoned in language has been 'sentenced' to the sentence.

The Unnamable is the critical turning point in Beckett's *oeuvre*. The realization that it is impossible for even that very strange hybrid, a fictional being, to escape the necessity of a human point of reference in language leads in the later works to a new style – a 'syntax of weakness' that might be able to express being. Key words such as nothing, being, and self will regain a more affirmative sense in the post-trilogy texts. Beckett said that he did not understand the distinction Heidegger and Sartre had made between existence and being; their language was 'too philosophical'[55] for him (a more polite form of the Unnamable's 'They must consider me sufficiently stupefied with all their balls about being and existing' [348]). In 'For Avigdor Arikha' (1966), in the remarkably short space of six sentences, Beckett does make just such a distinction between being and existence, one which is very important throughout the later texts: 'Siege laid again to the impregnable without. Eye and hand fevering after the unself. By the hand it unceasingly changes the eye unceasingly changed. Back and forth the gaze beating against unseeable and unmakable. Truce for a space and the marks of what it is to be and be in face of. Those deep marks to show.'[56] There is an open declaration here that the battle of consciousness for an object that could give it meaning has again been taken up. 'For Avigdor Arikha' is typical of the later texts in that it turns away from the within to the greater problem of devising means of integrating the within with the without. While the without is an impenetrable, hermetic surface, the perceiver is located in an irrefutable 'thereness' that brings him face to face with the world. The eye seeks the being of this existential reality, the unself that lies outside the subject-object division of perceiving agent and phenomenal world. Although the gaze cannot penetrate the essence of that which lies outside the concrete, it can nevertheless leave the 'deep marks.' Several images are suggested by the 'deep marks': a furrowed face worn down by 'eye and hand fevering after the unself'; hieroglyphic inscriptions which the gaze can leave on the surface of the 'impregnable without'; the 'marks' of the painting which may have served as the occasion for Beckett's own marks or words. All three combine to reveal 'what it is to be and to be in face of.' For, though man cannot overstep the mark, the boundaries of his situation in time, to apprehend being ('unseeable and unmakable'), he can create marks which are characterized as possessing depth. In *Proust*, Beckett made it clear that he conceived the artist's role as an 'excavatory' search for the 'core.'[57] *The Unnamable* showed that there were limits beyond which the search could no longer be sustained. The art of depth initiated in *Proust* has led to the Unnamable's 'stupid obsession with depth' (293). The 'deep marks' of the Arikha piece are indicative of a major revision of Beckett's aesthetic. They are the signs of a new acceptance of the limitations of the human and artistic situation. The siege of the will-to-power must give way to a sense of weakness that accepts the confrontation of self with the without and the unself, and does not try to impose an absolute identification in which the boundaries between self and other would be absolved. The vision that emerges is both Orphic and hermetic: grounded in the world, man opens up a horizon of signification ('deep marks') which must, however, acknowledge and accept the boundaries which enclose him ('truce for a space').

Beckett's post-trilogy fiction works towards an important reformulation of the Orpheus myth that is of central importance in a total reading of his own works and is of great relevance to the contemporary crisis in language, literature, and literary criticism. There is a renewed emphasis upon the first phase of the myth in which Orpheus, the archetypal artist, established with his art a relationship between man and world. It is only in this sense that the term Orphic can be legitimately applied to Beckett's later works. The problem is that contemporary speculations on the myth have stressed almost exclusively the negations involved in the descent into the being of language. A case in point is Walter A. Strauss's fine study *Descent and Return*. Taking his departure from Elizabeth Sewell's 'organic' model of the Orphic reconciliation of opposites, Strauss says that a modern account of the myth must take into account the infusion of Gnostic and nihilistic elements and adds that the defining characteristic of modern thought is not organicism but a dialectical coincidence of opposites.[58] This view is, he argues, best exemplified by Maurice Blanchot, who sees the artist's search for the ideal source of being and language (the 'Eurydice' that can never be regained) as a confrontation with the negatives of descent and destruction. Since this is essentially the reading Blanchot gives of *The Unnamable* in his article ' "Where now? Who now?" ' it is surprising to find Strauss denying the relevance of the Orphic in Beckett, if only in this very limited sense:

These two [Kafka and Beckett], because of their vision of a hopelessly fragmented and absurd universe, would surely render the Orphic obsolete were it not for the attempts of Maurice Blanchot to resurrect the Orphic attitude of the writer by a reinterpretation in light of a new understanding of literature in our time ... Most of the latter [the descendants of Mallarmé] have abandoned the Orphic ideal altogether – Kafka, Beckett, Robbe-Grillet are authors for whom it is utterly meaningless – or else like Blanchot, they have attempted to give the Orpheus myth a restricted and predominantly negative interpretation.[59]

Strauss is clearly uneasy with the Blanchot-type solution and concludes that 'the new Orphism has reached a point of no return.'[60] But Strauss has misread Beckett; grouping him with Kafka and Robbe-Grillet is, to say the very least, highly misleading.

Beckett reached the so-called point of no return in *The Unnamable*, but he does return in the later texts to an Orphic vision that involves an affirmation of the relationship between language, world and man. These later works testify that Beckett is more than a great transitional figure embodying central aspects of the postmodernist crisis of language; Beckett has, in fact, expanded the literary enterprise into an exciting new zone of ontological investigations.

2

The Rhetoric of Failure in *Texts for Nothing*

Beckett describes in a litany of negatives the status of language at the end of the trilogy: 'There's complete disintegration. No "I," no "have," no "being." No nominative, no accusative, no verb. There's no way to go on. The very last thing I wrote – *Texts for Nothing* – was an attempt to get out of this attitude of disintegration but it failed.'[1] Critics have for the most part simply accepted Beckett's designation of *Texts for Nothing* (1967) as failures, and not examined the ways in which they attempt to escape the impasse of *The Unnamable*.[2] In these short, dense texts in which the conventional props of narration have all but disappeared, there is a dramatic change of vision from *The Unnamable*. There is an unmistakable turning towards the world and the fundamental problem of relocating the self which has fallen into the no-man's land of fictional non-being. The vital question now is whether language and the rhetoric of fiction are capable of authentically integrating this self with the world. It is in this sense *Texts for Nothing* attempt to overcome the 'disintegration' of *The Unnamable* where the 'I' would repudiate all existence, fictional or otherwise. Disintegration cannot here mean a radical annihilation of language, but – more realistically – a dislocation in which the key components of language lack ontological significance. Indeed, there is an incredible profusion of subjects, verbs and objects in *The Unnamable* and *Texts for Nothing*; the central problem is that these words keep forming the same patterns of rhetoric which preclude an affirmation of the self's being.

There is much less emphasis upon the expression of the void in *Texts for Nothing* than the title has misleadingly led readers to expect. The 'I' who has undergone the 'fall into fiction' is termed 'below' and constantly labelled a 'nothing,' but it is clear that the term is used as an antonym to what is, the world of things and people, 'above,' in the light. Nothing cannot mean in this instance the absolute negation of which 'Three Dialogues' spoke. The 'voice' obsessively returns to the theme that some sort of identification must exist between the something that is above, and the nothing that is below. 'Text 11' comments openly on the need for a new concept of negation which would allow for the meaningful integration of self and world: 'No, something better must be found, a better reason, for this to stop, another word, a better idea, to put in the negative, a new no, to cancel all the others, all the old noes that buried me down here, deep in this place which is not one, which is merely a moment for the time being eternal, which is called here, and in this being which is called me and is not one, and in this impossible voice ...'[3] The 'old noes' of logic and dialectic are derived from a more fundamental nothing which, while it is dependent on the prior existence of the world, makes for the very awareness and understanding of that world. Or, as Heidegger phrases it in *Being and Time*, 'Nothing is grounded in the most primordial something ... the world.'[4] The tantalizingly evanescent glimpses of the world above in *Texts for Nothing* are founded upon an analogous conception of a nothing that reveals, that is full of potential signification. The narrator of 'Text 6,' for example, still clings to a hope that a 'way out' will be found: 'I know, if my head could think, I'd find a way out, in my head, like so many others, and out of worse than this, the world would be there again, in my head, with me much as in the beginning.' (102)

Why then, given that all the 'Texts,' in varying degrees, share the same vision – the need for a reintegration of self with the world – do they fail to escape 'the attitude of disintegration'? The refusal of the 'I' to accept any existential reality of his own could be attributed to the recognition that these are only patently fabricated pseudo-selves, pathetic effigies of a would-be genuine 'I' in an authentic social reality. Somewhere there is the historical author-figure who is responsible for the predicament of the 'I' in the fictional realm. As with Heidegger's nothing the fictional 'nothing' of the Beckettian 'I' is continually drawn towards the world and being in time. But Beckett cannot posit *Dasein*, since the creative act is always mediated. Words are no longer directly referential: they are at once 'there' and 'not there,' partly historical and partly fictional, at once above and below. The narrators also encounter in the sentence form itself a Cartesian syntax of subject and predicate that hampers an identification of the subjective and objective dimensions of self. The sentence form tends to perpetuate a false ontology of substance and attribute and continually forces the speaker to say something about himself rather than expressing himself as he is. Without a new language to corroborate the 'new no' of a vision redirected towards the world, the narrators are imprisoned by the rhetoric of language – a rhetoric of failure, moreover, since it only involves a surface rearrangement of language and does not alter the underlying structures.

While the first six 'Texts' are, for the most part, highly resourceful attempts to integrate the self with an existing reality, the 'Texts' in the last half of the collection progressively betray a preoccupation with form for its own sake, and are distinguished not by an *inventio* or search after truth, but rather by an *elocutio* or urge towards ornamentation. Failure in these instances should not be superficially identified with the ideal of failure outlined in 'Three Dialogues.' Recognizing the formal brilliance of some of these 'Texts,' the critic still has to point out that they fail to substantiate the new vision that is drawn towards the world and an art of living. Art may be the 'apotheosis of solitude,'[5] as Beckett wrote in *Proust*, but the 'moral integrity necessary for the artist' can hardly be sustained without an engagement with the real – a hunger for the words that will validate the ontology of fiction.

'Text 1' clearly sets out to break the impasse encountered in the conclusion of *The Unnamable*. The first sentences recapitulate the last phrases of the trilogy ('I can't go on, I'll go on'): 'I couldn't any more, I couldn't go on'; 'You can't stay here'; 'I couldn't stay there, and I couldn't go on.' The conditional tenses prepare the way for the description of a 'new' place the 'I' has moved to. That a significant change has indeed taken place is emphasized by the repetition of the query 'What possessed you to come?' (75; 77). Whereas the Unnamable began with the assertion that his predicament was due to the fact 'that one day I simply stayed in' (129), the narrator of 'Text 1' follows the statement, 'I could have stayed in,' with the summary judgment 'I couldn't' (75). As a result of the decision to 'stay in,' the Unnamable adds, 'You soon find yourself powerless ever to do anything again' (291). The narrator of 'Text 1' seems to be answering the Unnamable: 'I can do nothing any more, that's what you think' (75). This 'I' admits there is a unity among these different aspects of self and that 'we seem to be more than one, all deaf, not even, *gathered together for life*' (75–6, italics mine). Nothing could be further from the Unnamable's resistance to an imputation of life in the world (that is, his rejection of the fables that depict real existence) than this acknowledgment of the need for being.

The new place the narrator finds himself in – 'the top, very flat, of a mountain, no, a hill, but so wild, so wild, enough' (75) – is another of Beckett's versions of Dante's Terrestrial Paradise, a motif he has often turned to in order to depict the zone of creativity the artist must penetrate if he is to resolve the complex relationships of art and life. The narrator's turning away from his 'home' of conventional beauty and pleasures – 'the so-called golden vale so often sung' (76) – is closely linked to Dante's meeting with Ser Brunetto in Canto xv of the *Inferno*:

> And he [Ser Brunetto] began: 'What chance or fate has led
> thee ere thy last day dawn down into this pit?
> And who is this, whose guidance lends thee aid'?
> 'Up there,' I answered him, 'in the life lit
> by sunshine in a valley I went astray,
> before my sum of days was yet complete.
> From it I turned at dawn but yesterday:
> as to it I returned did he appear
> and leads me home now by this narrow way'[6]

Further parallels between this passage and 'Text 1' confirm Beckett's conscious manipulation of the Dantean model: 'To think in the valley the sun is blazing all down the ravelled sky' (76) calls attention yet again to the world that has been left behind; the narrator's answer to the second posing of the question, 'What possessed you to come?,' combines elements of Ser Brunetto's question and Dante's answer: 'To change, or It's not me, or, Chance, or again, To see, or again, years of great sun, Fate ...' (77).

'Text 1' shows Beckett skilfully combining his personal aesthetic of 'The Vulture' with the Terrestrial Paradise motif appropriated from Dante. 'The Vulture' is virtually repeated in 'Text 1' by means of direct reference and paraphrase in the section that finally answers why he has come to 'the top ... of the mountain.' The embedded elements of 'The Vulture' are concerned with the mysterious impulses behind the act of creation and the concomitant paradoxical relationships of art and life, language and being. Discussing how this new 'here' has been reached, the 'I' says, with startling literalness, 'my feet dragged me out that must go their ways, that I let go their ways and drag me here ...' (77). The repetition of 'drag' echoes the opening section of 'The Vulture'; the phrase, 'must go their ways' expresses the central thought of the second section, the compulsive nature of poetic genesis. That Beckett is consciously drawing attention to the parallels between the two works is clear from an allusion to the last two lines of 'The Vulture' only a few sentences later, 'eye ravening patient in the haggard vulture face, perhaps it's carrion time' (77). 'Carrion' effects a parallel with the 'offal' of 'The Vulture,' the substance upon which the imagination would prey.[7] The narrator is 'flat on my face on the dark earth' (76), the position of 'the prone who must / soon take up their life and walk,' and the 'den' which he leaves is, of course, a variation of Beckett's favourite image of the skull as the home the artist must leave in order to integrate it with an outer reality.

'Carrion time' is truly 'story time.' While the narrator has previously struggled along with the help of 'old stories,' the child's tale of heroic Joe Breem is now offered as nourishment for 'the eye ravening patient in the haggard vulture face.' An ideal identification of subject and object is the apparent result:

Yes, I was my father and I was my son, I asked myself questions and answered as best I could, I had it told to me evening after evening, the same old story I knew by heart and couldn't believe ... And this evening again it seems to be working, I'm in my arms, I'm holding myself in my arms, without much tenderness, but faithfully, faithfully. Sleep now, as under that ancient lamp, all twined together, tired out with so much talking, so much listening, so much toil and play. (79)

The decision in 'Text 1' to 'go out' and up the mountain has helped to mediate the 'old thing' – the breakdown of subject and object announced at the beginning of *The Unnamable*. But the narrator admits that he 'couldn't believe' the 'old story' he tells himself, thus seriously weakening the affirmation of a unified self. The old story is 'a comedy, for children' (79), not *The Divine Comedy*.[8] There is no ultimate Authority to appeal to in order to guarantee a teleological progression towards an integrated self; there is no Virgil or Beatrice to act as surrogate parents. (The mother is dead in Breem's story and in the narrator's own.) Dante cannot accompany the Beckettian 'I' to the end of his journey – like Virgil his vision is finally deemed incomplete. As a modern artist, the 'I' of 'Text 1' has to be a self-creator: 'I was my father and I was my son.'

The narrator of 'Text 1' has made a heroic advance beyond *The Unnamable*, but he has not succeeded in creating a new story in present time for himself. Instead of fabricating an adult fable to meet his present needs, he has returned to a childhood recollection that nostalgically suspends the great paradoxes of language and being. Being in present time is still a very confused issue. The 'here' varies and all calculation of time depends 'on what I meant by here, and me, and being' (76); 'All mingles, time and tenses, at first I only had been here, now I'm here still, soon I won't be here yet, toiling up the slope, or in the bracken by the wood ...' (78). These different perspectives need a story of more substance than that of Joe Breem to bind them together. 'Sleep now, as under that ancient lamp' fuses two distinct points in time by means of the rest well-earned after the labour of completing this 'Text,' the toil up the mountain, and the toil of writing it down. If the toil up the mountain results only in child's play, the strenuous efforts involved have at least ensured that in this 'Text' the play of language has not ended in a rhetoric of failure.

Whereas 'Text 1' concludes with a poetic synthesis of subject and object, 'Text 2' begins with a series of parallel and symmetrical phrases that formalize the split between above (the light) and below (the darkness): 'Above is the light, the elements, a kind of light, sufficient to see by, the living find their ways, without too much trouble, avoid one another, unite, avoid the obstacles, without too much trouble, seek with their eyes, close their eyes, halting, without halting, among the elements, the living' (81). The two worlds are, however, viewed by a detached observer who can stand aside sufficiently to make judgments about both. 'Here you are under a different glass, not long habitable either, it's time to leave it' (81). As in the opening 'Text,' the main theme is the interrelationship between these two worlds which is necessary if the creative process is to continue. 'Text 2' sets itself the extremely difficult task of showing how the imagination, reluctant to accept its natural aliment – the world above (in which, however, 'nothing showed of the true affair') – can still find a mode of expression.

Words are failing: 'The words too, slow, slow, the subject dies before it comes to the verb, words are stopping too' (82). This is only true, however, as long as the narrator tries to confine himself to this world below. But, as acknowledged at the beginning of the 'Text,' it is necessary to 'depart.' Disgusted with life in the 'miserable light,' the self is still irresistibly attracted towards it, as if by tropism, and words only regain life when used to describe the world above. Simple declarative sentences are used in the brief glimpses of Mr Joly and Mother Calvet.[9] These naturalistic recollections do not, however, effect a true connection between above and below. Mother Calvet, 'creaming off the garbage,' is really only a burlesque version of the true artist-scavenger. A true naturalist, she digs in the muck for what Beckett in *Proust* termed the 'offal of experience' – 'beauty, strength, intelligence, the latest, daily, action, poetry, all one price for one and all' (82). Interspersed with these memories are attempts to describe the other 'here.' An image of a 'ragdoll rotting in a head' (82) underlines the sterility of the material the imagination must now work with in its attempt to bring about an authentic mediation between self and world.

In the final extended memory of Piers, the representative man, a solution to the aesthetic dilemma is found in a revised Proustian 'participation between the ideal and the real.' The story of Piers' tortuous journey between cliff and sea answers the question 'where would you go, now that you know' raised at the beginning of the 'Text.' Fiction, in other words, resolves the contradictory injunction, 'Go then, better stay,' and renders the compulsory departure of the 'I' to the world coexistent with that of his surrogate, Piers. The boundaries between art and life, fiction and being, have temporarily been broken down. Piers' 'brief halt' and subsequent movement echo the description of the 'living' in the opening sentence. The narrator exists, it is clear, only as long as his memory. A first-person pronoun enters for the first time in order to stress the narrator's identification with the impersonal process of fiction-making, 'There, it's done, it ends there, I end there' (84). 'Text 1' answered the question 'what possessed you to come?' with a profoundly disturbing literalness, 'my feet dragged me out.' The creative process in 'Text 2' is described in similarly physical terms, 'it's possible, the legs still seem to be working' (84). The emergence of a fiction is clearly as much a physical as a mental act. The narrator has skilfully manipulated a few residual images in order to establish for a brief spell a connection between the two glass enclosed worlds. Whereas in 'Text 1' there was an ideal fusion of a subject and object under one encompassing glass ('under that ancient lamp, all twined together'), in 'Text 2' there are two distinct worlds divided from each other by a glass barrier.[10] Even the 'artistic' solution in the last memory emphasizes a duality: Piers is outside in the winter's night, 'opposite the lamplit window.'

While the Unnamable perversely tried to maintain integrity by rejecting all attributes, the narrator of 'Text 3' willingly embraces all predication. 'Let us be dupes, dupes of every time and tense, until it's done, all past and done, and the voices cease, it's only voices, only lies' (85).[11] Through a sheer act of will, this 'I' is going to depart for life above, a departure which is also described as an inescapable compulsion: 'this time it's I must go.' Embracing with mock gusto all the grotesque contingencies of life in the body, the 'I' literally allows the narration to run out of control: 'Just the head and the two legs, or one, in the middle, I'd go hopping. Or just the head, nice and round, nice and smooth, no need of lineaments, I'd go rolling, downhill, almost a pure spirit, no, that wouldn't work ...' (89). The flow of memories is abruptly terminated by the narrator who seems to have been temporarily engulfed by their factitious circumstantiality but now returns to the question of whether any trace of himself is to be found there: 'See what's happening here, where there's no one, where nothing happens, get something to happen here, someone to be here, then put an end to it, have silence, get into silence, or another sound, a sound of other voices than those of life and death, of lives and deaths everyone's but mine, get into my story in order to get out of it, no, that's all meaningless' (89). Language in the form of an alien, disembodied voice still drags the 'I' from his 'nowhere' to a 'somewhere' in the world. The voice in this 'Text' seems to have lost control over its rhetoric, and seems capable of digressing endlessly in meaningless anecodotes of possible incarnations. The narrator periodically attempts to impose order on his discourse by repeating items like 'leave all that' and using the refrain 'it's not me.' However, language loosed from the restraints of a fixed 'I' flounders aimlessly, and immersion in a welter of physical detail does not constitute a true revelation of either the world or the self.

The question of to whom the voice belongs is raised in the first sentence of 'Text 4': 'Where would I go, if I could go, who would I be, if I could be, what would I say, if I had a voice, who says this, saying it's me?' (91). A perfectly balanced formal construct, any content it might express is drained away by the final query: 'who says this, saying it's me?' While the 'I' functions grammatically as the subject, it is ontologically the object of the 'someone' mentioned in the next sentence. The anguished appeal to this indefinite pronoun to answer the question 'who is speaking' dramatizes the growing linguistic confusion. The sentence, by being uttered, confers a spurious substantiality on the word 'I' of which it cannot get free. The proposed answer to the opening sentence reveals itself to be only a circumlocution: 'It's the same old stranger as ever, for whom alone accusative[12] I exist, in the pit of my existence, of his, of ours, there's a simple answer' (91). The sentence tries to render the 'I' simultaneously as both subject and object. But the voice is unable to surmount the logic of language, the syntactical division of subject and object, in order to effect an ideal union.

A new 'I' emerges in the subsequent series of pronoun references: 'That's how he speaks, this evening, how he has me speak, how he speaks to himself, how I speak, there is only me, this evening, here, on earth, and a voice that makes no sound because it goes towards none' (92). Here at last the voice seems to have found a home, an acknowledged narrator, an 'I' who admits that his original tactics were mad, since to name the silence is necessarily to destroy it. He also admits to 'having my figments talk,' thus granting the request of the first 'I' to be dignified 'with the third person, like his other figments' (92). Once the voice becomes attached to a pronoun, life with all its multifarious connections miraculously appears. But a fall back into linguistic chaos, however rhetorically patterned, is prompted by the invocation of yet another vaguely defined pronoun, a 'he who somehow comes and goes, unaided from place to place, even though nothing happens to him' (93). The multidirectionality of these different pronominal forms undermines the linear notion of conventional syntax and makes impossible the establishment of a referential context for them. It is true that the last sentence of the 'Text' pretends to resolve this problem: 'That's where I'd go, if I could go, that's who I'd be, if I could be' (94). But the pronoun 'that' is no longer demonstrative since it lacks any clear antecedent. Does 'that' refer to reasonable existence on earth, the speechlessness of a *via negativa* of non-being, or to 'he who somehow comes and goes'? While these alternatives are, in logical terms, mutually exclusive, the narrator emotionally considers them to be a unity, hence all the confusion. 'Text 4' is in fact a parody of the syllogism. The reasonable 'I' is the common term that relates 'he who neither speaks or listens' and 'he who moves.' As a consequence, this 'I' becomes literally an 'excluded middle,' not refined out of existence as in the Joycean ideal of the artist, simply reasoned away as a logical impossibility.

A discordant medley of competing voices is avoided in 'Text 5' by a concentration upon the image of a trial: 'To be judge and party, witness and advocate and he, attentive, indifferent, who sits and notes. It's an image, in my helpless head, where all sleeps, where all is dead, not yet born, I don't know, or before my eyes, they see the scene, the lids flicker and it's in' (95). This old dispute over the ontological status of the image renders problematical any identification between the subject and object. 'To be judge and party, witness and advocate' establishes only a formal relationship between parts of the image. This apparent fusion of subject and object must be clearly differentiated from that found in 'Text 1' in which the union was grounded in the phenomenal concreteness of being in the world, of being both above and below. Deprived of any such base in the world, the image in 'Text 5' does not come to life: 'where all sleeps, where all is dead, not yet born.' The inability to establish a connection between outside and inside prevents a true poetic genesis. Whereas in 'The Vulture' the creations of the imagination 'must / soon take up their life and walk,' the narrator's inability in 'Text 5' to substantiate any type of organic aesthetic makes the workings of the imagination appear mechanical: 'I'd be better advised to take a little turn, the way you manoeuvre a tin soldier' (96).

While the extensive use of the judicial image inevitably brings to mind *The Trial*, 'Text 5' owes much more to 'A Hunger Artist,' where Kafka's penitent explains his fasting by stating, 'I couldn't find the food I liked. If I had found it, believe me I should have made no fuss and stuffed myself like you or anyone else.'[13] The speaker of 'Text 5' would similarly 'lap up the rest,' if only he could believe in his existence. Beckett brilliantly distinguished his own art from Kafka's, whose 'form is classic, it goes on like a steam roller, almost serene. It *seems* threatened all the time – but the consternation is in the form. In my work there is consternation behind the form, not in the form.'[14] The delineation in 'Text 5' remains meticulously patterned throughout since it is regarded as nothing more than a conceit, a convenient trope to bring about a rhetorical heightening of effect. A reflection of this is the self-conscious commentary which underscores the rhetorical nature of the language employed: 'I trust the orator is not forgetting anything' (97); 'What do I do when silence falls with rhetorical intent, or denoting lassitude, perplexity, consternation ...' (97). The 'consternation behind the form' of the courtroom image stems from the effort to discover an ontological basis for what has now become only a rhetorical exercise for the narrator. Denied authentic sustenance from the world above, the narrator returns to his image, to his rhetoric of failure: 'Yes, one begins to be very tired, very tired of one's toil, very tired of one's quill, it falls, it's noted' (99). 'Play' and 'toil' are no longer united as they were in 'Text 1.'

In 'Text 6' the 'I' has obviously been found guilty and sentenced to some form of imprisonment, perhaps in a mental asylum. He has the same concern for his keepers' welfare as Kafka's hunger artist had for his 'night watchers.'[15] He wonders if they 'play cards, the odd rubber' or take a break 'with something cold ... in the interests of their health' (101). Enclosed by an 'infinite here' that is severed from the world, word-hunger remains unsatisfied and necessitates a further continuation of the fast. The image of the prisoner, forgotten for much of the 'Text,' is finally openly abandoned as it no longer even remotely approaches a true portrayal of the self's position: 'Apparitions, keepers, what childishness, and ghouls, to think I said ghouls, do I as much as know what they are, of course I don't, and how the intervals are filled, as if I didn't know, as if there were two things, some other thing besides this thing, what is it, this unnamable thing that I name and name and never wear out, and I call that words' (104). This hunger artist will not be able to satisfy his appetite for meaning, for 'a little story, with living creatures coming and going on a habitable earth' (105), until he can discover or create images which can identify his position within the 'Text' with his being 'behind the form.' Only then will he be able to name his 'unnamable thing,' which is indeed 'two things,' since his 'I' is a hybrid of fiction and reality.

'Text 7' is the mathematical centre of *Texts for Nothing*, and at this pivotal juncture the whole undertaking appears to have ended in failure. The opening question as to whether the search for the lost self has thoroughly exhausted all the possibilities seems answered in the affirmative by the 'Text' itself. The narrator confides, the 'search should be made elsewhere, unless it be abandoned, which is my feeling' (110). Although he immediately qualifies this judgment, it is obvious that the decision to go on is more indicative of an obsessional 'obligation to express' than of the discovery of a new line of thought that might extricate the self from its suffocating rhetoric. When the narrator attempts to speak directly of what he regards as his authentic self, the language becomes increasingly abstract. In 'Text 1' the narrator was in 'troughs scooped deep by the rain,' 'down in the hole the centuries have dug' (76); in this 'Text' the speaker is simply said to be 'in the trough of all this time' (108). A sense of calm is only restored when the narrative focuses on a scene in which a character reminiscent of Watt waits endlessly at the South Eastern Railway Terminus. As the narrator is no longer speaking directly of himself, the description takes on the naturalistic coherence of ordinary social reality. While this 'lump' may once have been the narrator, he is no longer equivalent with the 'I' trapped in the timelessness of a fictional world. The last sentence is thus especially ironic. While the 'I' literally has no time to lose, 'night is at hand and time come for me too to begin' (110).

In 'Text 8' the narrator's sense of any previous existence is irrevocably lost: 'I burrowed my way out alone, to linger a moment free in a dream of days and nights, dreaming of me moving, season after season, towards the last, like the living, till suddenly I was here, all memory gone' (112). This sounds remarkably similar to Murphy's description of the 'Belacqua fantasy' in which 'he would have a long time lying there dreaming, watching the dayspring run through its zodiac, before the toil up hill to Paradise.' But this latest avatar appears to have lived through the 'Belacqua fantasy' and erased all traces of life in the world. The hope which the narrator harbours of being able to regain the world is a recognition that the only honest way to silence is through an acceptance of mortality within time. The last part of the 'Text' toys briefly with the affirmation of an existential self parading through the Place de la République, but ends with an anticipated negation, for to accept this self would be to deny the priority of the other self, 'blind and deaf and mute,' in relation to whom the grotesque above is a pathetic impostor. As long as the conception of a pure self postulated in *The Unnamable* is upheld, 'Text 8' can only make more balanced and orderly the rhetoric of failure. Only a murmur that flows 'like a single endless word' (111) could be equivalent to the speaker's 'infinite here' in which 'time has turned into space' (112). One could say of 'Text 8' what Beckett said of a Denis Devlin poem, 'If only the 8 ... had been left on its side. So: ∞.'[16]

'Text 9' makes a powerful emotional impact through the narrator's plea for a way out of the word-mess, a way back to the earth. While the dialectic impasses of 'yes or no' and 'it's me, it's not me' are commented upon, they do not in this instance constitute the main topic: 'The way out, this evening it's the turn of the way out ...' (117). Whereas the previous 'Text' stated 'my past has thrown me out, its gates have slammed behind me' (112), this narrator skirts 'the gates of the graveyard' (121), vainly seeking admission. The central image of the road of life that leads to the graveyard raises the question of the verifiability of existence on earth. The speaker is therefore preoccupied with the problem of whether others have seen him. If to be is to be perceived, as Berkeley said, the testimony of others will resolve the confusion of 'the here of then, the then of there' (120) by fixing the 'I' as a particular spatio-temporal entity. Life will then be able to pursue its relentless course towards death, which will be the ultimate proof one has existed. But the speaker has not forgotten that the question of existence is finally one of giving life to words. Whereas the narrator of previous 'Texts' discovered that it is impossible to kill words, this speaker comments on the equally disturbing corollary that he cannot be obliterated by the word-shit. As long as words exist, there will be an endless need for talk of 'a world to reach, in order to have done, with worlds, with creatures, with words, with misery, misery' (118).

In the last section of 'Text 9' there is an interweaving of the central themes of hunger, word-hunger, and rhetoric. The initial discussion concerns the self-cancelling nature of a language determined by the interplay of yes and no. Dismissing the facile solution that one has only to wait until the 'others' come in order to prove his being, the speaker is confronted with the failure of language clearly to represent any idea of what being actually is: 'Then it goes and I see it's not that, but something else, difficult to grasp, and which I don't grasp, or which I do grasp, it depends, and it comes to the same, for it's not that either, but something else, some other thing, or the first back again, or still the same, always the same thing proposing itself to my perplexity, then disappearing, then proposing itself again, to my perplexity still unsated, or momentarily dead, of starvation' (121). Language dominated by the logical conception of being will never, it is clear, be able to satisfy the appetite for meaning. In desperation, therefore, the narrator turns to the affirmative world-oriented dimension of language. The thinly disguised pun in 'borne by my words' (121) underscores this new direction: 'if I could get out of here, that is to say if I could say, There's a way out there, there's a way out somewhere, to know exactly where would be a mere matter of time, and patience, and sequence of thought, and felicity of expression' (121). The subordinate clause, 'if I could say,' establishes here the priority of *inventio* over *dispositio* ('sequence of thought') and style ('felicity of expression'). Rhetoric in its authentic role never aimed merely to persuade, but to induce belief. In the opening sentences of 'Text 9,' the narrator says that he is waiting to believe that there is actually a way out. To create this belief, Beckett must, however, find a new form of thought, a 'new no.'

'Text 10' makes imperative ('give up') what was more tentatively expressed in 'Text 7' ('unless the search be abandoned'). Unless a new no is found to answer the 'new question, the most ancient of all, the question were things always so' (111), this 'I' will not be able to return to his being in a world that existed before the engulfment in language and fiction. The exercise has now become merely intellectual in nature; the head has gone on its own way: 'slobbering its shit and licking it back off the lips like in the days when it fancied itself. But the heart's not in it anymore, nor is the appetite' (123). Words issue forth from the mouth, fail to connect with any outside reality, and finally spill back to their source. Utterance is composed of 'inanities' (124) – vain, empty words that lack substance and lead to a state of 'inanition.' A tautological exercise, in other words.

'Give up' implies, however, that there once was something. Unable to return to this previous condition, the narrator can only console himself with the manipulation of an image. The cliché 'I'm in good hands' (123) flowers into a conceit. But the image of fingers like tentacles closing off the senses of the narrator is presented in a very self-conscious manner that exposes the development of the trope as only another empty formalist construct. This figure gives way to further speculation concerning the space between silence and babble that the narrator occupies. The refusal to accept the fact that the self is among the living is motivated by a perverse sense of moral integrity. If no revelation of the truth of affairs is possible within language, the narrator can only opt for the 'voice of my silence' (125), and the calm that descends at the end has an affirmative quality strangely reminiscent of 'Text 1': 'I'll go to sleep, so that I may say, hear myself say, a little later, I've slept, he's slept, but he won't have slept, or else he's sleeping now, he'll have done nothing, nothing but go on, doing what, doing what he does, that is to say, I don't know, giving up, that's it, I'll have gone on giving up, having had nothing, not being there' (125). Although this fusion of 'I' and 'he' is clearly the antithesis of that found in 'Text 1,' it produces the same peaceful effect. If the self cannot be grounded in an existence that does not blind the participant to the illusions mankind has created for itself, the decision to remain in a state of non-being represents, however perversely, a sense of integrity.

The speaker in 'Text 11' repeats the exact words of his predecessor in 'Text 1,' 'I shouldn't have begun' (75; 124), thus indicating just how little progress has been made in the intervening 'Texts' to make an utterance about the self that will not be immediately denied by a negative. Nevertheless, the speaker accedes to the compulsion to go on and is able to gain at least a measure of aesthetic satisfaction by reaching a conclusion that provides answers to the ellipses of his stuttering beginning:

When I think, no, that won't work, when come those who knew me, perhaps even know me still ... it's as if, come on, I don't know, I shouldn't have begun. (127)

And that is why, when comes the hour of those who knew me, this time it's going to work, when comes the hour of those who knew me, it's as though I were among them, that is what I had to say ... between two parting dreams, knowing none, known of none, that is finally what I had to say, that is all I can have had to say, this evening. (131)

The all too neat circular form disguises the fact that in the body of the

'Text' the narrator has patently failed to express a relationship between himself and the self that exists in time.

The penultimate 'Text' tries to clarify the problematic existence of a self in the world by transferring the burden of proof to the third person. As long as the speaker is among the 'true others' (133) who possess movement and hence are undoubtedly in the realm of space and time, there is no need for him to turn inwards the search for the self. But the last words deny the existence of a so-called true other: the quest for an absolute verification would only lead to an infinite regression, 'you'd need a god, unwitnessed witness of witnesses' (135). The dichotomy of a detached 'I' who projects himself into the memory of an existential self is now modified to reveal the reciprocal nature of the relationship. The studied repetition of 'it's a far cry to morning' (133) by both the 'I' and the 'he' identifies them as parts of the same self: 'It's me in him remembering' is quickly inverted to 'he thinks of me' (133). As in the earlier 'Texts,' time is a primary obstacle to effecting an integral connection of the two selves. On 'this winter night, without moon or stars' (133), a self on earth is haunted by the memory of a being freed from the ravages of time, an old dream of Beckett's, expressed by his Descartes in 'Whoroscope' as a 'second / starless inscrutable hour.'[17] In this winter's tale, there is, however, no reconciliation of 'I – he.' The multiplication of voices renders the whole question of self hopelessly confused: 'And this other now, obviously, what's to be said of this latest other, with his babble of homeless mes and untenanted hims, this other without number or person whose abandoned being we haunt, nothing. There's a pretty three in one, and what a one, what a no one' (134). Without the ability to determine a central subject, a stable 'I,' the state of the self is plunged into the chaos of an interregnum. A Shakespearean tone echoes in the rhetoric of mutual incrimination as different selves wrangle over the 'usurp[ation]' – 'wasn't I always there, like a stain of remorse, is that my night and contumacy, in the dungeons of this moribund' (134). Without specific referents for the pronouns, language becomes a system of signs emptied of meaning.

'Text 13' refers to itself as 'coda,' a musical term for an independent and often elaborate passage introduced after the natural conclusion of a movement, and is orchestrated around the central image of the 'weak old voice' (134). The key phrase, 'it says,' is employed with various combinations which all lead to the fundamental duality of Texts for Nothing – the alienation of self from language. The impersonal 'it' construction strikingly places in relief the irreconcilable opposites (being and nothing, words and silence, and time and timelessness) which have prevented a successful operation of the imaginative process from 'Text 3' onwards. Although the 'narrator' (if such a word can now be legitimately used) states that 'there is nothing but a voice murmuring a trace' (137), it is important to note that after the first mention of a first-person pronoun there is an inexorable movement towards an intermingling of first-person and 'it' forms – 'it's ended, we're ended who never were' (139). The 'last images' (139) of 'Text 13' derive a great deal of their effectiveness from a contrapuntal opposition with those of 'Text 1.' The literalization of metaphor in the opening piece is reversed in the last. Joe Breem's knife, for example, has become a metaphor for an essential opposition within language: 'the screaming silence of no's knife in yes's wound' (139). While the first narrator was plagued by nature, 'the cold is eating me, the wet too' (77), the last one is tormented by having to use a language that is a stain on the silence: 'unslakable infinity of remorse delving ever deeper in its bite, at having to hear, having to say' (139). The 'all is noise' (77) of 'Text 1' has become a murmur that trails off into the silence that follows the end of this last 'Text.' Whereas the first narrator could follow 'all the voices, all the parts' (77), there is now, through the 'it' construction, an objectification of the gulf between the voice and the self. The birth of the image in 'Text 1' ('we seem to be more than one ... gathered together for life') has finally led to an aesthetic based on the extinction of all signs of life.

'The Vulture' aesthetic of 'Text 1' accepted the paradoxical conjunction of the claims of reason and imagination as the centre of art, and embraced the idea that reality lies in the process of becoming. 'Text 13' replaces this balance with a series of opposites which are felt to constitute a whole, but can only be expressed within the logic of language as contradictions: 'It's not true, yes, it's true and it's not true, there is silence and there is not silence, there is no one and there is someone, nothing prevents anything' (139). The narrator's incantatory denunciation of the voice does not, however, finally convince him that there is only a self that is one with the void that language obviously cannot express. There is a 'no one' that is still somehow inexplicably connected with a 'someone.'

'Text 13' should not be regarded as an example of Beckett trying to implement the aesthetic of nothingness in 'Three Dialogues,' for it is, if anything, a criticism of those views. The echoing of phrases from 'Three Dialogues' in the last 'Text' suggests that Beckett was consciously drawing a comparison. The manifesto speaks of the 'dream of an art unresentful of its insuperable indigence and too proud for the farce of giving and receiving';[18] 'Text 13' speaks of the 'end of dream ... the end of the farce of making and the silencing of silence' (139). Beckett declared at the end of 'Three Dialogues' that he would not circumvent the 'fidelity of failure' by turning it into 'an expressive act, even if only of itself, of its impossibility, of its obligation.'[19] Yet this is just what he has done in the 'silencing of the silence' in the last half of *Texts for Nothing*. The variation on the phrase from 'Three Dialogues' in 'Text 13' is a recognition on his part of the rhetoric of failure. Even failure can become a habit, which is anathema in Beckett's theory of art. The Unnamable said, 'I don't mind failing, it's a pleasure, but I want silence' (310). The narrators of *Texts for Nothing* do mind failing, it's become a habit, they want being. Beckett has not been able 'to submit wholly to the incoercible absence of relation.'[20] To do so would make it impossible to write at all. However dislocated and turned against itself, language survives; there is still an 'it' that murmurs.

The relationship between metaphor (which effects a connection between disparate entities) and logic (which presents basic differences as contradictions) is a central issue in *Texts for Nothing*. Although *Texts for Nothing* possess an abundance of metaphors whereby aspects of one object would be carried over to another object, so that the second object is spoken of as if it were the first, the whole metaphorical process of 'transference' (referred to throughout the 'Texts' as a 'departure') is denounced as 'only voices, only lies.' The metaphorical process is called into doubt because Beckett is aware of the equal and opposing force of logic which denies such a synthesis. The self is depicted as both a static thing in the void and as a part of the process of life. How can the two dimensions be united? The absence of a true relation between above and below cripples the normal work of metaphor. Even the deictics above and below are spatial metaphors that do not accurately picture the position of the self.

Texts for Nothing exhibit the salient characteristics of Roman Jakobson's concept of the 'similarity disorder' in which the normal functioning of metaphor is severely impaired. The incredible profusion of metaphors only serves to underscore the failure to relate below with above. For example: the narrator of 'Text 11,' in a desperate effort to locate the position of the self and the voice, proposes a series of possible metaphorical identifications:

Or it's in the head, like a minute time switch, a second time switch or it's like a patch of sea, under the passing lighthouse beam, a passing patch of sea under the passing beam. Vile words to make me believe I'm here, and that I have a head, and a voice, a head believing this, then that, then nothing more, neither in itself, nor in anything else, but a head with a voice belonging to it, or to others, other heads, as if there were two heads, as if there were one head, or headless, a headless voice, but a voice. (128)

This passage should be compared with similar ones dealing with a proliferation of metonymic detail ('Text 3,' for example). In both instances, metaphor and metonymy remain separate worlds in themselves. Neither linguistic operation is able to grasp the essence of the reality it tries to convey. The resultant defect in the capacity of naming is a failure of metalanguage, the inability to use language in order to talk meaningfully about itself. The narrator of 'Text 6' cries out, 'with what words shall I name my unnamable words?' (105). Aristotle, who, 'Text 10' says, 'knew everything' (94), believed that 'midway between the unintelligible and the common place, it is metaphor which produces knowledge.'[21] In *Texts for Nothing*, metaphor is suspended between the unintelligible and the common place and reveals the impossibility of attaining knowledge.

A further characteristic of the similarity disorder is that 'words with an inherent reference to the context like pronouns and prenominal adverbs, and words serving mainly to construct the context such as connections and auxiliaries, are particularly prone to survive ... whereas key words may be dropped or superseded by abstract anaphoric substitutes.'[22] This is an apt description of the prose in 'Text 4' in which the futile attempt to reconcile via logic various conceptions of the self results in a total disruption of the semantic, meaning-giving role of language and produces only formal interrelationships of words in a context. 'Text 4' also illustrates that it is not possible to do away completely with metaphor without having recourse to metaphor. As the Unnamable astutely remarked: 'it's entirely a matter of voices, no other metaphor is appropriate' (325). In 'Text 4,' however, no subject, no pronoun accepts similarity with the voice. Instead of a substitution set in which terms are meaningfully interchangeable, there is an involuted syntax and a labyrinthine series of pronouns which lack any defining context.

In the similarity disorder, 'the main subordinating agent of the sentence, namely the subject, tends to be omitted ... Sentences are conceived of as elliptical sequels to be supplied from antecedent sentences uttered.'[23] The subject as a grammatical category is not omitted in *Texts for Nothing*, but, in what amounts to an omission in the ontological sense, it is replaced by vague unnamed entities, usually indefinite pronouns. There is in 'Text 9,' for example, an omission of the subject as unspecified pronouns replace references to a determinate reality: 'it's not that either, but something else, some other thing, or the first back again, or still the same, always the same thing.' 'Text 13' is the prime example of sentences employed as elliptical sequels to previous ones. The very last sentence of all is composed of a series of clauses which only constitute a whole with the addition of the formulaic phrases, 'it says, it murmurs.' To break out of the rhetoric of failure and to discover new connections within language that will allow for an affirmation of the self which has 'fallen into fiction' is a guiding theme in Beckett's post-trilogy texts. *Texts for Nothing* is an important and unjustly neglected first step towards a confirmation of the Orphic vision of an engagement of the imagination with the world.

3

Rhetoric and the Sublime in *From an Abandoned Work*

Written in 1954–5, *From an Abandoned Work* is Beckett's only published prose work between *Texts for Nothing* and *How It Is*. Set apart from the stories, texts and residua of *No's Knife* (1967), *From an Abandoned Work* seems to be a fragment which even Beckett found difficult to identify with either his earlier or subsequent experiments. However, this view needs to be modified in the light of the collection entitled *Têtes-Mortes* which was published at the same time as *No's Knife*. *D'un ouvrage abandonné* appears there with the residual pieces. Perhaps it is best to see the work as pointing both backwards and forwards; above all, this odd fragment makes it clear that the development of Beckett's prose is by no means straightforward.

In *From an Abandoned Work* the narrator tries to counteract an obsessive concern with the intractable problem of origins which so dominated the trilogy and *Texts for Nothing* by reverting to a number of aesthetic tenets first elaborated in the poem 'Alba' (1931) and in the unpublished novel 'Dream of Fair to Middling Women' (1932). But the failure of this narrative strategy finally compels the old man who is ostensibly recounting trivial and unrelated incidents from his distant past to confront once again the perplexing problem of creating a fictional identify for himself. The abortive ending of this neglected text underlines the fact that an impasse encountered in preceding works has once again undermined the very continuation of the narrative. No wonder Beckett said he abandoned the work because 'there was simply nothing more to be said.'[1] It had already been said many times before: the confused rhetoric of fiction inherited from 'The Vulture' aesthetic has yet again forestalled a solution to the 'sublime' question of the narrator's being.

'Alba' represents an alternative mode of transcendence to that which

Beckett pursued from *Murphy* to *Texts for Nothing*. It avoids the dangers of the descent into 'the dark gulf'[2] by restricting itself to a restructuring of the surface reality – 'the tempest of emblems.'[3] The poem strives to place 'the white plane of music' between the self and the cosmos with all its contingent spiritual and moral dilemmas ('and Dante and the Logos and all strata and mysteries'); the whiteness and music are employed to blank out the rituals of being in time represented by the endless unveiling of the sun. As in *From an Abandoned Work*, there is a movement in 'Alba' from the particular (the woman whose name expresses her essential whiteness) to the general (whiteness itself – the 'plane' and 'sheet'):

> whose beauty shall be a sheet before me
> a statement of itself drawn across the tempest of emblems
> so that there is no sun and no unveiling
> and no host
> only I and then the sheet
> and bulk dead

From an Abandoned Work appears at first to be only an ironic version of this transcendence, since it begins with one more unveiling – 'Up bright and early that day.'[4] In place of the white goddess 'Alba,' there is the 'helpless love' of the narrator's mother, 'white and so thin' (140); instead of the beauty which is 'a statement of itself' there is the figure of the mother, who is 'always changing.'[5]

The ideal tautology ('a statement of itself') obviously cannot be fashioned when there are a multiplicity of terms which appear totally unrelated. The focal image of the story (which is more properly seen as a series of digressions) is the white mother 'waving and fluttering and swaying in and out of the window' (140). The narrator is frustrated by the fact that all his encounters with whiteness (with the exception of his dream animals, 'white mostly' [142]) are part of the 'tempest of emblems' – his mother, the white horse, the stoats. A quintessential vision of whiteness is denied him. Alba does not come 'before morning' to erect a 'sheet' between self and world. While there is no need in 'Alba' to continue the journey, since 'there is no sun and no unveiling,' in *From an Abandoned Work* a negative version of this 'no unveiling' serves to emphasize just how much this narrator is still trapped within a repetitive cycle: 'Not wet really, but dripping, everything dripping, the day might rise, did it, no, drip drip all day long, *no sun*, no change of light, dim all day, and still, not a breath, till night, then black, and a little wind, I saw some stars, as I neared home' (146, italics mine). 'Before morning you shall be here,' says the poem; because no such loved one ever appears in *From an Abandoned Work* the 'I' must continue on his travels: 'I shall fall as I go along and stay down or curl up for the nights as usual among the rocks and *before morning be gone*' (145, italics mine).

The 'I' still harbours the dream of a state of perfect peace: 'a long unbroken time without before or after, light or dark, from or towards or at, the old half-knowledge of when and where gone, and of what ...' (148). There is, however, no hint in *From an Abandoned Work* that life in the flux is actually tending towards the ideal stasis of 'all going, until nothing' (148). Sleeping among the rocks is the closest approximation of this state of quietude to be found in the work. Beckett first used the motif in 'Dream of Fair to Middling Women' in a passage which relates the loss of stillness with anger:

Nobody can hold it. Nobody can live here and hold it. Only the spirit of the troubadour, rapt in a niche of rock, huddled and withdrawn forever if no prayer go up for him *raccolta a se*, like a lion. And without anger. It is a poor anger that rises when the stillness is broken, our anger, the poor anger of the world that life cannot be still, that living things cannot be active quietly, that the neighbour is not a moon, slow wax and wane of phases, changeless in a tranquility of changes. (21)

The troubadour/vagabond of *From an Abandoned Work* cannot remain hidden among the rocks since he is unable to compose an aubade ('Alba' is etymologically cognate with aube) to end all unveiling. It is precisely the absence of changelessness 'in a tranquility of changes' which exacerbates the violent feelings he mentions in the opening sentences. Anticipating the erratic way in which the day will end ('blue and sun again a second, then night' [139]), he is compelled to stop and seek out all those things which violate his sense of order and stillness, including even relatively immobile things – 'snail, slug or worm' (139). His repugnance at motion of any sort is particularly ironic, of course, when we compare it with his own erratic movements – 'with me all is slow, and then these flashes, or gushes' (142).

The prose paraphrase of 'Alba' in 'Dream of Fair to Middling Women' makes explicit the association of whiteness and stillness that is so prominent in *From an Abandoned Work*: 'Plane of white music, warpless music expunging the tempest of emblems, calm womb of dawn whelping no sun, no lichen of sun-rising in its candid parapets, still flat white music, alb of timeless light. It is a blade before me, it is a sail of bleached silk on a shore, impassive statement of itself drawn across the strata and symbols, lamina of peace for my eyes and my brain slave of my eyes, pressing and pouring itself whiteness and music through blindness into the limp mind' (162). In *From an Abandoned Work*, the narrator is unable to fuse his ideal vision of whiteness with either stillness or music. The 'music' of his words contradicts the 'stillness' of an ideal whiteness: the often beautiful rhythms of the words are based on a motion that is at cross-purposes with the pure whiteness he would ideally desire to apprehend. The words that express whiteness are referential – almost ludicrously so in the context of a would-be beatific vision: the mother, the horse, the stoats, the slugs. The 'tempest of emblems' cannot be a 'statement of itself' since this narrator (unlike the lyrical poet of 'Alba') is distanced in space and time from his narration.

The failure of the different aspects of the narratorial 'I' to coincide in a single indissoluble unity results in rages far removed from the 'impassive statement' of which 'Dream' speaks. The rages produce a 'really blinding' effect, quite opposite to the blindness of the 'limp mind' as it experiences a blanking of consciousness in the approach to a transcendent state: 'All well then for a time, just the violence and then this white horse, when suddenly I flew into a most savage rage, really blinding. Now why this sudden rage I really don't know, these sudden rages, they made my life a misery' (141). The suppression is by means of what 'Dream' termed 'the violent voiding and blanking of his mind so that the gush was quelled' (2). But the 'blanking' process is much less effective in *From an Abandoned Work* and leads to more drastic measures being taken. Here the metaphors of 'voiding' and 'blanking' are taken crudely and literally: 'I tried to get relief by beating my head against something' (141–2).

What is wrong, what is this something that recurrently forces itself into the narrator's consciousness and drives him into rages? At the first occurrence, the narrator denies any knowledge of the phenomenon: 'why this sudden rage I really don't know.' But the strange episode upon which the text ends suggests that the narrator does indeed know what is wrong, and does not want to admit it: 'Extraordinary still over the land, and in me too all quite still, a coincidence, why the curses were pouring out of me I do not know, no, that is a foolish thing to say, and the lashing about with the stick, what possessed me mild and weak to be doing that, as I struggled along' (148). The cause of the rage is a recurrence of the 'fall into fiction,' the original loss of peace that is endlessly repeated throughout Beckett's works of the trilogy period.

Throughout *From an Abandoned Work*, the narrator tries to resist the pull towards story or coherent narration, as is most simply seen in the concentration upon images of himself which are widely distant from each other in time ('skipping hundreds and even thousands of days in a way which I could not at the time' [145]). Somewhat in the manner of 'Dream' the narrator tries to manipulate these memories and images in a way that prevents the formation of a unified narrative. In 'Dream' the narrative fell apart because the author could not coerce his characters into performing predetermined roles: they refused to be 'pings' who would 'squawk on tune.' The recalcitrance of the characters was, however, also a means of releasing creative energy, since the author was not seeking to write a work 'strong on architechtonics,' but striving to express the freedom of the creative consciousness in its attempts to mirror 'the passional movements of the mind charted in light and darkness.' The catharsis of creative energy in 'Dream' prevents the frustration that leads to the 'poor anger' of *From an Abandoned Work*: 'The mind suddenly entombed, then active in an anger and a rhapsody of energy, in a scurrying and plunging towards exitus, such is the mode and factor of the creative integrity, its proton, incommunicable; but there, insistent, invisible rat, fidgeting behind the astral incoherence of the art surface' ('Dream', 13). The narrator of *From an Abandoned Work* is always conscious of his lack of 'creative integrity,' since his 'I' is only a fabrication or 'figment.' The narrator is plagued by 'these awful fidgets[6] I have always had' (147), and his restless movements are determined by an awareness that there is no 'exitus' for a fictional being. Instead of a 'rhapsody of energy' there is only the 'I' pouring out 'filthy language' (148) and madly beating the bracken with his stick. In the struggle for authority the fiction is a helpless victim of impotent rages. 'Did I ever kill anyone?' (144), he asks himself; the answer must be no: a fiction cannot kill anyone except another fiction, and how can you kill a fiction except by creating another fiction to replace it?[7]

To be born as a fiction is to be given a voice. The thoughts of an ending which torment the narrator are stated as not belonging to him – 'not mine, no matter, shame upon me' (143). But the phrase 'my voice' is used twice (143) to suggest an interrelationship the narrator cannot clearly convey as it depends upon a simultaneous acceptance and rejection of the voice – 'and the sound of my voice all day long muttering the same old things I don't listen to, not even mine it was at the end of the day' (143). The important passage on his 'reward' (in which he envisages a state of unbroken time where 'there was never anything, never can be, life and death all nothing' [148]) still admits the presence of a voice: 'only a voice dreaming and droning on all around, that is something, the voice that was once in your mouth.'

Why, we must ask ourselves, is a situation resembling that found in 'Text 13' ('Whose voice, no one's, there is no one, there's a voice without a mouth') presented as a fitting end to the fictional process, a just reward? It is desired by the narrator because it would be an ending to sweep away the pretence that he possesses his own voice when he knows (the 'horrid,' 'awful' thoughts) that he is only a mouthpiece for the Author's unfathomable ends. Such a reward would be preferable to 'this night here among the rocks' where there are 'perhaps just moments here and there still, this little sound perhaps now that I don't understand' (147). As long as he is constrained to perform as a fiction, he will have to try to understand this 'little sound.' To salvage at least a pretence of his own being, the narrator must resist the full power of the pull towards fiction by relating incidents 'so bygone they can be told.' His reasoning is that these ancient memories could not possibly be mistaken for his actual situation which lies somewhere between the incidents narrated and the longed-for release of a 'voice dreaming and droning on all around' without his participation.

Detailed analysis of the last section of *From an Abandoned Work* will show that the emergence of 'The Vulture' aesthetic raises once again questions about the relationships between the different aspects of the voice, in which the role of Balfe[8] (anagram of fable), whom this narrator meets on the last day of his journey, is bound to be central, since only by the means of a story can the voice be unified.

The work ends with a 'rage,' analogous to that earlier said to be 'like a great wind,' a common trope for the sublime moment with its 'divine afflatus' or inspiration. It is interesting to find Barbara Hardy commenting on how Beckett's 'natural images frequently approach the sublime,' and saying of *From an Abandoned Work* that it 'even presents a scene (almost but not quite sublime) of nature's vastness, in the striking sentence, "One day I told him about Milton's cosmology, away up in the mountains we were, resting against a huge rock, looking out to sea, that impressed him greatly." '[9] Hardy has clearly located the sublime in the wrong elements of this sentence; the truly sublime element is Milton's cosmology, the literary expression of the bridge between the ways of God and man. Hardy's failure to recognize this results in her misinterpreting the conclusion of the work: 'a cruel nature ... joins monstrously at the end, to confirm the abandonment.'[10] Hardy is here reading Beckett much too literally, as if he were a nineteenth-century naturalist. Throughout the text, the narrator has referred to the difficulty of getting properly settled in a specific location, and the intensive use of deictics has expressed this stylistically: 'day after day, out, in, round, back, in, like leaves turning' (148). The narrator even imagines himself in hell, cursing his parents, a parodic version of Lucifer's fall, and an archetype of the romantic sublime. A subsequent, more realistic vision of the after life – 'just under the surface I shall be, altogether at first, then separate and drift, through all the earth ...' (145) – further confuses the distinction between art and reality: 'Where did I get it, from a dream, or a book read in a nook when a boy, or a word overheard as I went along ...' 'Leaves turning' and 'book read in a nook' remind the reader that the journey is framed throughout by the metaphor of world and book and that the question of getting in position ultimately concerns the relationship between the narrator and his narration. When the narrator comes to 'this night here among the rocks,' he is in possession of 'my two books, the little and the big' (147), where the little may be regarded as the narrator's own story[11] and the big as the story of the world. The narrator's problem is to unite these two stories so that the self is meaningfully related to the whole. The two books mentioned by name, the Bible and Milton's epic, achieved, as *From an Abandoned Work* very clearly does not, precisely this synthesis.

The last scene in *From an Abandoned Work* is in fact one of Beckett's most inventive revisions of one of the most sublime moments in literature: Dante's ascent of the purgatorial mountain to the Terrestrial Paradise. Careful repetition and variation of phrases from previous works of Beckett where this motif has been used alert the reader to its presence here. In his 'Belacqua fantasy,' Murphy imagined 'he would have a long time lying there dreaming ... before the toil up hill to Paradise.' Later, Mercier and Camier's 'toil up hill' takes place 'unsuspected[ly] ... imperceptibly'; later still the narrator of 'Text 1' begins *in medias res* at 'the top, very flat, of a mountain'; still later the narrator of *From an Abandoned Work* leaves home and 'the next thing I was up in the bracken' (148). This narrator's sudden transposition is directly preceded by his own version of the 'Belacqua fantasy' – 'only a voice dreaming and droning on all around.' But the Paradise this narrator finds himself in offers even less solace than those of his predecessors. As 'Text 1' showed, a series of temporal and spatial dislocations occur when the self enters that zone of creative consciousness represented by the Terrestrial Paradise: 'All mingles, times and tenses, now I'm here still, soon I won't be here yet, toiling up the slope, or in the bracken by the wood' (78). To forestall an investigation of these problems, the 'I' of *From an Abandoned Work* follows the advice of the narrator of *Mercier and Camier* who, after describing the sleep of the two old men, comments, 'Here would be the place to make an end' (103).

The narrator of *From an Abandoned Work* knows that failure to heed this advice would lead again to the incredibly complex investigations of the trilogy and *Texts for Nothing*. He knows that the 'extraordinary still over the land, and in me too all quite still' (which would seem to satisfy his quest for stillness) is really only the 'dead calm' at the heart of which will only be another frenzied search for the meaning of 'here, and me, and being.' This inner stillness prompts a rage that manifests itself both verbally and physically ('my stick making the drops fly and cursing, filthy language, the same words over and over'). Beckett's Terrestrial Paradise is not (as Beckett considered Dante's to be) 'the carriage entrance to a Paradise that is not terrestrial.' The description of the ferns, stalks, and bracken emphasizes just how down-to-earth Beckett's version of Dante's sublime is. Dante's Paradise 'with its static lifelessness' is the only place in which the narrator could find his ideal of 'all things still and rooted,' but he is definitely still 'on this earth that is a purgatory.' In 'Dante ... Bruno . Vico .. Joyce,' Beckett stated that the purgatorial cycle was perpetuated by the opposition of 'any pair of large contrary human factors.' *From an Abandoned Work* reveals that these 'contrary factors' are art and life: the 'vicious circle of humanity' is inextricably compounded with the vicious circle of fiction-making. As a result of this opposition, Beckett, in his 'last word about the purgatories,' says: 'the explosion duly takes place and the machine proceeds.' In *From an Abandoned Work*, the explosion or 'flood of movement and vitality'[12] has become a rage. The 'I' who doubles as both author and character can no longer hold the two parts of the creative act together. The fable ends with the buffoon wildly thrashing about with his stick, while the narrator remains at some undefined further remove from the text proper. The question of voice has indeed become incredibly complex since 'Assumption': somewhere behind the narrator's dreaming resides the Author-organist whose 'dreaming and droning' is the real reason for the creation of this text.

In Chapter 7 of *Mercier and Camier* and in the first of the *Texts for Nothing*, Beckett combined his variants of the Terrestrial Paradise with

'The Vulture' aesthetic, because only by means of the latter could he deal with the complex questions of identity raised by the former. In *From an Abandoned Work*, the narrator, realizing the inefficacy of 'The Vulture' aesthetic, refuses to play this game of fiction-making. The 'white plane' of 'Alba' has failed to shield him from art and life: 'and Dante and the Logos and all strata and mysteries' are still very much in evidence in the final scene. Although the narrator cannot deny their presence, he can (and does) refuse to deal with the problems they raise. The proferred synthesis of the Terrestrial Paradise motif with that of 'The Vulture' is no longer viable; it merely serves to underline the conflict between fiction and being felt throughout the work. The narration and the narrator, the big book and the little book, are not truly identified in an ontological sense; they are at best only tenuously and perilously joined by a literary equation which (in its present form) is quite unable to serve the quest for an authentic mode of being.[13] The work ends in an abandonment, a resigned acceptance of an apparently insuperable dualism – 'just went on, my body doing its best without me.'

New fables of identity must be found whereby the self can believe in metaphors for his own voice. The state of 'being over' will never be attained until the multiple questions of being have been satisfactorily answered. An abandonment is no solution: the relationship between abandoner and abandonee remains. This unjustly neglected work reminds us once again of Beckett's need for a radical reappraisal of the whole problem of fiction and being. Without an abandonment of the quest for an absolute transcendence, there will indeed be nothing more to say, only more repetition, more regression and more rhetoric – with no possibility of ever obtaining a new conception of the sublime that sees man's transcendence in his acceptance of being in the world.[14] To convey this vision a new language will have to be invented. From the 'decay of eloquence'[15] Beckett must seek the 'carrion' of words necessary for the self's being. The problem has become particularly urgent by the time of *From an Abandoned Work* because another temptation towards non-being has surfaced in this work. As early as 'Alba' and 'Dream,' the colour white has offered a way of blanking out the relationship between self and world, author and character. In the works after *How It Is*, there is a major conflict between the hunger for whiteness, *'une couleur si intense qu'elle a dévoré toutes les couleurs,'*[16] and the hunger for words that will validate being. The problem of voice is truly 'revised' and 'corrected' in *How It Is*, the first fragment of which in English was entitled 'From an *Unabandoned* Work' (italics mine).

4

Rituals of Syntax in *How It Is*

How It Is (1964) explores in revolutionary new ways the relationships between author and character, art and life and, ultimately, language and being. The essential drama of *How It Is* involves a struggle for being which turns decisively upon the issue of the ontological status of fiction, that is, what being can a character actually be said to possess? Previous discussions have revealed that a narrator who participates in language as fiction (as distinct from language as being) is extremely self-conscious about how his stories are distanced from the real self, and instead expressive only of an essential 'otherness.' The following discussion of *How It Is* will show that only when the character as 'narrator/narrated'[1] takes possession of the 'voice' and proceeds as if it were his own do his words take on a meaning beyond the purely formal contrivances necessary for the fabrication of a text. This bizarre fictional world in which the narrator crawls tortuously through an excremental underground containing, so we are told, a great chain of victims and torturers, each supplied with his own sack of provisions, etc., is fundamentally concerned with a far more strange and profound question than those spuriously raised by the grotesque literary paraphernalia. *How It Is* details the struggle of the narrator, trapped in an absurdly logical fictional world, to authenticate his historical being by breaking away from the formal structures imposed by the authorial voice.

Despite periodic disclaimers to the contrary, this narrator does accept the need for some type of relationship with the voice, thus avoiding the proliferation of indeterminate pronoun references which characterized the most difficult sections of *The Unnamable* and *Texts for Nothing*. The initial rejection of the 'ancient voice in me not mine'[2] has to be carefully distinguished from apparently similar ones made by his predecessors.

For although the narrator of *How It Is* seems at first to accept the role assigned him – 'no more searching not even for a language meet for me meet for here no more searching' (17) – he later makes a vital qualification: 'when shall I say weak enough later later some day weak as me a voice of my own' (35). This narrator does finally discover 'a voice of my own,' and thereby does radically transform the problem of fictional being which has led to an impasse in earlier texts.

The authorial voice is, however, primarily interested in writing a perfectly ordered fiction in which the characters are simply convenient ploys. But this most recent character creates more problems than the author of 'Dream' or *Murphy* could ever have anticipated. Although the dictatorial authorial voice still wishes to create a literary world 'strong on architechtonics' in which everything falls neatly into its preordained position, the narrator's 'weak' voice has other designs. Ironically enough, he gains an important measure of independence because of an inability to hear properly the authorial voice; words are 'ill-heard ill-recorded ill-understood' (139).[3] Since he is only able to grasp fragments, 'bits and scraps' of the discourse, he is, in effect, able to edit the voice and manipulate the words towards his own ends. As a result, *How It Is* is the first major example of the 'proper syntax of weakness' which Beckett deemed necessary if being is to be let into literature.

Many critics have rather simplistically adopted Beckett's statements to Tom Driver (1961) about 'accommodating the chaos' in order to support their formalist readings of *How It Is* and the following residual works.[4] A careful reading of Beckett's statement in context reveals, however, a much more complex and challenging dilemma: the conclusion that 'the form itself becomes a preoccupation, because it exists as a problem separate from the material it accommodates' *follows* the crucial insight that 'there will be new form, and ... this form will be of such a type that it admits the chaos and does not try to say that the chaos is really something else.'[5] But the form of *How It Is* does indeed try to say that the crawling creator is 'something else,' namely a mere cipher in a highly formalized literary construction. The 'narrator/narrated' is struggling against such authoritarian impositions of form in order to discover new patterns or rituals which might validate his own being, a quest which, in Beckett's own words, is 'ontospeleological'[6] in nature, necessitating an excavation beneath the surface of language to locate the bases of being itself. In *Man's Rage for Chaos*, Morse Peckham points out a creative paradox of human behaviour: the drive for order which enables man to cope with his environment loses its value when the primary interest is to correct orientation – 'to use an old expression the drive to order is also a drive to get stuck in the mud.'[7]

The narrator/narrated's quest for a language 'weak as me a voice of my own' is not, of course, gained simply by an abandonment or variation of normal sentence patterns. Intertwined with his weak voice is the strong voice of the author who is trying to impose a perfect structure on the 'mess' the narrator finds himself in. This conflict of interests is evident in the ritualistic nature of the word patterns of How It Is. Both the formal and ontological aspects of language are suggested in ritual: as well as designating the prescribed order of performing an action (with the connotation of a tendency towards excessive formalism), ritual can also refer to the effort to invoke a presence, to create a meaningful universe in which the self has a unique role to play. The second verset comments on both these needs. 'voice once without quaqua on all sides then in me when the panting stops tell me again finish telling me invocation' (4). Invocation is traditionally a calling upon God in prayer, and an appeal to the Muse for inspiration. Although both senses are ironically present in How It Is, this invocation refers more literally to the voice the narrator hears inside his head and the 'scraps' which he must work with to invoke his own being. The voice of the narrator in How It Is challenges the 'present formulation' of the authorial voice in which everything is meticulously, if ridiculously, organized, right down to the placement of sacks, can-openers, victims, scribes et al. If the rituals of syntax can impart a belief in the narrator's own being and yet also allow for the formal completion of the literary act with its emphasis upon order and form, Beckett will have accommodated the ontology of the fiction in a truly revolutionary modus vivendi.

The hunger instinct occupies a prominent position in this quest for being. An early declaration – 'no appetite a crumb of tunny then mouldy eat mouldy no need to worry I won't die I'll never die of hunger' (8) – is later varied to make explicit the relationship between words and hunger: 'a murmur a few mouldy old reliables' (95). But there is a drastic alteration of the implications of the hunger drive in How It Is that serves to set the novel apart from earlier works. Hunger is here identified with the voice of the author whose craving is for a perfectly ordered work. For the narrator, however, eating has become a meaningless ritual. The distribution of the sacks full of hermetically sealed tins of fish has made any search for food unnecessary. Towards the end of part three the narrator speculates upon the origins and significance of this allotment of provisions. If the fictional 'as-if' of the sacks is accepted, the voice will inevitably be imputed to a God-Author figure who pre-ordains every event within his creation: 'if we are to be possible our couplings journeys and abandons need of one not one of us an intelligence somewhere a love who all along the track at the right places according as we need them deposits our sacks' (137-8). The final rejection of an 'other' responsible for his well-being enables the narrator to break away from the would-be perfectly ordered fictional world and to declare the freedom of his own voice.

This fundamental change in attitude towards the nature of hunger can be most effectively illustrated by showing how the parable of 'The Vulture' – Beckett's most important model of the creative process – is modified in order to serve new ends. All the key elements of the poem are reworked in *How It Is*. The most significant variation is the change in point of view; the process of artistic genesis is now told by the 'prone,' and the narrator drags his hunger (as symbolized by the sack) through the cloacal wastes which have become his 'shell of sky and earth': 'then within the panting stops ten seconds fifteen seconds in the little chamber all bone-white if there were a light oakum of old words ill-heard ill-murmured that murmur those murmurs' (134). The author/voice has grown tired of dealing with the labyrinthine complexities contingent upon the implementation of the organic syntheses of 'The Vulture' aesthetic. Fed up with this disgusting spectacle in which the question of the self is hopelessly confused, the author/voice of *How It Is* has opted for the imposition of a purely formal order, the old dream of a 'chain-chant solo of cause and effect.'[8]

In the absence of a vulture-artist to give him life, the narrator must take on this function himself. However committed he may be to the formal order, the authorial voice cannot deny the narrator's participation in 'the voice,' the words which constitute *How It Is*. If the underground crawler can formulate his own being, the author-character problem may be solved in a radically new way. Each will be able then to have his own being without raising the insoluble problems of the subject-object dichotomy of author and character that has plagued all the narrators since at least *Mercier and Camier* and *Stories*. Certain conditions favour this new conception of the creative act. The last line of the poem, 'till hunger earth and sky be offal,' takes on new meaning in *How It Is*. Hunger, earth, and sky have become 'offal' in the sense that they are all identified with the mud or shit. Moreover, word-hunger has also become 'offal' – the scraps of the voice which the narrator manages to grasp. From the interaction of the mud and the voice the narrator must validate his being by creating a 'tissue' or script that will serve his purposes.

A full understanding of the central episode with Pim is dependent upon an awareness of this fundamental realignment of the creative process in *How It Is*. The physical nature of the creative act evident throughout Beckett's work is nowhere else so grossly visualized as in part two of *How It Is*. What seems a horrific vision of personal relationships is mitigated on the aesthetic plane by the fact that this is patently self-torture. As early as the middle of part one, it is stressed that Pim does not exist. Pim is the creative aspect of the self that can only be brought to life by the suffering that leads to communication. Although the ritualistic torture appears simply gratuitous and mechanical, this is merely the 'artisanal' dimension of the creative process and in no way accounts for the words that are emitted by the 'miraculous flesh' (51). Beckett has not renounced the anti-behaviourist stance of *Proust* in order to embrace a simplistic theory of stimuli-response. Indeed, *How It Is* savagely parodies the naturalist 'worshipping the offal of experience, prostrate before the epidermis.'

The grotesque coupling with Pim involves not so much ritual torture as rituals of syntax: 'and what but words could be involved in the case of Pim' (64). One of the most important features of these rituals of syntax concerns the interchangeability of different aspects of the self: 'I let him know that I too Pim my name Pim' (60); 'the day comes I come to the day Bom comes YOU BOM me Bom ME BOM you Bom we Bom' (76). Not until one is 'tortured' is the possession of a voice possible. In this regard it is important to note that the narrator, especially in part one, refers to his own words as 'soundless' (21), 'imprecations no sound' (40). Only when the narrator is brought to life by self-torture will he have a voice. This explains why there are two cries, Pim's voiced cry and the narrator's 'mute cry.'[9] The whole Pim episode shows the narrator applying to himself, in a strange but identifiable manner, the vulture aesthetic which the author/voice, obsessed with 'architechtonics,' would deny at all costs. The author/voice gratuitously tortures the narrator as it is concerned primarily with using him as a medium for the elaboration of an image having only formal and aesthetic properties. If the narrator can, however, convert the words he hears into his own, he will give voice to his 'mute cry' and be able to 'take up [his] life and walk.'

Until this ritual of being can be enacted, the temptation simply to lapse into states of unconsciousness is prevented by another ritual action: the use of the sack. The sack, to which more attention is given than to any other object in *How It Is*, is the key factor in creating the 'realistic' details or 'connexions' (30) of the underground journey. The first description of the sack employs a language with concrete metonymic details which contrasts markedly with the opening more abstract comments on the nature of the voice: 'the sack sole good sole possession coal-sack to the feel small or medium five stone six stone wet jute I clutch it it drips in the present but long past long gone vast stretch of time the beginning this life first sign very first of life' (8).[10] At last there is something solid to cling to. The phrase 'that hangs together,' which is used to comment on the plausibility of the various aspects of plot machinery, has its source in the original allocation of a sack to the narrator. Once an object is mentioned a host of other 'connexions' necessarily follows. The sack is still regarded as 'the crux of the whole affair' (122), to use the words of *Mercier and Camier*. But in *How It Is* the linguistic reality of 'sack' is never lost sight of and is given as much recognition as its more obvious physical qualities: 'my sack a possession this word faintly hissing brief void and finally apposition anomaly anomaly a sack' (17).

To halt the decline of the faltering imagination at the start of part three, the narrator turns in desperation to the sack:

a sack bravo colour of mud in the mud quick say a sack colour of its surroundings having assumed it always had it it's one or the other seek no further what else that thing could possibly be so many things say sack old word first to come one syllable k at the end seek no other all would vanish a sack that will do the word the thing it's a possible thing in this world so little possible yes world what more can you ask a possible thing see it name it name it see it enough now rest I'll be back no alternative some day (105)

As 'sole variable' (17), it is invested with an excess of symbolic meaning that ultimately causes the word to 'burst,' losing any meaning beyond that found in the formal rituals of syntax. This sack, full of the 'suffering of the ages' (38),[11] is identified with all the other components of the subterranean world. The equation 'my sack my life' (35) is amply illustrated. It contains the food; when empty it is filled with mud or else the narrator crawls inside; it takes the place of a loved one ('turn to it again clasp it to me again say to it thou thou' [17]); it is even compared to Pim ('he can't repel me it's like my sack when I had it still' [55]). The 'big scene of the sack' (36) gradually displaces the little scenes of life in the light. The narrator is reduced to the subordinate role of a 'utility-man' (52), the actor of the smallest parts.

The tribute accorded to the sack is a recognition well-deserved by the many leading roles it plays: 'no the truth is this sack I always said so this sack for us here is something more than a larder than a pillow for the head than a friend to turn to a thing to embrace a surface to cover with kisses something far more' (66). What is this 'something more'? The 'more,' the extra dimension of significance, is simply that the sack is 'something' that has consented to being named, and the name remains as a talismanic invocation of this would-be reality even after it has virtually disappeared as a physical entity: 'so many other things too so often imagined never named never could useful necessary beautiful to the feel all I was given present formulation such ancient things all gone but the cord a burst sack a cord I say it as I hear it murmur it to the mud old sack old cord you remain' (46). The sack is still, however, an anomaly. Whilst it is the possession whereby the narrator continues to convince himself of his reality, the 'pillow of old words' associated with the sack is inadequate for dealing with the new journey towards being. The self cannot be articulated by the material possessions which enclose it. The sack is only a means to an end; the arrival of Pim necessitates the 'death of the sack' (38). To free himself from his fictional status, the narrator must rid himself of the sack, the staple stock-in-trade of the writer trying to deny the 'deeper need.'[12] In *Mercier and Camier*, Beckett saw 'how worn out and thread-bare was the conventional language of cunning literary artificers,'[13] and deprived his characters of their sacks, thus leading the sack-less Mercier and Camier to the zone of fictional creativity. The voice as author in *How It Is* would, however, prefer to reverse his former decision and willingly accept the conventional order conferred by the sacks. But the narrator will not go along with this plan and divests himself of the sack. He has seen through the trick – 'the light through the worn thread strains' (88). He tears shreds from the sack but the 'oakum of old words' (134) will not mask any longer the awareness of his lack of being.

The 'last reasonings' of part three make a final concerted effort to explain this business of the sacks. If the concept of sacks is maintained, a God-Author figure responsible for their distribution and the 'perpetual revictualling narrations' (148) will need to be invoked. To accept this supreme fiction is to absolve the self of commitment to its own world. Only the self as 'sole responsible' can sustain a fundamental belief in a world disclosing 'thereness.' The difficulty of breaking the habitual identification of self with objects is very neatly caught in the narrator's words after he has rejected the whole business of sacks: 'only me in any case yes alone yes in the mud yes the dark yes that holds yes the mud and the dark hold yes nothing to regret there no with my sack no I beg your pardon no no sack either no not even a sack with me no' (146). At the end of the novel (which is truly the beginning), the character spurns the sacks and takes control of his only real possession, the voice which, though it can never actually be owned, can be made to serve his needs as soon as he acts as if it were his.

The acceptance of the voice as his own does not immediately confer being on the narrator: the voice is still that of a fiction until it is directed to someone or something other than itself. The authorial source of the voice was self-reflexively regarded as both mouth and ear – 'who listens to himself and who when he lends his ear to our murmur does no more than lend it to a story of his own devising' (139). If the voice the narrator takes as his own is in turn directed solely towards himself, it too will become a meaningless set of rituals. For the voice to gain a referential significance beyond a merely formal interrelationship with other words, it must be directed towards something: the mud.

The relationship between the voice and the mud cannot be regarded simply in terms of the subject-object paradigm. What makes possible the connections between the two is a commitment by the self to a world design in which he is able to choose his own fictions or 'as-if' transformations. Although mud and voice remain separate entities, they are accommodated by the being conferred on them by the narrator who accepts his 'thereness.' The mud (in contrast to the sacks which are burdened with an excess of meaning bordering on the allegorical) possesses a rich potential for the development of meanings implicit in the text.[14] The mud appears as an extension or projection of the self rather than as an imposition upon the self as was the case with the sacks which were finally deemed expendable. A series of images identify the mud with the body of the narrator: the 'yawning' or opening of the mud to reveal images of the world above is coordinated with the opening of the narrator's mouth and eyes as he struggles to state himself and see himself. The problem of discriminating between the real and the imaginary is exemplified by the mud, not resolved by it. At one point the mud is 'splendid' (26); at another it is 'hog's wallow' (69). An authentic self must take into account the truth expressed in both these views. To fail to do so would, ironically enough, lead to the same debilitating concept of purity being applied to the mud as had previously been applied to the silence in *The Unnamable* and *Texts for Nothing*, thereby emptying the word of meaning. The spectre of purity does in fact appear briefly in *How It Is*, where the idea of a 'pure mud' (81) leads inevitably to a God figure who can end all the journeys and abandons 'and nothing on its surface ever more to sully it' (142). This is reminiscent of Malone's description of his narrative approach: 'to look at myself as I am ... After that mud-bath I shall be better able to endure a world unsullied by my presence' (189). *How It Is* underlines that a world cannot exist unless it is 'sullied' by a presence who is engaged in determining the truth of the fictions by which reality is apprehended.

The revelation of being requires a fixed 'there' in conjunction with a 'now,' that is, an 'is' that can relate past and future. If *How It Is* does lead to an affirmation of the being of the fiction, it must be shown that the novel concludes with this 'is.' The state of 'no time' is apparent in the qualifications made in relation to the original plan to follow a conventional temporal progression: 'the natural order more or less ... not all a selection natural order vast tracts of time' (7). This scheme is constantly violated. As a fiction, the narrator does not possess time; words like now, after, before do not belong to him: 'various times mixed up in my head all the various times before during after vast tracts of time' (107). There is even the suggestion that the book can be read in reverse order: 'once studied from left to right its course can be retraced from right to left no objection' (132). All these problems stem from the fact that the so-called natural order is actually a division of a 'single eternity' (89). The narrator's timelessness is only an ironic version of the being outside time traditionally attributed to the Deity. All conventional units of chronometry lose significance within the context of infinity, where the very large and the very small add up to the same total: 'vast stretch of time before Pim with Pim vast tracts of time a few minutes on and off added up vast stretch eternity same scale of magnitude nothing there almost nothing' (104). As the subsequent developments in part three illustrate, an 'almost nothing' can, if endlessly repeated, approach infinity. Hence the conflation of periods of time of vastly disproportionate size. While the narrator avowedly has 'centuries of time' (14), he is concerned 'not to lose a second' (26). An 'old infant' (96) with an 'ageless body' (92), he will only have being in time when the eternal present of narrative time ceases and a new historical time begins.

The anticipation of last things is continually frustrated by the return to a timeless present. All three sections begin with an attempt to establish a past that will lay the foundation for a normal progression of time. This problem is most clearly seen in part two in which the narrator begins 'here then at last part two where I still have to say how it was' (51). The words of the voice are here in the present tense and prevent any permanent consignment of an action to the past: 'his cries continue that clinches it this won't work in the past either I'll never have a past never had' (54); 'the song ascends in the present it's off again in the present' (63). The narrator tries to convince himself of his temporality by comparing the quality of his present state with previous ones (the time before Pim is, for example, seen as 'heroic'[15] from the vantage point of part two). Repetitions of the banality, 'good moments,' negate any genuine appreciation of what is good. Within a timeless present, everything is actually of equal value, that is to say, of no value. Value belongs to the world above where things can be measured and time moves inexorably towards death; below there is only a formal sense of the future tense: a 'boundless futurity' (137) is equivalent to a timeless present.

The last few pages of *How It Is* will radically reverse this situation. The movement towards the historical realm at the conclusion of *How It Is* is evident in two opposed capitalized phrases. The first, 'NEVER SUFFERED' (146), denies the historical reality of the narrator, but makes a kind of literal sense – after all, how can a fiction, made of an arrangement of words, actually suffer? The second, 'I SHALL DIE,' reflects a countermovement towards historical being in time. As Robert Champigny in *The Ontology of the Narrative* points out: 'I shall die one day. But, historically, I cannot consider my life as accomplished, since I am not yet dead. To adopt a historical perspective, I have to project my death into the future.'[16] At this point the full significance of the title begins to emerge. Concerned throughout with achieving an end, *How It Is* is really only a beginning, as the French title *Comment c'est* punningly suggests. The very last words of the novel, 'how it is,' have a dual significance. Whilst they obviously refer to the literary artifact that has been assembled before the reader's eyes, they also contain an 'is' pregnant with potential meaning because the narrator is breaking away from the structures that have determined his fictional status. The vulture aesthetic is vitally present in the last pages and helps the reader to realize imaginatively that the voice now also belongs to the narrator. The narrator likens himself to the 'prone who must soon take up their life and walk': 'flat on my belly yes in the mud yes the dark yes nothing to emend there no the arms spread yes like a cross no answer LIKE A CROSS no answer YES OR NO yes' (146). Christ on the cross is the human moving towards the divine. The narrator with his cross of words is the fictional being moving towards historical being. In the former, the flesh is becoming word; in the latter, the word is becoming flesh.

The language of *How It Is*, characterized as it is by 'losses,' effects, however, an affirmation of being which was not possible with the classical rhetoric of *Texts for Nothing*. Why is the 'weakened' language of *How It Is* actually stronger than that of its predecessors? The answer lies ultimately in the change of vision that allows for a new evaluation of the terms strength and weakness. The juxtaposition of the terms appears initially in Beckett's writing as little more than an opportunity for a neatly turned phrase: Belacqua's 'strong weakness for oxymoron,' Murphy as a 'hank of Apollonian asthenia.'[17] In *Molloy*, strength and weakness are brought together in a new kind of creative synthesis: 'Where did I get this access of vigour! From my weakness perhaps' (84), The Unnamable's last words, 'I'll go on' echo the last words of 'The End,' 'the strength to on on.'[18] In 'Text 13', the voice is 'weaker,' although still characterised by the strength of its syntax which prevents either a return to the world or a plunge into the void. The change of vision in *How It Is* allows for a radically new relationship between strength and weakness. The strength of language is now recognized to be in its referential qualities; the weakness now sought concerns the breakdown of the subject-predicate structure of the sentence in order that the words used in depicting different aspects of the self can unite to affirm the body of language and the body of the world. At first it may appear as if strength and weakness are still irreconcilable; after all, the very first page announces that the narrator is 'too weak' even to question his identity. His weakness is usually related to the problem of time – 'all this vast stretch of time all that beyond my strength' (66); words like 'day and night' are 'too strong' because they draw him towards a being in time which his fictional status makes it impossible to accept. The development of the 'syntax of weakness' in *How It Is* paradoxically involves the narrator's ability to accept the strength of words with their tropism towards being.

Before the syntax of weakness can be articulated, the self in the world below has to undermine or weaken the pseudo-realistic language which would stifle his own voice. The 'underground' language seems at first to be based solely on contiguity, the interlocking of realistic detail. The 'demented particulars' (13) and 'petty cash of current events' (178) of *Murphy*, 'the wealth of filthy circumstance' (65) of Molloy's narrative are inconsequential when compared to the realistic impulse of *How It Is*.

The outrageous parody of the extent to which fiction will go to create an illusion of verisimilitude that will gull the reader is a major source of humour in a work that is more or less accurately described by the phrase 'deterioration of the sense of humour' (18).[19] There are 'things things always' (7), and a novel that proposes to tell it 'how it is' must find ways of accommodating them. 'Details for the sake of something' (33): 'something' turns out to be the consistency of the narrative itself.

While the narrator is able to congratulate himself on how the 'connexions' fit together, he is ironically enough barely able to 'cling to species.'[20] The details are easily manipulated with regard to contiguity in space but contiguity in time poses much greater difficulties, as the persistent interjection 'something wrong there' underlines. Still, the assembly of details in a fiction does have certain advantages, one of the most gratifying being the remarkable way words can act as agents of a self-fulfilling prophesy: 'better a big ordinary watch complete with heavy chain he holds it tight in his fist my index worms through the clenched fingers and says big ordinary watch with heavy chain' (58). These circumstantial details are finally only a confirmation of the formal status of the fiction. Even this formal 'pseudo-realism' is stretched to the breaking point in part three in which the amount of detail proliferates to a point at which it becomes almost unmanageable. Just as the profusion of metaphors in *Texts for Nothing* pointed to a failure of metaphor as a means of connecting above with below, the profusion of metonymy in *How It Is* points to the failure to fit all the would-be realistic detail of below into a meaningful whole.

Essential characteristics of what Roman Jakobson calls the 'contiguity disorder' are evident throughout *How It Is*. Jakobson's analyses show how the contiguity disorder diminishes the extent and variety of sentences: 'The syntactical rules organizing words into a higher unit are lost; this loss, called agrammatism, causes degeneration of the sentence into a mere "word heap".'[21] Some qualification of Jakobson's view is, of course, required, since, if the discourse is at times aptly described as 'midget blurts grammar past' (76), the versets never become 'mere word heaps.' While the stringing together of phrases has in large part replaced the sentence, the sentence is still a recognizable feature, especially in part one where the narrative flows quite easily even upon a first reading. Repetition of these set sentences in the rest of the book reveals their status as 'ready-made sentences,' the use of which Jakobson states as characteristic of the contiguity disorder.[22]

Another major characteristic of the contiguity disorder is that 'ties of grammatical coordination and subordination, whether concord or government, are dissolved. As might be expected, words endowed with purely grammatical functions, like conjunctions, prepositions, pronouns, and articles disappear first, giving rise to the so-called "telegraphic style." The less a word depends grammatically on the context the stronger is its tenacity in the speech ...'[23] This agrammatism (or syntax of weakness) is most easily seen when set in contrast with a passage from *Texts for Nothing*:

... who is this raving now, pah there are voices everywhere, ears everywhere, one who speaks saying, without ceasing to speak, Who's speaking?, and one who hears mute, uncomprehending far from all, and bodies everywhere, bent, fixed, where my prospects must be just as good, just as poor, as in the firstcomer. ('Text 12, 134)

rags of life in the light I hear and don't deny don't believe don't say any more who is speaking that's not said any more it must have ceased to be of interest but words like now before Pim no no that's not said only mine my words mine alone (21)

The example from *How It Is* does not completely dissolve 'the ties of grammatical coordination and subordination,' since, quite clearly, if punctuation ('no commas not a second for reflection' [70]) were added, the passage would be very similar to the one from 'Text 12.' But in the contiguity disorder 'the kernel subject word is least destructible,'[24] whereas in the similarity disorder the subject is most easily lost. The passage from 'Text 12' lacks a subject in an ontological sense; the section from *How It Is* asserts possession ('my words').

The contiguity disorder predictably results in a counter-movement towards similarity and metaphor, the meaning giving dimension of language. When the narrator accepts the voice, the identification is, of course, metaphorical. The Unnamable's words are still relevant here: 'it's all a question of voices, no other metaphor is appropriate.' The acceptance of the voice by the narrator enables the words to combine through him by virtue of an intertwining of their meanings, through the trading of metaphor. Self and world are, in the last analysis, the 'tenor' and 'vehicle' of any metaphorical equation. What matters is not the manifest meaning of each word and each image, but the lateral relations, the kinship patterns that are implicated in their transfer and exchanges. An important word in this connection is family, which has a merely formulaic role until the conclusion when the relationship between the various word families (most significantly 'day and night family') becomes possible. A lateral relationship has, for example, been established among the different contexts in which the key word 'sole' is employed:

sack sole good (8)
me sole elect (13)
sleep sole variable (36)
to the sole and that there may be white on white (110)
me ... sole responsible (144)

The last phrase does not so much supersede the previous ones as draw them into a more meaningful perspective within the encompassing concept of being. The words 'sole responsible' do not resolve the long wrangle over the existence of others in favour of solipsism as the words 'me sole elect' tend to do. There is no such thing as private property or private salvation in language; everything is socialized.

Strange as it may at first seem, *How It Is* could be regarded as a highly original postmodernist exploration of the nature of the sublime. It is, of course, a radical departure from many of the rhetorical techniques that writers such as Longinus say are required for the art of the sublime. While *How It Is* 'lacks the arrangement of words in due order'[25] in the structure of the sentence, it does have the 'proper syntax of weakness' necessary for the invocation of being. The poetic ellipses of *How It Is* are, however, in Longinus's own terms, 'properly used' for they are not 'entirely broken up into fragments and thus frittered away.'[26] Beneath Longinus's sources of sublimity, 'there lies as a common foundation the command of language, without which nothing worthwhile can be done.'[27] The ultimate paradox of *How It Is* is that the syntax of weakness enables the narrator to find a language that has the strength to command being. Longinus's final source of grandeur, and the one that includes all the rest, is 'the total effect resulting from dignity and elevation.'[28] Crawling through the slime, the narrator of *How It Is* may appear as yet another embodiment of the modern fascination with the grotesque and absurd. But, at the end of his journey, he has gained his own voice and is ready to 'take up [his] life and walk' – the rituals of syntax have succeeded in their invocation of being.

5

The Nature and Art of Love in *Enough*

Critics have tended to regard *Enough* (1967) as a beautifully crafted anomaly that is peripheral to more experimental works like *Imagination Dead Imagine* and *Ping* which are somehow felt to deal more uncompromisingly and accurately with Beckett's vision of 'how it is.'[1] Beckett's own startled reaction to the text – 'I don't know what came over me'[2] is often cited in support of the argument that *Enough* lies outside the main development of his work in the post-*How It Is* period. On the contrary, *Enough*, along with *Lessness*, *Still* and *Worstward Ho*, constitutes a central line of development, one in which there is a progressive movement towards an Orphic series of balances between word and world that would vindicate language as a means of being. The natural order of *How It Is* – journey, couple, abandon – is complemented in an affirmative way by the art of the narrator in *Enough*. The solitary journey after the abandonment by her companion leads the old woman to a realm where language allows for a reconciliation with her mentor/lover via a new understanding of the nature of her art and craft.

Through the medium of art this 'Eurydice' has regained her lost one by herself becoming an 'Orpheus.'[3] The victory is, however, realistically qualified: she is now old, 'entering night I have kinds of gleams in my skull, stony ground, but not entirely.'[4] The golden age of *saturna regna* has obviously passed; Chronos, that 'double-headed monster of damnation and salvation,'[5] now holds sway. The cycle is, however, regenerative, for it is from the union of Eros and Night that the heavens and earth emerge from Chaos in Orphic cosmology. Other elements in the text are uniquely Orphic and contribute to the vital theme of reconciliation. The only exclamation mark directly attributed to the old man is brought forth by the sighting of the Lyre or the Swan.[6] The Lyre is the sign of Orpheus and contains Vega, 'the falling vulture.' If Orpheus was finally raised to the stars, the myth retains as its abiding centre the creative juxtaposition of the self's yearning for an assumption with an awareness of man's terrestrial nature. The amazing statement 'We lived on flowers. So much for sustenance' (159) is much more, however, than a declaration of an ideal Orphic harmony with nature. The mere tabulation of Orphic elements in *Enough* does not explain how the text develops the major insights of *How It Is*. The most important clues for an answer to this question are found in the last paragraph. 'He halted and *without having to stoop* caught up a handful of petals ... They had on the whole a *calming action* ... Nothing but the *two of us dragging* through the flowers' (159, italics mine). Instead of the solitary vulture 'dragging his hunger through the sky,' there are 'two of us dragging through the flowers.' The narrator's head is still 'my skull shell of sky and earth,' but it is no longer a scavenger of corpses. Hunger in the fundamental physical sense is no longer a motivating factor and can be quickly passed over. For the old man there is no need to 'stoop.' Instead of an 'eye ravening patient in the haggard vulture face' ('Text 1' [77]), there is the human and sentimental – 'I felt on my eye a glint of blue bloodshot apparently affected' (156). The notion of calm (never fully achieved in 'The Calmative' and subsequent works) has replaced the inhuman intensity and patience of 'The Vulture' revision of 'Text 1.' The calmness is due to the fact that the intervention of a third person, a vulture-artist, is not required; the couple have already 'take[n] up their life and walk[ed].' Nor is this narrator any longer 'mocked by a tissue that may not serve / till hunger earth and sky be offal.' The last words of her story are 'enough my old breasts feel his old hands.' Beckett's own consternation before *Enough* is more readily understandable if rephrased – 'I know what did not come over me.' The vulture-artist as a predatory force compelling fictions to take up roles that hopelessly complicate the questions of being and authority is conspicuously absent in *Enough*.

As outlined in the prologue paragraph on her 'art and craft,' *Enough* is an investigation of the reciprocal nature of the voice/pen relationship. Sometimes her voice is too weak to continue, at other times the 'pen stops.' A syntax of weakness is not important here, as it was in *How It Is*, for there is no internecine warfare between different functions of the voice or language. The point is that her way of writing follows her ex-companion's way of speaking: 'He sometimes halted without saying anything. Either he had finally nothing to say or while having something to say he finally decided not to say it' (56). Art does, in this instance, imitate nature. The crucial difference is that now a reversal of roles has occurred: the woman has replaced the man as the central speaker. The artistic situation is more complex than the natural one. Whereas she always willingly complied with her companion's need to communicate ('I bowed down as usual to save him having to repeat himself' [156]), the pen, representing the craftsman aspect of her new role as artist, often balks at recording her utterances. The first paragraph comments elliptically on the fact that the piece of writing called *Enough* is the product of the times at which 'art and craft' were able to combine their efforts. Numerous silences are to be assumed during the creation of the work. What is new is the emphasis upon the need for cooperation between art and craft in order to overcome the tautology 'too much silence is too much. In Three Dialogues,' Beckett asserted 'to be an artist is to fail, as no other dare fail, that failure is his world and to shrink from it is desertion, art and craft, good housekeeping, living.'[7] There is something to express in *Enough*. Although only briefly discussed, art and craft are not here contemptuously dismissed. They are the means of expressing the central theme – living: 'it is then I shall have lived or never' (154). Furthermore, it is the 'good housekeeping' of the last sentences which affirms that art need not be identified with failure but can successfully recapture in the present the essence of all that has gone before and cannot be forgotten – 'Now I'll wipe out everything but the flowers' (159).[8]

The assertion of a single unified voice rather than a list of competing 'I's allows for new possibilities in the depiction of the creative act (or, perhaps more accurately, allows Beckett to succeed in the more traditional ways he has denied himself). It is fitting that in this most traditional of Beckett's works, a pastoral of love lost and regained, the time-honoured description of tropes as flowers should receive such prominence. There is an acceptance of the ability of language to express, a notion which Beckett has challenged since 'Dream of Fair to Middling Women.' *Enough* could be seen as a direct refutation of this passage from Beckett's first novel: 'The experience of my readers shall be between the phrases, in the silence, communicated by intervals, not the terms, of the statement, *between the flowers that cannot coexist*, the antithetical (nothing so simple as the antithetical) seasons of words, his experience shall be the menace, the miracle, the memory of an unspeakable trajectory' (9, italics mine). Compare this with the remarkable passage in *Enough* where the flowers do coexist: 'I see the flowers at my feet[9] and it's the others I see.

Those we trod down with equal step. It is true they are the same' (156). The power of her art is evidently capable of literally transporting her back in time so that the present vision of the flowers is superimposed or merged with the earlier. The first paragraph alerted the reader to 'silence' and 'intervals.' But the experience of the reader in *Enough* is not primarily focused 'between the phrases.' One of the reasons for the absence of commas may in fact be to forestall any possibilities of experiencing the pauses between phrases as being more important then 'the terms of the statement.' The miracle of *Enough* is the memory of a speakable trajectory. However painful the revisiting of the scene of her abandonment may be, it is capable of being voiced for it contains a truth that is uniquely human.

For Beckett to achieve this statement in *Enough* – and it is, despite its distinctive qualities, the expression of the oldest hope of the writer, that art can somehow redeem the withering of time – his whole conception of the question of authority had to be radically altered. For the trajectory to be expressed effectively the 'I' must have a sense of integrity, an ontological status that has been absent since at least 'The Calmative.' *How It Is* played a decisive role in moving towards a resolution of the conflict between an Author-God figure and the narratorial 'I' who strives to create a language of his own suitable for the expression of his own being. Each must be allowed to go his own way or form a partnership that serves both their needs. *Enough* carries further this parable of authority with its need for a demarcation of responsibilities. When under the tutelage of the nameless man who has guided her since her sixth year, there is obviously no questioning of authority since she effaces herself before 'all his desires and needs' (153). Once forced upon her own, all that has gone before has to be forgotten. She has a free hand. The implications of her forced freedom are apparent in her second statement on aesthetics: 'All I know comes from him. I won't repeat this apropos of all my bits of knowledge. The art of combining is not my fault. It's a curse from above. For the rest I would suggest not guilty' (154). 'Curse from above' is intriguingly ambiguous: it can be associated with both her companion (who originally appears as a giant towering above her) and with a Divine punishment (the words 'mansion above' immediately precede this paragraph). The ambiguity serves to conflate the role of the man (who appears in many ways to have authored her life) and the role of God. In any case, the 'curse' is a sentence of excommunication which paradoxically necessitates another form of communication. A force above has compelled her against her will to be free. Away from the range of the man's voice, she must pursue her own 'art of combining.' Whether or not it is her fault, she must accept responsibility for her words.[10]

Even in Beckett's works, where there is increasingly less social background in any directly recognizable sense, Enough stands out in that there is not even a mention of the family situation. It is laconically stated that the woman 'belonged to an entirely different generation': 'I cannot have been more than six when he took me by the hand. Barely emerging from childhood. But it didn't take me long to emerge altogether' (154). If their relationship begins as that of a father and daughter, it quickly blossoms into that of man and wife. But the central focus of Enough is upon their separation, the man's command for her to depart. Without discounting the simple human aspects of this abandonment, it is also possible to see the separation as a parable of the origins of a writer who is compelled to make her way after being guided by a precursor, a 'spiritual father,' the relationship to whom is for the artist necessarily 'sensuous.'

The new concept of authority that results is in fact a most traditional one, and one moreover that Beckett has up to this point rejected. A fundamental requirement of the new view is to see the father-complex with its contingent problem of origins as an essentially religious function that has formerly been misinterpreted in terms of biological and family relationships.[11] There is no longer the Unnamable's paranoiac fascinations with notions of forebears and the vexed image of 'windows lit at night' – indications that the 'I' is haunted by the thought of his true author's inaccessibility – nor is there the compulsion to spy on this deus absconditus as at the beginning of How It Is: 'life in the light first image some creature or other I watched him after my fashion from afar through my spy-glass sidelong in mirrors through windows at night first image' (9). In contrast, the old man in Enough is fascinated by the beauty of the 'mansions above': 'In order from time to time to enjoy the sky he resorted to a little round mirror. Having misted it with his breath and polished it on his calf he looked in it for the constellations' (157). The spirit and the flesh are balanced once God the Father is transformed from a tyrannical authoritarian figure to a source of creativity with which the individual can willingly identify himself. His 'broken paternosters' are 'poured out to the flowers at his feet' (155). The narrator also gives voice to a paternoster when she makes the flowers coexist. Enough is a religious work in the sense Beckett termed the only intelligible one in Proust – it is both an assumption and an annuciation. If the old man is approaching an assumption, the woman is the chosen vehicle of the annunciation, the announcement of an incarnation.

In *Enough*, there is no 'anxiety of influence.' Harold Bloom's thesis is that the newcomer (or 'ephebe') is enslaved by his precursor's system and is consequently engaged in a lifelong struggle to establish his own authority. Such a 'victory' can only be gained at great cost, for it is a repression of various ways and solutions arrived at in the tradition the newcomer must strive to rewrite. Bloom puts forward the view that 'every forgotten precursor becomes a giant of the imagination,'[12] that is, a force which must be opposed by the would-be 'strong poet,' whether he consciously admits it or not. The determining factor in the 'ephebe's fantasia' is to 'quest antithetically enough, and live to beget yourself.'[13] What is forgotten in *Enough* is not the teachings of the old man but the very attempt to beget oneself. The memory of the precursor may be distorted in *Enough*, but it is not forgotten in the sense of repressed with its host of pejorative Freudian implications. The old man does at first appear as a 'giant' (154), doubtlessly of her own imagination. The stress is, however, upon her progress towards an equal status – 'it didn't take me long to emerge altogether' (154). They walk with 'equal step' (156). During the last period of their travels there is no conflict of generations – 'That part of it at least we were to make past of together' (156).

As an artist, she has to remember that her position is no longer subservient. He is on his 'last legs' (153; 158); 'I had only to straighten up to be head and shoulders above him' (156). In marked contrast to Bloom's theory, the narrator's 'misinterpretations' in *Enough* are not designed to resolve a competition for ascendancy with the precursor. Rather they are intended as a means of reconciling her own needs with a sense of indebtedness to her mentor whose voice is now 'spent' (158). Her words now carry on this tradition and, as it is a living tradition, there will necessarily be changes in emphasis. These changes do not, however, destroy the essential continuity. Tradition no longer carries the burden of guilt. 'The art of combining is not my fault. It's a curse from above. For the rest I would suggest not guilty' (154). What, then, is to be made of the obsession with 'disgrace'? It is important to note that at one point she refers to 'the day of my supposed disgrace' (157). Taken in conjunction with the verdict of 'not guilty' and the various ways the scene of the disgrace is presented (on a 'crest' and then 'on a flat in a great calm'), it appears that she is aware of her innocence and as an artist cannot hide from her new obligations by invoking the always convenient myth of an original sin. If the disgrace is a fall from favour, it is a fortunate fall, as it forces her to create her own values and meaning from the past.

The new integration of self is realistically founded upon a prior period of losses and suffering. The Golden Age landscape seeks by means of a mythological language to become a beatific vision of divine perfection. The weather was 'eternally mild' and 'windless' (158). The 'endless equinox' is paralleled by another state of equilibrium – 'we walked in a half sleep' (159). But the celebration of the Golden Age is not simply a wistful and deluded reconstruction of a time when everlasting spring prevailed and the earth provided for a man's needs. On the contrary, its meaning is wholly metaphorical, 'as if the earth had come to rest in spring' (158). The 'as-if' nature of this pastoral 'soulscape'[14] – the fluctuation between trope and assertion of an imminent reality – is especially apparent in the description of the 'mounds.' For while it is stated that the old man 'clamoured for the steepest slopes,' the narrator insists 'we were not in the mountains however' (157). The patently contradictory geographical details indicate an attempt to grasp meta-phorically the idea of the Terrestrial Paradise where conventional desig-nations of time and space are no longer adequate. This confusion is cleared up in the final paragraph – 'Now I'll wipe out everything but the flowers. No more rain. No more mounds.' Whereas previous works (most notably 'Text 1' and *From an Abandoned Work*) invoked a variant of 'The Vulture' aesthetic in a vain attempt to resolve the confusion engendered by the Terrestrial Paradise motif, the problem is solved here by the narrator herself. In the final paragraph, the 'I'-'he' dualism that has predominated gives way to a 'we' and "us" that creates a new collective unity. The 'my' and 'his' of the last sentence convey a whole-ness that has not been present since the 'his' and 'my' of the first two lines of 'The Vulture.'

Words are finally for this narrator also her 'only love,' but in a sense quite different from that in *From an Abandoned Work*. Since all she knows comes from the man, her words are also in a very real sense his own. Through these words combined in her own way, they do meet again in the image of the flowers that coexist. The word love is used only twice: 'he loved to climb,' 'love of the earth and flowers' thousand scents and hues' (157). Words are a whole, just as the old man, her teacher, had taught that 'anatomy is a whole' (155). Words are drawn towards the summits and towards the concreteness of the flesh with its 'cruder imperatives of an anatomical order' (157). This 'doubleness' of words was earlier pointed to in reference to the old man's 'vision' and 'sacral ruins,' words which draw together the anatomical and the prophetic. The family of words with all their connections unites the physical and spiritual, and only through a critical and poetic use of words can what Freud termed the family romance with its attendant questions of authority be successfully worked out.

'How far this was not a delusion I cannot say' (156): the narrator's doubts about the old man's vision can be applied equally to her own final vision and to the critic's interpretation of it. My reading of *Enough* is so radically at odds with the traditional views that it may appear as an idealization – a delusion. But it should be obvious at this point in my argument that I am not simply endorsing a 'pro-art'[15] stance in opposition to the 'art of failure' school of Beckett criticism – the whole question of fictional being is still, of course, highly problematical and riddled with perplexities. My more affirmative reading can, however, be accommodated by the text, if not by the more usual interpretations of Beckett's so-called pessimism, nihilism, scepticism ... It is much more difficult to discuss love than the void and the aesthetics of self-cancellation with their attendant fashionable rhetoric. For a writer who has always masked his thoughts on love the simplicity of *Enough* is overwhelming. No wonder Beckett was amazed: 'I don't know what came over me.' As the narrator of *First Love* ruefully commented, 'either you love or you don't.'[16]

The movement towards an affirmation of an Orphic relationship between language and being is also evident in the recently published *Fizzles* (1976), many of which were written in the early sixties. The Gnostic dualisms of 'Fizzle 4' ('I gave up before birth') with its rhetoric of failure and litany of hate ('he'll never say I anymore, he'll never say anything anymore ... because of me')[17] give way to the Orphic atonement of 'Fizzle 6' ('Old earth') whose opening sentence admits that all the tortuous, guilt-ridden denials of life in the world were lies: 'Old earth, no more lies, I've seen you, it was me, with my other's ravening eyes, too late.'[18] As in 'Text 1,' engagement with the concrete real is conveyed by the image of the eyes of a vulture ('des mes yeux grifanes,'[19] in the original). *Enough* is an even more affirmative development of the Orphic dimensions of 'The Vulture' aesthetic.

6

'Tempest of Emblems': Elements of Allegory and Naturalism in *All Strange Away* and *Imagination Dead Imagine*

As Georg Lukács very thoroughly points out, 'the rejection of a selective principle must lead the modernist writer to naturalism, even where the experimental form would lead one to expect the opposite,'[1] which is, for example, a valid critique of those *Texts for Nothing* in which details do not fit into an encompassing reality because of the absence of a fixed perspective, a selecting 'I.' Naturalism and allegory, ostensibly so different, can theoretically converge: allegory involves an alienation from objective reality as a result of a denial of the assumption of immanent meaning and, in turn, this tends to reduce art to naturalistic description. In *All Strange Away, Imagination Dead Imagine*, and *The Lost Ones*, Beckett's inability to reconcile the conflicting claims of the authorial voice and the 'someone' discovered in the 'place' of the imagination once again entangles his experiments with new forms with the old questions of naturalism and allegory.

The first sentences of *All Strange Away*, 'Imagination dead imagine. A place, that again. Never another question. A place, then someone in it, that again. Crawl out of the frowsy deathbed and drag it to a place to die in,'[2] describe a fundamental split between creative consciousness and the 'someone' which, if it cannot be mediated, will inevitably lead towards either naturalism or allegory. Dragged to the place of fiction or image-making, words no longer mean the same as they did in the extra-fictional, historical world. Beckett remains true to his realistic principles by declaring that in this realm words do not belong to a speaker in the same way as they do in the normal world – the 'he' discovered in the 'place' cannot speak: the phrases 'no sound', 'no true image' punctuate the text with a refrain-like insistency. The transition from one realm to another has clearly resulted in a potentially allegorical bifurcation of meaning. This is reflected in the fact that although large sections of the text are preoccupied with catalogues of physical details they singularly fail to substantiate the presence of a living being. Pseudo-naturalism cannot mediate the sundering of reality in the literary act and will only lead to what Beckett's early poem 'Alba' calls a 'tempest of emblems.'

All Strange Away, written in 1963 but not published until 1976, is an important missing-link for a critical appraisal of the subsequent residual works. While the title is really an ironic misnomer, *All Strange Away* does help to remove some of the strangeness of the works which were written after it by clearly establishing the basic issues which they attempt to elucidate. More important than the use of phrases which will figure prominently in later works (for example, the first sentence, 'Imagination dead imagine') is the delineation of a context, a set of 'signifieds,' to which the 'signs' of the later works (often regarded by critics as divorced from referents) are also drawn in the attempt to reveal the meaning of the creative act.

The work begins with Beckett's most startling opening sentence since 'The Calmative,' but startling in a very different way. In *All Strange Away*, the never explicitly named 'I' is not directly involved in the action at all. There is indeed a rejection of the earlier method of *Stories, Molloy* and *From and Abandoned Work,* in which the exercise of the imagination involved a physical engagement, 'Out of the door and down the road in the old hat and coat like after the war, no, not that again' (39). Beckett is now intent on dismissing this strategy as a clever trick that masks an essential unreality, an 'I' masquerading as both author and character. 'Imagination dead imagine' indicates an attempt to dispense with this more conventional role-playing and to substitute at last a true image of the self's predicament in the act of creation. What results, however, is a failure by the undesignated 'I' to substantiate the reality of any of the images used to portray the 'he' and his various personifications. The presence of a first person is strongly felt in the first five sentences and is further implied by the antithetical 'last person' which the character uses to refer to himself. The authorial consciousness moves to a new position, a new state of the imagination ('Crawl out of the frowsy death-bed and drag it to a place to die in'), and his hunger for words once again compels him to create 'a place, that again.' But if he fulfills the ancient command to 'take up thy bed and walk,' he refuses to 'take up [his] life and walk' in the sense that 'The Vulture' made of it, or as exemplified by the narrator of 'The Calamative' who satisfies his hunger through a story. The unnamed narrator of *All Strange Away* will admit his initial implication in the creative process but, in furthering the realistic impulse of *How It Is*, will not pretend that what is depicted after that point is literally identifiable with himself.

There is in *All Strange Away* a fundamental duality that must be recognized if the literary realities of the situation are to be apprehended: 'him' is distinct from the authorial self and stands for an ontological otherness. For Beckett, a 'he' of some sort undeniably does exist in the very nature of the creative act. But the problem is that an authorial self who refuses to admit his own identification with the 'he' cannot be sure of the nature of this strange being. The first reference to 'him' establishes the sense of doubt and tentativeness that envelops the piece, 'try for him there' (39). Logically, the 'he' should be easily located since both occupy the same space: 'no way in, no way out.' But they cannot be identified because they belong to different realms of discourse. The 'he' communicates only self-reflexively – 'talking to himself in the last person murmuring, no sound' (39). Is the suppressed 'I' trying to still the turmoil or trying to release it? For the latter to occur the 'he' must become fully human and abrogate the imposition of fictional categories such as speechlessness and timelessness – 'all being well vented as only humans can' (62). It would seem that this authorial 'I' is secretly willing to follow a course that will relieve him of this terrible paradox that is the essential strangeness of literature for Beckett. Rather than pursue the reality of the situation as outlined in the opening sentences of the work, he is drawn more and more to a formal structuring of the 'tempest of emblems,' thereby obscuring the central problems of the 'unstillable turmoil' (63). The truth is indeed stranger than fiction.

The rigid authorial control which is characteristic of the allegorical displacement of the image emerges as a geometrizing obsession: 'Call floor angles deasil a, b, c, and d and ceiling likewise e, f, g, and h, say Jolly at b and Draeger at d, lean him for rest with feet at a and head at g ...' (42). The hypostatized 'someone' has been turned into an emblem with a purely diagrammatic role (indeed the word 'Diagram' is later prominently featured in the text). The search of the 'he' for the pin, paper and shroud are obviously ornamental rather than realistic details. The problem is that these details, when they appear, do not combine to create a representative reality. Isolated from a normal human context and restricted to the inferno of the imagination ('all six planes hot when shining'), the details only serve to elaborate mental conceptions rather than a living human reality. Anatomy is definitely not the whole it was in *Enough*. Able to grasp only parts, the artist becomes a sort of vivisector-

cum-pornographer. The various positions and 'play of joints' is dominated by sexual elements: 'First face alone, lovely beyond words, leave
it at that, then deasil breasts alone, then thighs and cunt alone, then arse
and hole alone, all lovely beyond words' (43). The triteness of this
repeated phrase 'lovely beyond words' is further emphasized by a
parodic variation on a famous line of Henley's: 'he' quite literally cannot
'wince nor cry aloud' as long as he is merely an object at the disposal of
the 'fell clutch of circumstance'[3] controlled by the author.

The mute language theme debilitates even the puerile attempts at
creating a semblance of a crude physical reality – 'Imagine him kissing,
caressing, licking, sucking, fucking and buggering all this stuff, no
sound' (44). 'He' disappears and a figure called Emma becomes the
central character. The statements 'all that most clear' and 'all strange
away' refer to the descriptions of the space this character fills, but fail
to engage the question of language and being which the character's
problematical existence persistently raises. A 'he' or 'she' might be said
to exist, but until allowed to speak for themselves the language that tries
to speak of them will lack any ontological validity: 'Say again though
no real image puckered tip of left breast, leave right a mere name' (49).
Only the ability to speak will confer a true particularity on details and
make them the embodiment of a meaningful reality.

The problem of the two voices is the central topic again in the conclusion of *All Strange Away*. But here the irreconcilability of the 'He could
have shouted and could not' conundrum of 'Assumption' is clearly
regarded as a thing of the past. It is circumvented, never properly
confronted or vented: 'All gone now and never been never stilled never
voiced all back whence never sundered unstillable turmoil no sound ...'
(62–63). A 'last look' is sentimentally invoked and details of geometry
and physique are duly repeated in condensed form. In a last indulgence
of this 'amateur soliloquy' (63) in which the author unsuccessfully tries
to imagine the murmurs too faint for his mortal ears, he plays the
ventriloquist again: 'faint sighing sound for tremor of sorrow at faint
memory of a lying side by side[4] and fancy murmured dead' (65). These
last three words are in decisive contrast to the first three, 'Imagination
dead imagine.' Rather than creating a work in which a new imaginative
function could give voice to the murmurs, *All Strange Away* reveals a
reduction of the imagination to the mechanical collocations of fancy.
The gerund 'murmuring' and the present tense 'murmurs' which domi-
nate the text are only fancifully placed in the past tense in the last
sentence's 'murmured.' The tense is disingenuous in that the murmurs

have not been 'murmured' at all, but only smothered by the officious narrator's conventional fictional machinery. In his rummaging in the cube, rotunda etc., the narrator is dealing only with hearsay, unverified statements of doubtful accuracy. Only in a formal sense has anything been 'murmured.'

The question of the ontology of the fiction in *All Strange Away* turns upon the use of capitalization. The use of capitals throughout the work shows a vain attempt at establishing the reality of the 'something there' – or at least the possibility of keeping 'it' distinct from the author's narrative. The first use of capitals within a sentence establishes the rules for this new convention: 'murmuring, no sound, Now where is he, he, no, Now he is here' (39). Whenever the 'great confusion' engendered by 'no sound' appears in the discourse, a capital begins the next word to emphasize that it is not the 'he' who is really speaking. But the attempt to clarify the relationship of the two aspects of being involved in the creative act only results in further confusion. The author cannot have it both ways. The 'he' cannot be recognized as both a separate entity and a something for whom the narrator is authorized to speak. Rather than validating the 'he,' the capitalization serves ultimately to confuse further its status.

Are 'he' (and 'she') personified abstractions, allegorical agents, or real people? The fluctuation between the major and minor case finally tips the piece towards allegory and the admission of the unreality of the image. The use of *figurae* indicates the author's reluctance to employ allegorical agents: 'Since in figural interpretation one thing stands for another, since one thing represents and signifies the other, figural interpretation is "allegorical" in the widest sense. But it differs from most of the allegorical forms known to us by the historicity both of the sign and what it signifies.'[5] Giving a proper name to the 'she' (Emma) and creating a historical past ('evenings with Emma and the flights by night' [44]) does not alter the fact that the author's interpretation of the 'something there' is still essentially allegorical. Nor does the use of topical allusions, 'Pantheon at Rome or certain beehive tombs' (54), Diogenes, and Greek place-names. Christ, Mother, Praeger, and Jolly[6] may or may not have been historical entities, but within the imagination of *All Strange Away* they are only shadows on the wall. Angus Fletcher reminds us that allegories 'may have very human agents' and that 'we should make no automatic assumptions about the "unreality" of allegorical personifications': 'Such personified agents are of course intended to represent ideas, not real people; they could not, like the characters in a young author's first novel, be traced to their particular "originals." This point can be easily misunderstood – allegorical agents are real enough, however ideal their referents may be. They have what might be called an "adequate representational power." '7 In *All Strange Away*, the personifications may be intended to represent real people, but the conventions of the literary process transform them into mere abstractions. 'The allegorical hero,' Fletcher adds, 'is not so much a real person as he is a generator of other secondary personalities, which are partial aspects of himself.'8 It is this essentially conventional view of the creative process which the first sentences of *All Strange Away* challenge. The 'author' is real and cannot be simply regarded as a secondary personality. Although the 'I' that 'drags' its 'deathbed' is itself a daemonic agent of the imagination, the 'I' is not so totally possessed by this force that it can be identified with the 'he' that is being sought in this place. Hence the images in this skull completely lack Fletcher's 'adequate representational power.'

The determination of the ontological status of this 'something,' the question of whether it differs in degree or in kind from the implicit authorial 'I,' involves Beckett in confronting the old Romantic distinction between Fancy and Imagination. Imagination in *All Strange Away* is associated with the authorial presence; Fancy is associated with the occupants for whom 'She' is the 'only hope.' Imagination is pictured as a servant of the author's fantasies ('Imagine what needed,' and the desired objects appear); Fancy is the last recourse of the 'last person.' The Imagination (discounting its use in 'Imagination dead imagine') is an agent of conscious will ('some reason yet to be imagined' [47]). Employed in these ways, Beckett's Imagination and Fancy both would fall into Coleridge's category of Fancy, which is judged to be decidedly inferior to Imagination: 'Fancy, on the contrary, has no other counters to play with, but fixities and definites. The Fancy is indeed no other than a mode of Memory emancipated from the order of time and space; while it is blended with, and modified by that empirical phenomenon of the will, which we express by the word CHOICE. But equally with the ordinary memory the Fancy must receive all its materials ready made from the law of association.'9 Schemes which promise an artificial memory, says Coleridge, 'in reality can only produce confusions and debasement of the fancy.' Fancy is 'always the ape, and too often the adulterator and counterfeiter of our memory'10 (which is an apt description of the sexual fantasies in *All Strange Away*).

Instead of developing further the 'syntax of weakness' of *How It Is*, Beckett is forced back into rhetoric in *All Strange Away*. Faced with

'soundlessness,' the authorial agent of the imagination can only discourse with himself (a situation which he attributes to the 'someone' in
the 'place' – 'talking to himself in the last person'). The words continually
fall into rhetorical patterns divorced from their ostensible subject matter.
This is evident in the breakdown of the central metaphor of body and
language. The beings in the place are identified with words: 'tattered
syntaxes of Jolly and Draeger' (39), 'syntaxes upended in opposite corners' (45). There is, however, no real identification between words and
flesh (as in *How It Is*) for in this instance the body is only 'silent flesh.'
Hence a more objective attitude is taken to all this 'stuff' or 'meat.' The
segments are merely toys for the author's enjoyment, puppets with
human characteristics: 'this body hinged and crooked as only the human
man or woman living or not' (58). There is no life in the 'he' or 'she'
because they are not, as is constantly repeated, on earth, but rather
confined to the timeless zone of fiction. No wonder the flesh is 'quite
expressionless, ohs and ahs copulate cold' (52). There is in fact no
employment of the copula 'to be,' except in the often repeated phrase
that denies any being in time: 'never was.'

The central irony of *All Strange Away* is that, since the narrator cannot
detect the 'sounds too faint for mortal ears,' he increasingly formalizes
his own 'sounds' or words. In the very last sentence, the narrator tries
to impose his own formal harmony upon the work: 'all is dark' and
there is a 'simple sighing sound black vowel a' (64). But it is clear that
these projections are only perpetuated to satisfy 'old mind's sake.' The
narrator's rhetoric points to the need to satisfy his own desire for form
in spite of the 'turmoil' of 'soundlessness' which remains 'unappease-
able.' The imagined words of 'she' are even at one point criticized for
manifesting the 'tailaway so common in untrained speakers' (52). Just
before the work ends, there is a reference to 'dying fall of amateur
soliloquy' (63), but the narrator of *All Strange Away* is no amateur; he is
a very professional rhetorician. The last sentence is indeed a masterly
exposition of how to execute a 'dying fall.' But in terms of the fundamental issue of the two languages, it is indeed an 'amateur soliloquy.' The
authorial presence is in love with his own voice.

The last pages of *All Strange Away* veer away from the drama of being
that is enacted in the last pages of *How It Is* and instead focus on the
object in Emma's hand. This object ('fingers tighten as though to squeeze,
imagine later' [49]) is duly expanded upon – 'and so arrive at though
no true image at small grey punctured rubber ball such as on earth
attached to bottle of scent' (57). As Roman Jakobson has pointed out, 'It

is still insufficiently realized that it is the predominance of metonymy which underlies and actually predetermines the so-called "realistic" trend ... Following the path of contiguous relations, the realistic author metonymically digresses from the plot or the atmosphere and from the characters to the settings in space and time. He is fond of synecdochic details.'[11] The concentration on the object in Emma's hand is comparable to Jakobson's example of how Tolstoy focuses attention on Anna's hand-bag in the suicide scene, and Beckett is undoubtedly fascinated by 'synecdochic details' in *All Strange Away*. But the 'long black hair' and the 'ivory flesh,' for example, are details which are emblems which stand for the characters; they are not just the stock-in-trade of naturalistic authors. In fact, the concern with the 'rubber ball' tends naturally towards allegory rather than an authentic realism. Beckett's blatantly allegorical comments in the Schiller Production Notebook of *Krapp's Last Tape* on the rubber ball Krapp gives to the dog and the 'sin' it signifies may suggest a similar intention in *All Strange Away*.[12] But the 'grey punctured rubber ball' in this work involves a different sin. The author, in his own interest, tries to reduce all to whiteness, darkness, or greyness, and, consequently, sins against the living human and literary complexity with its irreducible admixture of darkness and light, other and self. The narrator of *All Strange Away* finally dismisses this object which (like the sack in *How It Is*) promises to take on too much allegorical value: 'So that henceforth here no other sounds than these say gone now and never were sprayer bulb or punctured rubber ball and nothing ever in that hand lightly closed on nothing' (59). The only sounds left are the imagined 'sop to mind' of the 'dead imaginings.' The pull towards allegory has been resisted. But there is a concomitant denial of any true sounds from the 'someone' in the 'place.' What remains, then, is little more than a 'tempest of emblems.'

In *Imagination Dead Imagine* (1966), naturalism in a form of pseudo-scientific objectivity checks the trend towards allegory so evident in *All Strange Away*.'[13] The authorial presence is not initially concerned with the 'strangeness' of the characters he finds in his refuge; he is more concerned with the fixing of stable points of maxima and minima. Thermodynamics has replaced the correlation of light and darkness with voice and 'no sounds' which was so important in *All Strange Away*: 'At the same time the temperature goes down, to reach its minimum, say freezing-point, at the same instant that the black is reached, which may seem strange.'[14] In the first half of the text (marked by a departure and return, 'rediscovered miraculously after what absence in perfect voids'

[163]), very little attention is given to the occupants. They are almost forgotten in the preoccupation with the dimensions and characteristics of the rotunda (and there are no sexual fantasies for this would-be scientific observer). For the reader of *All Strange Away*, what is most strange is the silence of this new place. Instead of the stuttering start of its predecessor with its 'try for him there,' everything seems established and known from the beginning. Concentration upon the rotunda allows, indeed, for a 'rotundate' style, a balanced rhetoric of ostensibly objective description. In addition to the author's words, there are only two sounds to disturb the piece: the 'rap' that produces a 'ring as in the imagination the ring of bone' and the final 'only murmur ah, no more, in this silence' (164).

The second part of the work does, however, reintroduce some of the strangeness of *All Strange Away*. This is because the focus is increasingly on the occupants: the woman is singled out for attention – 'merging in the white ground were it not for the long hair of strangely imperfect whiteness, the white body of a woman finally' (163). An important contrast is thus established between 'the perfect voids' and the 'imperfect' void of a rotunda that contains a couple.[15] There is a marked increase in unordered activity in the second visit to the rotunda. The scientific tabulation of vibrations in which 'uncertain passage is not common' (162) is replaced by the more poetic 'storm.' There is now a 'convulsive light' (164) and 'never twice the same storm' (163). The question of the 'soundless storm' referred to at the conclusion of *All Strange Away* returns, though here the narrator is not certain about the final state that the couple will find themselves in, 'the black dark for good, or the great whiteness unchanging, and if not what they are doing' (164).

The crucial distinction between the authorial presence of *All Strange Away* and that of *Imagination Dead Imagine* is that, whereas the former intermittently struggles with the question of the language and being of the 'someone' that is discovered in the creative process, his successor simply departs when the question becomes too pressing. A formal harmony is therefore salvaged, but the ultimate effect is to trivialize the fundamental literary problem that has obsessed Beckett since 'Assumption.' Whereas the death or metamorphosis at the beginning of *All Strange Away* dramatizes a short-lived attempt at clarifying the realities of the creative process without denying the existence of an external world, the situation in *Imagination Dead Imagine* is virtually the opposite: 'Island, waters, azure, verdure, one glimpse and vanished endlessly, omit' (161). Accepting that the normal fare of the imagination no longer exists ('no trace anywhere of life'), and yet compelled to imagine, the author, after an initial scepticism, takes up the challenge. The final result is 'all whiteness in the whiteness the rotunda,' an echo of the 'sole end white on white' of part three of *How It Is*. As in 'Alba,' a 'white plane' has been interjected between the self and the world.

Brian Finney interprets the 'omission' sentence thus: 'the second sentence describes naturalistic images which belong to the kind of imagination which the reader has been told to discard.'[16] Finney's use of the word naturalistic here confuses the issue because, in the literary sense of the word, it is the description of the rotunda which is naturalistic: the observer is, in fact, a naturalist 'worshipping the offal of experience.' ('Experience' is actually a key word in his calculations.) It is, moreover, a very odd kind of naturalism that does not exclude the supernatural ('rediscovered miraculously after what absence in perfect voids'). The term is definitely not much help in determining the ontological significance of the realities in *Imagination Dead Imagine*. The 'islands, waters, azure, verdure' are or were real; the 'ground, wall, vault, bodies' are now equally real. 'One glimpse' is granted to the first set; two glimpses of the 'little fabric' are vouchsafed. The rotunda itself is finally 'omitted' – 'there is nothing elsewhere, and no question now of ever finding again that white speck lost in the whiteness' (164).

The ideal alternative to this rotunda is the 'perfect void' in which there would be silence and no 'thousand little signs.' In such 'perfect voids,' the ideal tautology of art would be possible, and the 'whiteness' that obliterates all distinctions would then be like that sought in 'Alba': 'a statement of itself drawn across the tempest of emblems.' But this ideal tautology possesses only a formal significance. As in 'Alba,' the attempt at transcendence raises a host of ontological questions. How can there be 'only I and the sheet' unless the 'I' becomes a self-contained god-like being? As Beckett put it in *Proust*: 'if this mystical experience communicates an extratemporal essence, it follows that the communicant is for the moment an extratemporal being.' This is the impossible situation that the narrator of *Imagination Dead Imagine* finds himself in when he abandons the rotunda. An extratemporal being is no being at all.

The drama of the last two pages concerns the nature of the relationship between the observer and the observed, the author and his characters. The nature of the relationship between these two unquestioned realities of the literary act is ultimately a question of language and being. The narrator's contact with the occupants in the second part of the work proceeds from a geometric description to more subjective evaluations and these reach a climax with 'Only murmur ah, no more, in this silence, and the same instant for the eye of prey the infinitesimal shudder instantaneously suppressed' (164). The ambiguity of reference has produced several readings of this crucial sentence. Finney, for example, thinks that the 'ah' is spoken by the narrator, while Ruby Cohn regards the 'ah' as spoken by the couple. J.E. Dearlove places 'the burden of interpretation ... on the reader because a deceptively analytic prose refuses to mean.'[17] It is difficult to see how the sentence beginning 'Only murmur ...' could be described as 'analytic prose,' since the repetition of groups of words in mechanical fashion diminishes throughout the second part, resulting finally in this complex subjective statement which is full of potential meaning. The 'ah' is surely spoken by the narrator in lieu of some of the 'thousand little signs' that he could have recorded, and represents a more resonant emotional response that replaces his original 'pah.' But if the sound 'ah' is one of the signs, then the narrator's recording of it raises the whole question of the relationship between author and character. The 'ah' makes the observer act out of character. From a would-be neutral observer, he has turned into a vulture-artist with an 'eye of prey' that is quite alien to the whiteness of 'Alba.'

In *Imagination Dead Imagine* the couple's eyes 'at incalculable intervals suddenly open wide and gaze in unblinking exposure long beyond what is humanly possible' (163). Earlier the narrator had commented on 'pauses of varying length, from the fraction of the second to what would have seemed, in other times, other places, an eternity' (162). Entrapped in the fictional 'no time' of the imagination, the couple can indeed keep their eyes open 'beyond what is humanly possible.' The 'pale blue' of the eyes reintroduces the 'azure' that was originally 'omitted' and is one of the 'signs' that life has not truly ended. These fictions may be real, but have not been fully brought to life, are not yet fully human. For this to occur, they would have to speak. Nevertheless, an 'infinitesimal shudder' does take place, and it is a moment of living time that contrasts dramatically with the vague pseudo-scientific calculations ('say twenty seconds') and with the timelessness of 'what would have seemed ... an eternity.' While the author may prefer the 'perfect voids,' it is a fact of their coexistence in the imaginative act that, once brought together, the literary problem is one of language and being. But the narrator of *Imagination Dead Imagine* opts out of this complex situation: the shudder is 'instantaneously suppressed.'

The turmoil which the couple's existence creates is, of course, stilled by the author's departure. The 'infintesimal shudder' of communion is impossible to duplicate in the 'now' he occupies after leaving the rotunda. He has inadvertently corroborated that there is in fact a 'trace ... of life,' but he has not discovered the source of the light and heat 'of which still no trace' (163). He fails to realize that the source is ultimately himself. He is the source that links heat and light, just as he is the source that links the authorial voice and the 'voice' of the occupants. Rather than explore this 'great confusion,' he ends his narrative. Without an engagement with the real, any so-called imaginative acts are as hermetic as the 'literature of notations' of naturalism, as Beckett stated in *Proust*.[18] Once he leaves the place of the imagination, the ability to imagine is, of course, logically impossible: 'Imagination, applied – a priori – to what is absent, is exercised in vacuo and cannot tolerate the limits of the real.'[19] After he leaves, he can speak with no authority, only wonder 'what they are doing.' No Proustian 'reduplication' is now possible. The return after the first visit was itself 'miraculous.' For this narrator, a departure (even though it signifies the irrevocable death of the imagination) is preferable to remaining and attempting to make sense of the turmoil of contradictions. Has the narrator left the rotunda for Murphy's 'pure forms of commotion'? Such 'absolute freedom' is worthless if it involves an attempt to deny the necessity of art which is always occupied with the real. Moreover, pure forms do not admit to being expressed in literature. If the storm is to be weathered, the relationship between authorial voice and the voice of the other discovered in the creative act needs further investigation. If not, the turmoil will turn into a 'tempest of emblems' that is amenable to control only by means of a greater emphasis on naturalistic and allegorical elements.

7

The Nature of Allegory in
The Lost Ones, or the Quincunx
Realistically Considered / *Ping* as
a 'Hieroglyph' of 'Inspired Perception'

The Lost Ones (1966; completed by the addition of Section 15 in 1970)
may initially appear to be a type of 'closed garden' (or paradise) in which
the fictional world seems to possess an order that can be easily identified
with the world outside it. The 'cultivation' is, however, unsuccessful
and only produces a *hortus siccus* or arrangement of 'withered ones.'
Discounting the 'words of the poet' on 'nature's sanctuaries' and the
allusion to Dante's 'sun and other stars,'[1] the images not directly derived
from the cylinder itself also depict a wasteland:

The bodies brush together with a rustle of dry leaves. (8)

This desiccation of the envelope robs nudity of much of its charm as pink turns
grey and transforms into a rustling of nettles the natural succulence of flesh
against flesh. (53)

The ladders 'planted' (20) in the 'bed' (18) of the cylinder do not afford
'a way out to earth and sky' (21). The band of searchers is finally 'rooted
to the spot' (37). Nature and art are not truly compatible within this
hermetically sealed world. Or, to formulate the central issue in terms
that Beckett adopted from Proust, tree and building, the natural and
artificial, cannot both flourish within the structure of a fiction.[2]
    What is at stake in *The Lost Ones* is a determination of the relationship
between world and book. In the hermetic tradition, the world was
regarded as a book, and a series of allegorical correspondences established a realm of meaning in which the natural and artificial were
reconciled. *The Lost Ones* rewrites this equation: the book is its own
world, the cylinder is a world unto itself. What then is the reader left

with after he has 'rustled' his way through the 'dry leaves' of *The Lost Ones*? Is he confronted only by a formally self-sustaining verbal construct that tantalizingly holds out the promise of meaning, but finally forces the reader to conclude that the verbal riddles (like the cylinder 'riddled with niches' [21]) lead nowhere? This is surely not the case. *The Lost Ones* is not cut off from all realms of meaning. On the contrary, what gives life to the 'dry leaves' is a series of questions that are raised concerning the ontology of the fiction. If the dual realities of author and character cannot coexist, the authorial presence is inexorably drawn towards an allegorical form in which the characters mean what he wants them to mean. But to impose an outright allegorical form deprives the work of any life and goes against many of Beckett's most strongly held views about the integrity of the creative act. The following discussion will show that Beckett was led towards allegory as a result of the failure to find a *modus vivendi* between the narrator and the narrated.

The Lost Ones is immediately distinguished from preceding residua, *All Strange Away, Imagination Dead Imagine,* and *Enough,* in that it does not begin with a prologue describing the aesthetic that governs the creation of the work. *The Lost Ones* begins *in situ:* the abode has already been discovered or created. All that remains is a description of its workings. The cylinder and its occupants are the given realities, *les données.* A careful reading reveals that the often repeated phrase 'if this notion is maintained' never calls into question these basic realities. The word notion refers always to the question of time, and it must be emphasized that, given the cylinder or 'abode,' the narrator is willing to abide by all its rules, except those that require him to bide his time. After only ten sentences, he is ready to speculate, 'It is perhaps the end of their abode' (7). The narrator (like Beckett) is trapped by the cylinder, by the realities of his own creation or discovery. Section 15 attempts 'a way out' of this dilemma by imagining the end of the searchers. The epilogue is, however, a patent falsification of the reality of the work in the interests of a rhetorical closure that will satisfy the narrator's need for order. Once again Beckett presents two irrefutable realities – those of the author and 'others' – in an apparently irreconcilable situation.

In her discussion of allegory in *The Lost Ones,* Susan Brienza says that, although the narrator questions his own creation, 'the searchers do not dare to question the consequences of their absurd system ... and Beckett's question for the reader becomes "Do you dare to face the real conditions of your own world?"' [3] The question might more properly be rephrased as, 'does the critic dare face the real conditions of this fictional world?'

The larger question of relevance to 'our world' cannot be broached until this question is resolved. Beckett makes it a paramount point that the cylinder is not our world from which it is hermetically sealed (though, of course, narrator and reader are miraculously allowed access – 'no way in, go in,' to use the words of *Imagination Dead Imagine*). The real conditions of this fictional world involve a struggle for authority between the narrator and 'the little people' (15). In short, whose story is *The Lost Ones* to be – the story of the narrator, or the story of the inhabitants? Brienza says that the 'if' formulations 'undercut any authority the narrative may have had'[4]; but they are, in fact, the narrator's main means of asserting his authority, for only by speculating on the 'unthinkable end' can he escape from the almost timeless present in which his narrative has trapped him along with the searchers.

There is a great deal of sardonic humour in the narrator's comment. 'That a full round should be authorized is eloquent of the tolerant spirit which in the cylinder tempers discipline' (49). The narrator's own authority is anything but tolerant. Rather than put up with the indecisive nature of the quest (will pandemonium reign? will the searchers miraculously escape?), he ruthlessly jumps to the conclusion (knowing full well that 'all has not been told and never will be') that vanquishes all the inhabitants to 'cold darkness motionless flesh' (15–16). There is a price to pay, however, for winning the battle against the 'little people.' The reality of the inhabitants' world and quest is undermined by the narrator's *deus ex machina* solution. Until the last section, the narrator, although evaluating and reporting upon the system in the cylinder, does not presume to speak for its inhabitants. But in the last section he does speak for them and the price to pay is a fall into allegory. Denied a 'natural end' (61), the inhabitants are made to mean something else for the benefit of the narrator's message. The narrator has adapted the reality of the cylinder to his own system, a move that leads directly to allegory which Beckett has pejoratively termed 'a threefold intellectual operation: the construction of a message of general significance, the preparation of a fabulous form, and an exercise of considerable technical difficulty in uniting the two ...'[5]. But Beckett adds that if a myth or story is considered allegorically 'we are not obliged to accept the form in which it is cast as a statement of fact.' Throughout *The Lost Ones*, there is an implicit 'message of general significance' (the narrator's obsession with darkness and stasis) and a 'fabulous form,' the cylinder itself. But when Beckett realized that he could only remain faithful to the realities of the work by abandoning the narrator to a time without end, he opted finally (and, from the four year pause after section 14, it would seem reluctantly) for allegory. This 'exercise of considerable technical difficulty' does not, however, really succeed in uniting the 'message' and the 'fabulous form.' Consequently, the reader is definitely not obliged to accept *The Lost Ones* as a 'statement of fact.'

The narrator dogmatically asserts that 'in the cylinder alone are certitudes to be found and without nothing but mystery' (42). But the statement can only be read ironically. The question of time, for example, is surely just as much a mystery within the cylinder as it is in the world outside. Moreover, maintaining the notion that all will ultimately be vanquished does not so much demystify the nature of the quest as make it explicitly more mysterious ('mystery' comes from the Greek for closing the lips or eyes – the identifying signs of 'the vanquished'). The narrator in his conclusion shows that he is literally trying to turn the cylinder into his idea of a utopia. For the truly vanquished their surroundings no longer exist and have become a 'no where,' a negation of reality which complements the earlier assessment, 'No one looks within where none can be' (30). The 'best of all possible worlds' for the narrator of *The Lost Ones* is one in which everyone, Murphy-fashion, enters a trance that negates both the inner and outer worlds. This conclusion is undoubtedly meant as an ironic self-indictment, for it is as absurd and unwarranted a manipulation of cause and effect as anything fabricated by a Pangloss. The pretense that the final conclusion is the natural one, merely abetted and hurried on by art, is unacceptable in terms of the narrator's own description of the life in the cylinder and the possible courses it could pursue.

Until the fifteenth and final section, the most remarkable characteristic of *The Lost Ones* is its attempt to view patterns of order realistically in terms 'as far removed from the mystical as it is possible to imagine.'[6] *The Lost Ones* is, indeed, best seen as a reinterpretation of the hermetic tradition as exemplified by a work like Sir Thomas Browne's 'The Garden of Cyrus or, the Quincuncial Lozenge or Net-Work Plantations of the Ancients, Artificially, Naturally, Mystically Considered.' *The Lost Ones*, like 'The Garden of Cyrus,' takes as its fundamental principle of order the quincunx (an arrangement of five objects set so that four are at corners of a square or rectangle and the other at its centre): 'In the upper half of the wall disposed quincuncially for the sake of harmony a score of niches some connected by tunnels' (17). The quincuncial patterns of *The Lost Ones*, while similar, indeed often strikingly similar to the samples educed by Browne, have a dramatically different import.[7] For Browne, the world is 'the great Volume of nature,' and, ultimately, 'that intelligible sphere, which is the nature of God.'[8] Beckett's systematic strategy is to undercut the significance of Browne's celestial symmetries by confining them within a world hermetically sealed from nature.

Browne begins his survey with a description of the patterns of order in the gardens of the ancients, especially with reference to the arrangement of trees. And Beckett, as we have seen, ironically exploits the image of his cylinder as a 'garden.' The obvious example for Browne of the tree of knowledge in the midst of the garden of Eden is not without an ironic counterpart in Beckett's garden. Stricken rigid in the midst of the cylinder is one of the vanquished (31), a tree of non-knowing, at the centre of a quincunx formed by the other four vanquished (of which only two are described – both women – the white haired one with the child and the red haired one who serves as the north marker). The Lost Ones seems ironically to corroborate Browne's assertion of the primacy of quincuncial multiples in art: 'To omit many other analogies, in Architechtonical draughts, which art itself is founded upon fives, as having its subject, and most graceful pieces divided by this number.'[9] The total number of inhabitants (205) is based upon various multiples of the vanquished five. All bearings are taken from the woman who acts as the north, whose shape is itself a quincunx or 'fundamental decussation':[10] 'She squats against the wall with her head between her knees and her legs in her arms. The left hand clasps the right shinbone and the right the left forearm ... The left foot is crossed on the right' (56–7). An x, we might say, marks the spot.

The work is organized around multiples of fives. There are twenty niches or alcoves and fifteen ladders. The temperature falls by a 'regular variation of five degrees per second' (16). It is, however, quickly pointed out that this is 'not quite accurate,' thus creating another 'irregular quincunx.' Still there are enough examples from the thousand which the narrator assures us exist to confirm a quincuncial disposition 'for the sake of harmony.' Like Browne's examples, they seem to 'neatly declare how nature geometrizeth, and observeth order in all things.'[11] In reality, of course, this is far from being the fundamental characteristic of The Lost Ones. All the patterns have not been traced, and never will be. The narrator only recounts one point in time in which the five vanquished form an 'irregular quincunx.' To trace the progress of the other two hundred inhabitants to their imagined end would involve a reticulation or 'net-work plantation' beyond the capability of any cunning literary artificer.

The rules for climbing, etc., are obviously merely conventions and hence lack the authority which Browne is able to ascribe to the various correspondences of God's handiwork that he discerns. Section 14 ends with a description of the worst 'scenes of violence the cylinder has to offer' (60) and implies that, if anything, the ultimate state of this world is likely to be pandemonium. Order appears to be giving way to license and the allegorical hierarchy of physical, ethical, and spiritual is often collapsed in favour of a crudely naturalistic appraisal: 'The effect of this climate on the soul is not be underestimated. But it suffers certainly less than the skin ... ' (52). There is, admittedly, an ironic recognition here that the 'incessant straining' of vision leads to a 'concomitant moral distress and its repercussion on the organ' (38), which combines with the 'certain ethics' which states, 'not to do unto other what coming from them might give offence' (58). The latter is a variation on Robert Burton's so-called 'familiar example of Regulus the Roman' in the section on 'Anatomy of the Soul' in *The Anatomy of Melancholy*: 'Do not that to another which thou wouldst not have done to thyself'[12] and proves decisively that anatomy is definitely no longer the whole it was in *Enough*.

One reason for this is the obliteration of the divine faculty of vision – 'the eye with which the best will in the world it is difficult to consign at the close of all its efforts to nothing short of blindness' (52–3). The deterioration of sight effects a dramatic contrast between the quincuncial systems of Browne and Beckett. For Browne, the very laws of vision are based on the quincunx: 'It is no wonder that this Quincuncial order was first and still affected as grateful unto the Eye. For all things are seen Quincuncially. For at the eye the Pyramidal rayes from the object received decussation, and so strike a second base upon the Retina or hinder coat, the proper organ of Vision.'[13] But the power of vision in Beckett's cylinder is finally destroyed: 'And were it possible to follow over a long enough period of time eyes blue for preference as being the most perishable they would be seen to redden more and more in an ever widening glare and their pupils little by little to dilate till the whole orb was devoured' (38–9). The search for truth and divinely sanctioned harmonies is essentially seen by Browne as an exercise in perception. Hence the need to shelter the eye, 'Keeping the pupilla plump and fair, and not contracted or shrunk as in light and vagrant vision.'[14]

Browne's conclusion to 'The Garden of Cyrus' says that 'a large field is yet left unto sharper discerners' in which they can discover 'delightful Truths, confirmable by sense and ocular Observation which seems to me the surest path, to trace the Labyrinth of Truth.'[15] In *The Lost Ones*, a diametrically opposed situation occurs: 'There he opens then his eyes this last of all if a man and some time later threads his way to that first among the vanquished ...' (62). He takes his place and 'dark descends' (62). However similar the ending of Browne's treatise may seem – 'the Quincunx of Heaven, runs low, and tis time to close the five ports of knowledge' – its implications are radically opposed to those of *The Lost Ones*: 'All things began in order, so shall they end, and so shall they begin again; according to the ordainer of order and Mystical Mathematics of the City of Heaven.'[16] Browne's allegory ends with the conjecture that perhaps 'all shall wake again,' that, on the anagogic level, a time will come which will free man 'from everlasting sleep.' But Beckett's final picture of the cylinder shows all the inhabitants 'truly vanquished': there will be no awakening. The important point to be made about these two radically opposed visions is that they are both explicitly allegorical. In Section 15, Beckett's narrator abandons his realistic critique of the hermetic tradition and imposes a solution that actually is equivalent to Browne's. To say that all will never awake, will never escape to the world outside, is just as allegorical as to say that all will certainly awake in a heavenly world. The rage for order in Section 15 is as much in evidence as it is in Browne's concluding fifth chapter. To achieve his own 'mystical harmony,' Beckett abandons his realistic premises and commits himself to allegory. The final resort to allegory confirms that the narrator's much-vaunted objectivity is really a form of pseudo-naturalism designed to circumvent the realities of this 'abode' of the imagination. The vital issue is not what is real but what is the ontological status of the real, that is to say, what is the being of the fiction created from the relationship of author and character? Beckett is undoubtedly aware (even if many of his critical advocates are not) of the truth of Georg Lukács's judgment that experimental forms can paradoxically lead to highly conventional effects such as naturalism and allegory. All the narrator's '*aperçus*' are 'seen from a certain angle' (13), that of the author obsessed with the formal harmony of the literary construct. Although he says that he is 'far from being able to imagine their last state' (15), and that it would be 'idle to imagine' (22) the 'unthinkable end,' he does say that the light and temperature 'may be imagined extinguished as purposeless and the latter fixed not far from freezing point' (15). How engaged or committed, we must ask ourselves, is the narrator in relation to the reality of the cylinder? The narrator is obviously a 'thinking being coldly intent on all these data and evidences' (39) rather than an artist hungering after a transubstantiation of the real. All his 'detailed knowledge' and 'all these data' do not combine to depict a representative reality. The 'picturesque details' of the white-haired woman do not combine with the 'tedious details' (42) of the life of the cylinder to give an affirmation of the searchers' reality. What emerges instead is a sense that these details only exist for the affirmation of the narrator's reality and his need to order the fiction. The query of *How It Is* – 'details for the sake of what' – is clearly answered in *The Lost Ones* in terms of the author's presence: details for the sake of harmony, for the sake of literary order. The tedious and picturesque are combined in Section 15 to allow the author to end the work after discouragement had prevailed at a certain stage (for Beckett the hiatus of four years after Section 14). The result is not, however, realism, a living reality that possesses an immanent meaning, but rather allegory for the author's sake of harmony. The coy use of self-contradictory evaluations through-out the text leads away from realism to allegory: for example, 'the fact remains' (19), 'in reality ...' (26), 'nothing more natural' (27), 'so true it is ...' (32). But the inhabitants are dishonestly, not truly, vanquished. Surrounding the hypothetical last searcher are not really 'others in his image' (61), but others in the ideal image which this God-author has created for himself.

The true quest in *The Lost Ones* is for being, and being cannot be authenticated without an engagement with the temporal. But the prob-lem is that this work of art occupies a timeless, ahistorical realm. Beckett's narrator stresses that the inhabitants are cut off from the world of time outside and trapped in a hermetically sealed container, at the same time as he insists upon a passing of time in this container, even if the inhabitants are unaware of it – 'a languishing happily unperceived because of its slowness' (15), 'all should die but with so gradual and to put it plainly so fluctuant a death as to escape the notice even of a visitor' (18). The narrator is, however, himself only a visitor, managing in the first fourteen sections to describe only one specific moment in the cylinder's would-be history: 'But as to at this moment of time and there will be no other ... may it suffice to say that at this moment of time ...' (35). All his judgments and prognostications are abstracted from this one instant of time. Despite the assertions that time is slowly moving forward, the narrator, when straining for accuracy, confirms his entrap-ment in a timeless present: 'From time immemorial rumor has it or better still the notion is abroad that there exists a way out' (17–18). In the cylinder, everything is 'immemorial' without ever having been ' memorial.' The only authentic reference point for the measurement of time involves a conditional tense and a would-be existence in the world outside where 'the sun and other stars would still be shining' (18). An alternative system of measurement is posited in the cylinder: 'and so roamed a vast space of time impossible to measure until a first came to a standstill followed by a second and so on' (35). The woman who acts as the north marker cannot, however, be simply transformed into the 'bewitching Miss Greenwich'[17] of *Murphy*. When the last searcher supposedly abandons his quest, he finds a position in space not time: 'He himself after a pause impossible to time finds at last his place and pose whereupon dark descends ...' (62). The eschatology of the fifteenth section is thus purely a construct of the author's imagination. The pause between it and the preceding section is indeed impossible to time – 'So on infinitely until towards the unthinkable end if the notion is maintained ...' (60). The notion cannot be maintained, just as previous references to time cannot be maintained, because the narrator has restricted himself to an instant in a timeless present. Since the narrator is concerned primarily with a spatial arrangement of the quincunx at only one point in time, the reader cannot accept without protest the narrator's word for scenes that lie outside this particular moment.

The ideal or passion 'preying on one and all' is a hunger for being beyond their fictional status. The searcher's 'eyes burn' (46) not with lust ('Whatever it is they are searching for it is not that' [36]) but with a passion for a confirmation of their own being.[18] They are susceptible to the 'old craving' (31) – the eyes 'as famished as the unthinkable first day until for no clear reason they as suddenly close again or the head falls' (32). The negation of all desires seems here to be the only means of satisfying their insatiable hunger. Is this then another confirmation of what Beckett in *Proust* called 'the wisdom of all the sages, from Brahma to Leopardi'?[19] Not quite. The inhabitants of the cylinder are not historical beings who are able to pronounce evaluations of being: they are fictions in search of being. And a reader of Beckett must be aware of these facts before the fundamental complexity of his work reveals itself as founded upon a startlingly realistic appraisal of the creative act. A vital inversion has taken place in the course of Beckett's fiction: whereas Belacqua, for example, in the early short story, 'Dante and the Lobster,' was situated in the world outside and failed to read the faces of the people around him, which would decipher his own being and enable him to become an artist and shape his own meaning, [20] these seekers are trapped in a cylinder and avidly seek to read the faces of their compatriots, particularly the vanquished. But since these others are also fictions (and hence lack being) all that can be discovered is of no value in the search for selfhood. As long as they are able to search, they will be tormented by hunger – 'enough will always subsist to spell for this little people the extinction soon or late of its last remaining fire' (15).

The great themes of allegory are, according to Angus Fletcher, temptation and the quest for power; and this narrator has, indeed, succumbed in Section 15 to the imposition of his authorial power.[21] The final section is as far removed as possible from the syntax of weakness which Beckett has said is necessary if being is to be given form; instead, it is a masterly exercise in rhetoric, an act of persuasion designed to convince the reader that this scene could be an acceptable description of the end of the 'old abode.' But the major reason for the failure of this rhetoric is that it totally excludes the 'sounds' of the inhabitants in order to further the interests of the authorial voice. Although sounds were a prominent concern in the opening section, the references seemed even then intended to belittle their relevance. 'A kiss makes an indescribable sound' (8); a 'sound is scarcely heard' when a body or object is thrown against the walls of rubber; the 'only sounds worthy of the name' (9) come from the movement of the ladders, or the searchers beating each other or themselves. The 'happy few' (ironic shades of Stendhal) are those who can temporarily knock themselves unconscious. But the fury they 'vent' does not issue forth in words, as in *From an Abandoned Work*. The situation is literally 'unspeakably dramatic' (36); the narrator never records what (if anything) is said, even though the cylinder is evidently filled with a 'murmur' (37): 'Among all the components the sum of which it is the ear finally distinguishes a faint stridulence as of insects which is that of the light itself and the one invariable' (38). This important reference to sound is repeated in the last section: 'Hushed in the same breath the faint stridulence mentioned above whence suddenly such silence as to drown all the faint breathings put together' (62). This is the central mystery which the narrator never explores. Does the murmur emanate from the light that keeps the cylinder alive (throbbing like a pulse) or does it come from the inhabitants? The statement that the light seems to emanate from all the objects in the cylinder (and the added qualification that light is not quite the right word) makes the problem even more intractable. As in *All Strange Away*, the narrator of *The Lost Ones* is attracted by the conclusion that no sounds exist. Rather than risk a destructive flood of sound (as in Beckett's first published prose work 'Assumption'), this narrator hypothesizes 'such silence as to drown all the faint breathings.' But the reader need not be a silent victim of the author's designs; we are not compelled to accept the form in which the work is cast nor to believe it. If the reader is trapped in *The Lost Ones*, it is really a trap of his own making, not Beckett's. While *The Lost Ones* tells us next to nothing about the world external to the fiction, it does tell us a great deal about the nature of fiction, especially the question of authority. The quest for a meaning that is more directly relevant to the world at large must be postponed until the meaning of the book is fully explored, otherwise we will be entangled in an allegory that blinds us to our own reality.

Fizzle 5 ('Closed place'), 'a condensed version of a much longer work in French begun in 1968 and finally abandoned,'[22] shows Beckett trying to rework elements of *The Lost Ones* in a way that would not involve him in 'intractable complexities.'[23] The complexities of the story in *The Lost Ones* are absent here, especially the important question of time: 'The place is already old. The ditch is old. In the beginning it was all bright.'[24] Hence there is no need here to trace a progression; the narrator of this piece can be truly detached since there are no inhabitants left in this hermetically sealed world. So detached, in fact, that it is not difficult to see why Beckett abandoned the work. If all is known, why bother to say it? The original French title 'Se voir'[25] clearly means in context 'to be obvious.' But, as was the case in *The Lost Ones*, this narrator overlooks the obvious in his own quest for a perfect order. Although the narrator asserts 'Beyond what is said there is nothing,'[26] the reader is bound to point out that there obviously once was something. The desiccated leaves in 'Closed place' are 'a reminder of beldam nature.'[27] The exclusion of 'beldam nature' in *The Lost Ones* results finally in scenes of bedlam. While the narrator of *The Lost Ones* admits this, he intervenes in the last section to impose his own preferred alternative. But the formal solution cannot stifle the need for the imagination to rejoin the world in being and time. Beckett decided that it was better to conclude *The Lost Ones* (which at least reveals the inadequacy of a formal justification for closure) than to continue with the longer work from which 'Closed place' is condensed where the formal harmony is enshrined in the opening 'All needed to be known for say is known.'

If *The Lost Ones* offered a semblance of order and clarity, Beckett's next work, *Ping*, appears, even on first reading, as one of his most difficult and complex investigations of the nature of the creative act. While *The Lost Ones* was abandoned for several years because of its 'intractable complexities' of detail, *Ping* encountered no such impasse. The variants of the work reveal that it was the beginning of the work rather than the conclusion which gave Beckett the most trouble. In fact, the inability to complete *Le Dépeupleur* seems to have been the original impulse for the writing of *Bing*. Beckett appended an important note to the manuscripts 'abandoned' in 1966: 'MSS *Le Dépeupleur-Bing*. Though very different formally these 2 MSS belong together. *Bing* may be regarded as the result or miniaturisation of *Le Dépeupleur* abandoned because of its intractable complexities.'[28] Beckett began a new formulation of *Bing* in the summer of 1966 and the nine drafts of this new start reveal a further miniaturization. The first four variants contain a reduced image of the cylinder: while the space and number of inhabitants is greatly simplified ('4x2 + 2x1 = 10 mètres carrés originalement' and 'un corps nu d'un mètre'), certain details are still present (ladders, niches, tunnels).[29] The first four drafts of Beckett's new start on what became the published version of *Ping* are therefore in the same vein as his first jettisoned efforts – a miniaturization. But with the beginning of the fifth draft the differences are much more than formal; a whole new attitude to the creative act now emerges.

Beckett quickly realized that a mere reduction in scope would not alter the fundamental problems encountered in *The Lost Ones*. However stringently limited, the narrative machinery of niches et al. demands a degree of attention that detracts from the true beginning of what became *Ping*. The machinery of *The Lost Ones* then vanishes; *Ping* now becomes in some key respects Beckett's own version of Yeats' 'now my ladder is gone.' Its central concern, indeed, is the 'rag-and-bone shop of the heart' from which fictions originate. Beckett's circus animals have deserted – not merely the hunchback at the beck and call of a Malone but the very figure of an authoritarian self-fabricating narrator. The narratorial presence in *Ping* is a far cry from the ring-master in *Imagination Dead Imagine*.

What sets *Ping* apart from Beckett's works of the sixties (especially from its predecessor, *The Lost Ones*) is the absence of a struggle for authority between the author and his characters. Instead the work reveals a series of 'coefficients of penetration'[30] whereby these two irreducible dimensions of the creative act are identified. Beckett's long journey of exploration has again led to the realization that each possesses undeniable claims to the real. But that alone is not enough: 'the only reality is provided by the hieroglyphics traced by inspired perception (identification of subject and object),' as Beckett asserted in *Proust*. The oppositions of Murphy/Endon, Watt/Knott, Molloy/Moran revealed above all else that the question of subject-object identification cannot even be broached until the real status of the fiction is established. The above antinomies only serve to mystify the question because they are not the true subject or object, merely secondary derivations of a more fundamental author/character dynamic.

Ping's opening words, 'All known,'[31] would seem to indicate a version of the classical omniscience which Beckett saw Joyce tending towards – 'the more he knew the more he could do' – rather than the celebrated 'little zone of ignorance, impotence' that is Beckett's own preserve.[32] But the comparison with Joyce is essentially an ironic one. Only in 'Closed place' does Beckett actually posit omniscience *Ping* on the other hand, quickly undermines its initial claim to complete knowledge: 'All known' is countered by the last words of the second 'sentence' – 'never seen.' The point is that the 'all known' is continually qualified by statements taken from the other's point of view. From this view, the situation is much less clear, only 'almost white.' Failure to note this dichotomy will reduce a reading of the work to a mesmeric chant of repeated phrases. Unless the author/character poles are delineated, the 1030 words permutated through seventy 'sentences' can only at best appear to be a complex type of verbal music.

The question of the narrator's status needs to be very carefully formulated. Elisabeth Segrè suggests that the phrase 'one second' is 'unexpected because it implies an additional point of view (that of the author), a point of view which jars with the other points of view, those of the subject and onlooker.'[33] The presence of the author-figure is not, however, so surprising, for it has been implicit since the opening words of the text. The statement 'all known' implies more than a mere witness or onlooker: the point of view is clearly that of an organizing consciousness who would assert the perfect order of 'white on white' if the figure upon which the light shines did not, however minimally, contradict his drive to an ultimate clarity. If *Ping* is viewed solely from the perspective of an organizing consciousness, an irremediable dualism will be foisted upon it. A 'hieroglyphic' identification is only possible within the being of a language in which the distinctions subject and object are no longer decisive. This is what happens in *Ping*, where the language simultaneously affirms both points of view, those of the so-called figure and those of the so-called observer. There are in *Ping* two legitimate narratives, both of which must be comprehended at the same time, and both of which are a part of a larger unity. Hence the inadequacy of a conventional critical and metaphysical vocabulary.[34] The 'subject' in *Ping* does not 'die' before it comes to the verb (as in 'Text 2'), because there is no longer a subject, nor any verbs either. Rather there are two subjects apprehended simultaneously, thereby undercutting the Cartesian dualisms that are reflected in the structures of ordinary language. Prepositions and articles are very sparingly used, and by removing the 'little words' of speech Beckett creates a paratactic series of phrases in which coordination and subordination are abandoned. Habitual modes of linguistic perception are altered in order to allow for a new apprehension of reality that underlies the subject-object dichotomy. There are two presences within *Ping*: one presence (that of the 'author') seeks a perfect order in which 'all known'; the other (that of the 'character') is a fiction who seeks being in the world outside this 'box' or enclosure. The imagination cannot function successfully except through a conjunction of ostensibly contradictory impulses. The faint blue eyes testify to a presence in the whiteness. The body is 'fixed' in its container and yet is also described as 'fixed elsewhere.' The blue eyes are naturally drawn to the 'way out,' and to memories of an existence before their entombment. An imminent engulfment of consciousness by 'whiteness' brings to the fore the essentials of being – nature and image, signs and meaning. However minimal the 'traces,' they are still referential and not merely counters in a formal pattern. The language of the text itself, by admitting the potential reconciliation of the formal and ontological dimensions of the word, makes possible an identification that lies beyond the subject-object paradigm.

There seems little point in comparing *Ping*, as many critics have done, with abstract painting or aleatory music. The colours all belong to something; they are not qualities detached from referents, whether of the body or of the place. The often-made comparison between the language of *Ping* and music is perhaps particularly misleading because the theme of sounds has important repercussions that lie outside the limits of a musical comparison. The very title of the piece draws our attention to Beckett's early speculation on musical form in 'Dream of Fair to Middling Women,' where he sought (as conductor/author) to make his characters become pure notes who would supply on cue just the right 'ping.' The residual work *Ping* is not a work in which the author succumbs to the temptation for a pure linguistic form; rather it is a laying to rest of this quest for formal perfection. The title is a highly ironic one in view of the way the 'pings' operate in this latest work, for they are anything but pure.

Ping strikes the ear as a subtle complex of sounds, almost as a tone poem, but a preoccupation with the musical qualities of the sounds does not do justice to that aspect of language which is concerned with reference and meaning. In the contiguity disorder, there is, Jakobson says, a regression of sound pattern which 'involves an inflation of homonyms and a decrease in vocabulary.'[35] In *Ping* the use of the word light as both adjective and noun is an obvious homonymic pattern. The decrease in vocabulary is immediately evident in *Ping* even after a reading of the first few sentences. But the sound patterns also support Jakobson's view that 'the phonic equivalence of rhyming words prompts the question of semantic similarities and contrasts.'[36] The childish rhymes so prominent in *All Strange Away* are even more in evidence in *Ping* (indeed the first words of the French *Bing* establish the principle – 'Tout su'). Examples of outright rhyme are' 'known'/'sewn,' 'light'/ 'white'/'right,' 'elsewhere'/'there.' In all instances, the combinations serve to identify two disparate perspectives on the various scenes that the work depicts. There are two important half-rhymes, 'eyes'/'sign,' and 'scene'/'mean(ing),' and an 'inspired perception' obviously implies both sound (the breath upon which all language depends) and sight. For Beckett, synaesthesia is an important step towards establishing the hieroglyphic unity of language. The sound/sight identification (for example, 'murmurs'/'blurs') is a vital aspect of the question of meaning and helps to make the major point of *Ping*: that sense and sound can never be totally severed. Words can be self-referential, but words can also refer to other entities in the 'without.' For Beckett, the realist, these two aspects of language correspond to the very nature of the creative process – the image is both of the mind and of the world.

The ending of *Ping* contains a startling reference to a 'black and white' eye: 'Ping perhaps not alone one second with image same time a little less dim eye black and white half-closed long lashes imploring that much memory almost never' (167), after which the question of time immediately comes to the fore: 'Afar flash of time all white all over all of old ping flash white walls shining white no trace eyes holes light blue almost white last colour ping white over.' The more frequent distribution of 'pings' in these last sentences indicates that the imagination is indeed on the verge of extinction. Critical reactions to the ending have varied greatly. John J. Mood views the imploring look as derived from 'the tradition of melodrama' and as 'deliciously ironic.'[37] On the other hand,

David Lodge found the image 'the most human touch, the most emotive phrase, in the whole piece.'[38] The interpretative problem might be better understood if it were rephrased: does *Ping*'s ending exhibit merely a formal closure or a conclusion which the reader accepts as 'integral'? Near the end of *All Strange Away*, an image of a black eye also appears twice: 'long black lashes on white cheekbone ... hell gaping they part and black eye appears' (56), 'black bottomless eye' (57). In *All Strange Away*, there is no doubt that these are not real images, for they are explicitly termed only a 'sop to mind.' But in *Ping* a last memory lingers in the melodic 'long lashes imploring,' as the 'pings' draw closer together to emphasize an irrevocable sense of being 'over.'[39] It is finally impossible to decide whether or not the image of the 'eye black and white' is the most human touch in the piece or simply a melodramatic flourish. It is both: the ending exhibits both closure and conclusion, the formal and ontological dimensions of language united in a hieroglyph of 'inspired perception.'

8

Sense and Nonsense in
Lessness

Beckett advances in *Lessness* the revolutionary view that the 'other' is in
fact nothing less than 'human being' and not an intermediary fictive
self, a Molloy, Malone, or even an Unnamable. This affirmation of being,
whereby Beckett identifies his radical experimentalism with the artist's
traditional responsibility to make sense of both his art and his world,
may at first appear as nothing more than 'nonsense.' Yet it is a very
strange type of nonsense that affirms, even if in a radically innovative
fashion, the traditional view that fiction can, somehow or other, deal
with real people (and, after all, it is this ostensibly nonsensical view that
ultimately gives value and meaning to the study of literature). What
distinguishes Beckett's affirmation of the reality of the fiction is that his
endorsement only comes after a devastating critique of the conventions
by which the writer of fiction has conditioned us to a willing suspension
of disbelief. But this literal-minded exposure went too far in *The Unnamable* and ironically, if predictably, resulted in 'the same old nonsense'
about an entanglement with fictive selves. After encountering this *terminus ad quem*, Beckett realized that it was impossible to keep separate the
realms of story and life, and the central challenge then became the
creation of a 'true fiction.' Beckett's *Avant-Garde* experimentalism is anything but 'perverse,' as Lukács would have it[1]: on the contrary, it aims
for a more human content and strives for a corroboration of his belief
that 'Being *has* a form.'

More is known about the composition of *Lessness* (the 1970 translation
of the 1969 *Sans*) than any of Beckett's other works. Beckett described
in detail to Ruby Cohn his method of composition: the creation of six
'families' composed of ten sentences each and their 'decomposition' and
arrangement into a two-part structure of sixty sentences each by means

of a chance selection.[2] Tired of having other people's comments appear on the dust-jackets of his works, Beckett supplied the comments for *Lessness*.[3] His own authority for the 'categories formally distinguishable through which the writing winds, first in one disorder then another' are of little value, however, until the reader is able to sense the *raison d'être* of the work which these categories purport to describe. Knowledge of how the work was composed has in fact led critics away from considerations of the new vision which preceded Beckett's division into formal categories. Fundamental questions concerning the ontological status of the categories need to be posed before they can really be of use in the explication of *Lessness*. The most urgent question is to determine the subject of *Lessness* – the narrative centre around which the formal divisions 'wind.' Normal categories of literary criticism are of little value in this instance, because the lack of an 'I' around which the work could take shape is the most striking 'lessness' in the piece. Nevertheless, there is (as in *Ping*) a sense of two distinct points of view operating throughout the text. They are evident in the pun on 'eye'/'I': there is, on one hand, the 'he' with 'two pale blue,' the 'something' that is discovered in the excavation of the creative act; and, on the other hand, the subject, the creating consciousness proper, whose 'eye' is 'calm long last.'[4] The 'he' that is discovered cannot be effaced but demands 'to be and be in face of.'[5] The little creature with 'grey face features slit' is 'face to endlessness.' The artist cannot attain a pure impersonality: he, too, is 'Face to white calm touch close eye calm long last all gone from mind.' The 'refuge' has opened onto a world. Nature and void are contained in the 'without': 'Little void mighty light four square all white blank planes all gone from mind.' / 'All sides endlessness earth sky as one no sound no stir.'

This opening allows for Beckett's most radical revision of his poetic since *How It Is*. Instead of the internalized reality of Chapter 6 of *Murphy* with its solipsistic implications, a new dualism is possible that is itself incorporated by an encompassing sense of wholeness. Reality in *Lessness* is shown to be the combination of inside becoming one with outside; differences between the two are now effectively collapsed. 'True refuge' is the identification of these two realms, what in the old terminology of aesthetics and metaphysics would be termed the mental and physical, the ideal and the real. Fascinated by Proust's concept of the 'ideal real,' Beckett was, however, unable to accept the mysticism which enshrouded it and which went against an engagement with the concrete he so admired in Vico and others. The negative form of the 'ideal real' which impressed him in Bram van Velde ('bereft of occasion in every shape or form, ideal as well as material')[6] proved impossible to attain in language and, besides, the creative act for Beckett has always admitted the existence of an other who is struggling to assert his own being. In *Lessness*, the image-making faculty has gone 'out of mind' to find and to create a reality that renders obsolete the inside-outside dichotomy.

The 'facts' are clear enough – 'ruins, exposure, wilderness, mindlessness, past and future tenses denied and affirmed'[7] – but they cannot be kept within the formal categories. Each of the ten sentences in each category or family is unique. As the reader 'winds' his way through the two parts of *Lessness*, he is always reminded that the text is potentially endless. Each fact or statement is connected to everything else in an endless network of substitutions and permutations. The sixty 'facts' do not form a chain as in *How It Is*, but a reticulated web of proliferating resemblances. The 'disorders' which Beckett draws attention to are present in the very language of *Lessness*. The majority of sentences (all except the 'he will make it' family) reflect a 'contiguity disorder' on the syntactical plane. The 'scattered ruins' is obviously a description of the words themselves. Without the normal grammatical categories and hierarchies, the words potentially face on 'all sides endlessness.' Each word reflects other words. This characteristic is obvious in the phrases 'earth and sky as one,' 'sky mirrored earth mirrored sky,' where the words act out their import. While the 'contiguity disorder' is everywhere present syntactically, it is also evident that contiguity on the semantic plane is in fact increased. The prime example is the way that the various parts of the 'little body' are shown to constitute a whole: 'Little body grey face features slit and little holes two pale blue.' The 'block[s]' of his body are paralleled by the little blocks of words that are *Lessness* itself.

The contiguity disorder of *Lessness* with its chance collocation of different units from different families inevitably juxtaposes statements which appear completely contradictory. For example, the last two sentences of the seventh 'paragraph': 'Never but dream the days and nights made of dreams of other nights better days. He will live again the space of a step it will be day and night over him the endlessness.' Is this another version of the 'similarity disorder,' of the inability to formulate comparisons or metaphorical identifications between diverse elements? On the contrary. It is at points like this that the very categories of language disorders (as set out by Jakobson) and the two 'disorders' through which the text winds (as set out by Beckett) become irrelevant. The disorders do not derive from an essential order that could be termed logical or reasonable. The simultaneity of 'denied and affirmed' suggests a new vision that is no longer bound by the endless dialectic of 'yes or no.' This 'eternal tautology'[8] has been temporalized by the substitution of 'and' for 'or.' Both the denial of 'days and nights' and their affirmation coexist within the language of *Lessness*. The 'yes' and 'no' can further be identified with the two differing points of view felt throughout the work: for the 'calm eye' of the authorial presence time is merely a delusion, a word without significance; for the 'he' who has gained his freedom from narrative 'no-time,' movement on earth in historical time will be a testimony to his being. The 'never was ...' / 'he will ...' families are the key nodes in the network of *Lessness*. The 'he' and implied 'I' need each other, and are involved in a symbiotic relationship, however much each may pursue different ends in the endlessness.

Both the author and the character are located in the without, the sand of the true refuge. But while this might adequately express the truth of the situation from the authorial point of view in which 'all gone from mind,' the problem has just begun for the 'little body' who must create new fictions from this wasteland if he is going to take his first step. Truth thus becomes entangled with further 'imaginings,' 'dreams,' and 'figments.' The 'blue' eyes of the 'little body' are identified with the 'blue celeste of poesy' which for the 'calm eye' signifies the misleading and self-comforting illusions of the conventional imagination. For the detached 'I,' these new fictions (of religion – 'He will curse god again ...,' of love – 'old love new love as in the blessed days ...') distort the essential underlying reality of 'Earth sand same grey as the air sky ruins body fine ash grey sand.' The 'never was ...' family conveys the authorial denials of the reality of these fictional transformations.

But it must be kept in mind that the 'will-to-illusion' and its relevance for determining the truth of life in time is both 'denied and affirmed.' There is an even more absolute absence of absolutes in this work than in Beckett's other writing. The 'he will ...' group affirms the reality of the dream in passing time: 'On him will rain again as in the blessed days of blue the passing cloud.' Although the 'calm eye' perceives an essential underlying sterility in the human dilemma, an artistic or philosophical stance that pretends to see things as they are has to admit the 'as-if' nature of his own truth and the truth created by others, in this instance by the 'little body.' Moreover, art as a truth-seeking medium is always compromised by the ineradicable optimism of nature whose images of blue conspire with the 'two pale blue' to form a pathetic fallacy that is intensely compelling. The truth of the refuge must finally admit the untruth of fiction as an undeniable reality. To be in the world entails an ineluctable pull towards fiction. The last sentence of *Lessness* conveys the ambiguity of the 'living errors'[9] that are necessarily part of life and time: 'Figment dawn dispeller of figments and the other called dusk.' Figments are an essential feature of the 'true refuge' and any attempt to determine what is the fundamental reality must be able to hold their composition and decomposition, affirmation and denial together as part of one imaginative transaction.

Beckett's repetition and variation in different contexts of a number of key images used in earlier works are an especially important indication of his efforts to achieve a reconciliation in *Lessness* of apparent contraries. *Lessness* is obviously a radical reversal of the situation in *Ping* where the 'body' is enclosed by 'white walls' and 'white planes' – all is truly known in *Lessness* for without/within are conflated. But to note this shift between *Lessness* and its nearest predecessor is only the initial step in placing the work in context. *Lessness* is Beckett's most original fiction since *How It Is* – but at the same time his most derivative. In other words, *Lessness* is Beckett's reinterpretation and resolution of some of the basic issues which have been at the heart of his explorations since the impasse of *The Unnamable*. If the writer is 'the victim of all [he] has written,'[10] the only way he can free himself is to rewrite (in a type of continuous revision) those previous works. *Lessness* is a solution to many of the problems that brought about the impasse – most notably, the question of authority with the attendant issues of language and being, and the nature of fictions in determining a life or story.

Telling support for this contention comes from a comparative analysis of *Texts for Nothing* (which were not translated and published in English until 1967) and *Lessness*, works which ostensibly bear little relationship to each other. The most important difference between the two works is the nature of the relationship between the two 'I's, the creator and the created upon which the ontology of the fiction rests. The first of the *Texts for Nothing* establishes a paradoxical two-in-one unity. The 'I' with 'closed eyes' below is one with his other 'I' above with 'open' eyes. The image of a vulture with its 'eye ravening patient' manages to hold (at least temporarily) these different aspects together. But by 'Text 12' this *discordia concors* has become an unmanageable 'three in one and what a no one' (134). As the 'here' of these different aspects is not a common one, the question of 'me' and 'being' proliferates aimlessly. But in *Lessness* a new unity of voice is made possible by an abandonment of the insatiable drive for an organic synthesis of 'I' and 'other': 'Face to white calm touch close eye calm long last all gone from mind.' In *Lessness*, the 'other' 'I' has been granted independence from the creating 'I.' He is indeed 'dignified by the third person' and 'authorized to expiate' ('Text 8,' 113) to 'curse God again, 'whereas the self-creators of *Texts for Nothing* could only 'curse myself heartily' ('Text 11,' 131). The author and character dimensions are now granted separate status and this is what enables *Lessness* to achieve an ontological verification of the fiction which was not possible in *Texts for Nothing*, not even in the first 'Text.'

The 'mindlessness' category of *Lessness* ('out of mind,' 'all gone from mind') allows for a completely new approach to the subject-object problem that is at the centre of aesthetic speculation. The first sentence, 'Ruins true refuge long last towards which many false time out of mind,' could be taken as a commentary upon the 'endless' departures of *Texts for Nothing* that vainly try to give credence to images of a real body in a real world. 'Out of mind' punningly draws into a critical perspective the 'madness' of the Cartesian logic that posits a mind groping towards a world set in opposition to it. This 'light of reason' is also 'gone from mind' in *Lessness*. The 'ruins' are the 'true refuge' because they do not set up an antimony of without and within.

World and mind reflect each other. The 'sky mirrored earth mirrored sky' of *Lessness* is indebted to the account of 'the sky and earth' in 'Text 5' as the setting for 'many a story' – 'so that he finds himself as it were under glass and yet no limit to his movements in all directions' (97). The phrase 'slow black with ruin' that is applied to the true refuge is derived from 'Text 7' where a person waits 'erect and rigid' in a 'station in ruins' unable to see through 'the glass black with the dust of ruin.' Another striking parallel between the two works is the image of 'a mute, an idiot ... who stares at himself in a glass, stares before him in the desert' ('Text 9,' 117). But in *Lessness* the 'mirrors' do not set up impenetrable panes between self and world. The world itself is seen to involve a play of mirror reflections. What underlies the glass imagery in both works is a passionate desire to determine what is the truth. The 'eye' was originally 'sealed' by the contact with the light above in 'Text 2' where 'nothing showed of the true affair' (82). One of the great achievements of *Lessness* is to transfer the quest for being into the without (referred to as the 'lost without' in *Texts for Nothing*) without, however, relinquishing the distinction between truth and the 'blue celeste of poesy' with its wish-fulfilling chimeras. The acceptance of the ruins as a true refuge for the calm detached eye and for the little person's 'two pale blue' allows Beckett to fulfill the prophecy of 'Text 6' where the narrator promises that when the senses 'open again it may be ... to tell a story, in the true sense of the word ... a little story with living creatures ... with night and day coming and going above ...' (105). The enclosure of the imagination 'fallen open' supplies a sustaining (if 'endless') 'here' that can resolve the questions of identity posed in *Texts for Nothing*. The oxymora of the 'Texts' are now paradoxes pregnant with meaning. While the refuge is 'open,' it is still necessary to 'close' the eye in order to preserve a sense of its truth; it is also necessary to regard this world with the 'two pale blue' if the story is to deal with 'living creatures' in the 'true sense of the word.'

The key transformation from *Texts for Nothing* to *Lessness* concerns the new ontological status given to the 'lies' of space and time so that they become as it were 'true lies' or necessary fictions. The 'passing moment' ('Text 10,' 124) of the first work is evident in various forms in *Lessness* ('the passing cloud'; 'passing deluge'; 'passing hour long short'). Both works seem to dismiss the present tense as a dream – 'Never but dream the days and nights made of dreams other nights better days,' 'to linger a moment free in a dream of days and nights, dreaming of me moving, season after season, towards the last, like the living' ('Text 8', 112). While the present tense is conspicuously absent from *Lessness*, the extensive use of present and past participles does create a sense of an action taking place. Time is starting again. The work describes that instant in which all is about to begin. As the narrator of 'Text 9,' obsessed with the 'way out,' comments, 'the future will tell.' 'Past and future tenses denied and affirmed' does not destroy the sense of a living present. There is no 'yes or no' cancellation in *Lessness* as was the case in *Texts for Nothing*. Both exist together: this is the essential paradox of the work. Nor is there a 'timeless present,' as was the case in *How It Is*. In *Lessness*, there is a sense of both the timeless and the present (the 'passing' of the little body who is undeniably there – 'heart beating'). From the point of view of the 'calm eye' all time may appear as a delusion, and the wisdom of the sages may counsel the 'ablation of desire.'[11] But this calm eye is still that of an author figure who must recognize a 'he' that is striving for being, a being in time that will struggle to break away from any imposed pattern, whether it be the 'perfect order' of *How It Is* or the 'disorder' of *Lessness*.

The need to create a world which is engaged with the temporal is recognized in the very last sentence of *Lessness* – 'Figment dawn dispeller of figments and the other called dusk.' The sentence does not fall into any of the six formal categories and can be identified with both the affirmation and denial of past and future. The whole question of figments could either be dismissed as a delusion or regarded as an inescapable process of the 'passing moment.' This sentence appears to be a complex rewriting of the phrase 'disperser of phantoms' in 'Text 5' where 'the phantoms come back, it's in vain they go abroad.' The attempt to make the phantoms real fails in 'Text 5' because the narrator is caught in an endless 'evening'; there is no belief that 'night is at hand, bringer of rest' (98), nor that 'day is at hand, disperser of phantoms.' For a phantom or a fiction to be made real its truth and untruth must be seen as part of an antecedent sense of being in the world of time.

The 'imaginary head' of 'Text 5' has been made real in *Lessness*. There is no longer the all-or-nothing dialectic of *Texts for Nothing*. As the narrator of 'Text 1' said, 'in half-an-hour it will be night, and yet it's not, not certain, what is not certain, absolutely certain, that night prevents what day permits, for those who know how to go about it' (77–8). This prophecy is fulfilled in *Lessness* by breaking down the barriers between mind and world and making them coterminous. *Lessness* is thus able to give life to the 'last images' and 'figments' of 'Text 13.' The 'imaginary ashes' of 'Text 13' (138) have become the 'ash grey sand' of *Lessness*. There is once again 'something' in *Lessness*, as there was 'something once, in a head, in a heart, in a hand, before all opened, emptied, shut again and froze' ('Text 9,' 123). The 'imaginary ashes' and 'ash grey sand' commingle under a common sky. A phoenix-like myth outlining the recreative powers of the imagination holds out a promise of future fertility.[12] The 'ash grey' little body bears the mark of his imprisonment in the 'mighty light' of the false refuge – 'little block genitals overrun arse a single block grey crack overrun.'[13] But the 'two pale blue' testify to his strength to go on, to 'make it,' to create a life and a fiction. He will 'leave a trace ... among the sand, it's with that it would make a life' ('Text 13,' 137). Nothing no longer prevents anything, as in 'Text 13'; the 'never was ...' and 'he will ...' of *Lessness* coexist. *Lessness* contradicts 'Text 13''s 'you can't do with less' by constituting a 'less-ness'; Beckett has made a something that is also a nothing. The logically impossible conjunctions of 'Text 13' can be accepted in *Lessness* without the final self-cancelling denial: 'It's not true, yes, it's true it's true and it's not true ...' ('Text 13,' 139).

This new vision has been made possible by a new style, a new technique that makes language a means of expressing being. The disruption of syntax and grammar allows for the new meaning that is carried by the images of *Texts for Nothing* which Beckett has rewritten in *Lessness*. The rhetoric of failure and the dialectic of 'yes or no' that dominated the earlier work have given way to an intricate combination of sense and nonsense, order and disorder, whereby the grammatical distinctions of subject and object are no long set intransigently against each other. For the first readers of *Lessness*, the work must have indeed seemed nonsensical, and the linguistic dislocations certainly fit the definition of nonsense set out by Elizabeth Sewell in *The Field of Nonsense*:

The ordinary individual, who is neither scientist, logician nor philosopher, has nevertheless a clear working knowledge of what constitutes sense and nonsense. The latter will probably take one of two forms. First, it may be a collection of words which in their internal composition of letters or syllables or in their selection and sequence do not conform to the conventional patterns of language to which the particular mind is accustomed ... Or nonsense may appear as a collection of events or a verbal description of such a collection where the order and relationships differ from those held to be normal. Even though the ordinary mind may not be familiar with logic or higher thought in general, it uses exactly the same standard of reference, a fixed pattern of mental relations between letters, words of events.[14]

The next step in Sewell's argument is critical for an understanding of *Lessness*:

The appearance of nonsense – a lack of conformity in the material in question – may be due either to an absence of internal relations in the material or to the presence of a system of which the mind is unaware. (From this follows the notion of 'chance'). These two possibilities may look as if they amount to much the same thing since, for the conscious mind, a relationship which is unperceived is equivalent to there being no system at all. There is a difference, however, and one that has practical results. If you assume an absence of relations, you can get no further; but if you are ready to postulate relations as yet unperceived in the particular material, something may happen[15]

Enoch Brater and Susan Brienza's 'Chance and Choice in Beckett's *Lessness*' shows how the 'disorder' is itself governed by the choice open to Beckett within language's field of operation. This reading is a significant advance in facilitating access to *Lessness*, but the chance-choice paradigm is too closely identified with the artisanal aspects of Beckett's writing in *Lessness* and does not afford access to the new vision which is such a radical reappraisal of *Texts for Nothing*. Their descriptive linguistic analysis does not really lead any further than John Fletcher's impressionistic response. When Fletcher says Beckett's short fictions 'are far from being gibberish,' his only alternative is to label them 'formal exercises.'[16] Brater and Brienza want to show that *Lessness* 'is something more than a verbal game evoking a hermetic syntax.'[17] But they singularly fail to show this because their reading is unable to determine the subject of the text, which can only be identified by means of a vision that contains both sense and nonsense.

Beckett shows that he has once again run 'the gantelope of sense and nonsense'[18]: 'sans' puns on 'sens' in the sense of that which is perceived through the senses; 'lessness' is an anagram of 'senseless' in the sense of that which is not empirically apprehended. Both aspects must be held together if the 'ideal real' of *Lessness* is to be apprehended: the 'calm touch close eye' that is literally senseless and the 'two pale blue' that gaze upon the world. If 'our only chance of renovation is to open our eyes and see the mess,'[19] Beckett also paradoxically shows in *Lessness* that it is necessary for us to 'close our eyes' to see with complete clarity. As Beckett said at the conclusion of a hoax lecture on a non-existent group of poets, art is 'perfectly intelligible' and yet 'perfectly incomprehensible.'[20]

It is highly ironic that the critics of Beckett's later works, in their quest to find order among what is often ostensibly disorder, actually turn his works into nonsense. As the notion is developed in Sewell's study, order is the prime criterion of nonsense: 'It is important to differentiate between this type of disorder, fluidity, the synthesis of the running together of pictures in the mind, and the type with which nonsense works and which we have tentatively called a rearrangement in the series of word references. Throughout this work the term "disorder" will mean the first type, that of dream and madness. If we are right, the second is not disorder so much as a condition necessary for the playing of a game.'[21] Nonsense, in Sewell's view, is hostile to dream, emotion, beauty, and the quest for truth and seeks instead to confine itself to a realm where logic maintains the individuality of items in a series ('one is one is one ...'). These are just the dimensions of being the 'nonsensical' calm eye also seeks to deny in phrases like 'Never but in vanished dream ...' The principle of identity in *Lessness* precludes, however, any such simple designation of what is realistic in the common-sense meaning of the word. The reader has to accept both sense and nonsense: the 'calm eye' and the 'two pale blue' are distinct entities and yet also constitute a unity within language – a veritable two-in-one. It is not so much that 'one is one is one' as that 'one is two and two is one.'

Nonsense is essentially the mind's endless playing against the forces of disorder which threaten it, aiming at a dialectical opposition between these forces rather than a reconciliation as in poetry. The poetic logic of *Lessness* dispenses with normal syntax and grammar but is not, of course, without its own 'rhyme and reason.' 'Refuge'/'deluge,' 'reign'/'rain'/ 'again,' 'light'/'white'/'upright,' for example, set up a series of associations that draw together the two distinct perspectives offered in *Lessness*. Both 'eyes' belong to the artist who has created the work before our eyes. Beckett has escaped the sense of disintegration by making it the very basis of a new kind of unity. The breaking up of language into units that defy normal categories of thought enables Beckett to escape the rhetoric of failure. In *Texts for Nothing*, language tended (after the first two 'Texts') to become an elaborate form of nonsense – rhetoric as the elaborate game language plays with itself. The 'orator' of 'Text 5' is very much aware of how 'it's getting to be a game' (98), and his 'toil' with his quill is a far cry from the 'toil and play' of 'Text 1' where the game and the real are able to accommodate each other. Critics have obviously felt the 'nonsensical' nature of Beckett's writing. The unsettling nature of the term nonsense has, however, led them away from a direct confrontation with the problem. Ruby Cohn, for example, says that Beckett sends his narrators 'through the looking-glass' in *Texts for Nothing*, only to go on to discuss the 'lyrical qualities'[22] of these fictions. Such question-begging only further confounds the problem. Beckett is, of course, not aiming to write nonsense in the fashion of Lewis Carroll. For Beckett, nonsense results from the failure to make sense out of life. In *Texts for Nothing*, Beckett is trying to find a way of letting reality into the game, not desperately trying (as Carroll did) to ward off the threats of real life.

Nonsense exhibits 'exercises in dialectic which, like games, have nothing to do with such a notion as "truth",' and, Sewell adds, 'Perhaps there is no truth to find out, any more than there would be in a nightmare or a game of chess, the notion being out of place.'[23] But the remarkable conclusion of her study points to a realm on the other side of nonsense's order that must be accommodated if a view of man's being is to be presented. What is needed is a new form of thought that combines sense and nonsense, order and disorder:

One comes to see more and more clearly, not only in connection with games and nonsense but in many ways of thought and experience, that what we need is a way of managing that other side, the unreason and disorder and make-believe and magic. For thirteen chapters now we have been logical, only to find at the end that we need an insulation from our own logic ... We need some way of moving from the circle of logic to the world outside the circle, from manipulation to make-believe. Reason cannot supply it, for the game we have been studying and playing has been reasonable, and any further pursuit of logic will merely take us further into this side of the game and hence into this dilemma. The answer cannot be a rational one.[24]

A similar series of conclusions was forced upon Beckett after the failure of his thirteen *Texts for Nothing* to combine reason with imagination as long as he was bound by a dialectical 'yes or no' of logic, grammar, and rhetoric. This 'trivium' would have to be replaced by a syntax of weakness in order to explain both sides of the game of language – its sense and nonsense.

9

The Rhetoric of Necessity in
Fizzles and the 'Still' Trilogy

The revolutionary change in Beckett's vision and approach to language in *How It Is* afforded a way out of the impasse which he encountered in *The Unnamable*. But even for the critic writing from a vantage point in time that allows for a 'foreknowledge' of all Beckett's published prose since *How It Is*, the implications of the new relationship between the author as 'voice' and the fiction as 'voice' presented in the closing pages of that novel do not represent an equation of which the subsequent works can be regarded as predictable consequences. The conclusion of *How It Is* embodies just as impossible a situation as that found at the conclusion of *The Unnamable*. But while The Unnamable seeks to transcend his status as a fiction and claim an identification with either the historical author-figure or the 'someone' who resides outside the fictional realm – 'we'd be reunited, his story the story to be told, but he has no story, he hasn't been in story' (413) – the 'I' of *How It Is* proposes his independence from both authorial 'voice' and the historical author-figure who is felt to be ultimately responsible for the whole business of perpetuating the act of fiction-making. Both narrative strategies are impossible 'as-if' departures from the conventions of the novel with its demands for a willing suspension of disbelief about what is real and what is fictional. What needs to be determined is the relative value of those two 'as-if' as a means of depicting the reality of the fictional process. Although *The Unnamable*'s program temporarily opened up a most exciting area of speculation by challenging all the unquestioned assumptions of the novel, it was bound to end in a rhetoric of failure, for art can never be totally 'other' than itself, can never, in other words, be totally life or totally silence. The 'as-if' of *How It Is*, on the other hand, is a much more useful departure from the conventions of language and fiction; it expands the whole range of possibilities inherent in the creative act and does not deny (as *The Unnamable* tried to do) 'the necessity of art.'[1]

How It Is marks Beckett's decision to proceed 'as-if' there is something to express. This new 'as-if' does not so much reverse the situation in *The Unnamable* as return to basic premises evident in Beckett's first works. In 'Assumption' the 'something' that strives to break free from the flesh of the artist is recognized as having needs as real as his own. The 'other,' discovered 'pre-existent' in the poet (as *Proust* would have it) is an indispensable and necessary consequence of the very nature of the imaginative process for Beckett and is the 'thing' without which the life of the poet cannot be maintained. But to grant this 'something' complete independence would mean the death of the 'author,' as the final 'drunken scream' of 'Assumption' revealed. What then are the implications of the final screams of *How It Is*? Does the narrator's 'I SHALL DIE SCREAMS GOOD' mean that the authorial voice has been eliminated by the declaration of the 'fiction' of his own being? If this were the case, the situation would simply reverse the terms at the end of *The Unnamable* and result in an impasse equally crippling to the continuation of the creative act.

In his review 'Denis Devlin' (1938), Beckett elaborated upon the nature of the conflicting needs that determine his interpretation of the artistic dilemma: 'The Dives – Lazarus symbiosis, as intimate as that of fungoid and algoid in lichen (to adopt the *Concise New Oxford Dictionary* example). Here scabs, lucre, etc., there torment, bosom, etc., but both here and there *gulf*. The absurdity, here or there, of either without the other, the inaccessible other. In death they did not cease to be divided. Who predeceased? A painful period for both.'[2] What Beckett here calls 'this Gospel *conte cruel*' could also be taken to suggest the type of dilemma that 'caused' his works after *How It Is* to be written. The works after *How It Is* are indeed reflective of 'a painful period for both.' Here the different 'needs' of the authorial and fictional aspects which struggle to assert their own being are confronted by an unavoidable 'necessity' – their symbiotic relationship in the dilemma of the creative act. The common 'source of need' that both Dives and Lazarus seek is an affirmation of being through language. The initial reaction to *How It Is* was a swing back towards an assertion of the primacy of the authorial voice in the interests of self-survival. *All Strange Away, Imagination Dead Imagine*, and *The Lost Ones* testify to a detached, would-be objective narrative point of view that precludes the 'something there' coming to life and asserting its full potential for being. This authoritarian view resulted, however, in the introduction of an allegorical perspective that distorted the reality of the relationship between Dives and Lazarus. While the 'something there' is admitted, its claim to a life of its own is smothered by the author's own self-interests.

Beckett's first published poem in twenty or so years, 'something there' (1974), focuses upon precisely this problem. The third and last stanza reads:

> so the odd time
> out there
> somewhere out there
> like as if
> as if
> a a m nothing
> not life
> necessarily[3]

The poem is indicative of Beckett's 'confused' response to the realities of the aesthetic situation in his works after *How It Is*. The 'I see something out there, not life necessarily' is, however, a dramatic reversal of the 'I have no being' statement which Beckett made to Shenker in an effort to describe the position in which he found himself after the famous trilogy. This new statement clearly indicates a movement away from 'complete disintegration' and the aesthetic of nothingness. But the situation is still riddled with difficulties because of the problematical ontological status of the 'something there' discovered in the creative act. *How It Is* confirmed and developed the last words of 'Text 13' in which a something was recognized as an irreducible reality of the creative act, even if it could not at that point be reconciled with a nothing to corroborate a living human presence. In *How It Is*, the something approaches a radical break with the authorial needs in order to establish a life for itself by means of a series of radical 'as-if' transformations.

'Not life/necessarily' are the key words for an interpretation of Beckett's works after *How It Is*. While these two last lines of the poem reveal Beckett's genuine doubts about the nature of the 'something there,' they also indicate an opposition between the author's need for a life of his own and the needs of the 'something there.' Hence the lines 'not life/ necessarily' may allow for a way out of the dilemma for the authorial voice: if the something is not a human being, the 'as-if' transformation can be legitimately displaced by techniques of naturalism or allegory. A formal structure that satisfies the author's needs without having to recognize the need for being of the something could then legitimately replace a quest for the ontology of the fiction in which a symbiotic or mutual need must be accommodated.

But the most important development in Beckett's prose works after *Lessness* involves the fulfilment of the potential of language to draw the hermetic and Orphic aspects into a complementary, reciprocal relationship. These texts show Beckett exploiting both the formalist view of the work of art as a self-enclosed world (in *Abandonné* and 'For to end yet again,' for example) and the ontological view in which language discloses and sustains a human world (in 'Still,' 'Sounds,' and 'As the Story Was Told,' for example). The distinction between the two views is not, of course, absolutely clear-cut – for the artist. Even when drawn towards the hermetic or formalist view of language, the poet must still speak with a human voice. Even when the authorial voice is primarily interested in manipulating the 'something there' for his own ends (in *The Lost Ones* and *All Strange Away*, for example), he is still testifying to his own being. This approach may be life-denying for the someones or somethings, but it is not the killing opposition of 'no's knife in yes's wound,' as found in *Texts for Nothing*.

The hermetic aspect of language can now be more profitably discussed if considered as an authentication of the 'necessity of rhetoric,' that is, an acknowledgment of a fundamental need of the artist, the need to create a world, however formal, which testifies to his 'particular human identity.' On the other hand, the 'rhetoric of necessity' is now a more apt description of the Orphic dimensions of language. In the 'Still' trilogy, for example, the 'necessity' acknowledged encompasses the needs of both Dives and Lazarus. Whether viewed as a relationship between aspects of the same self or as a relationship between two independent beings, the essential point remains that the old subject-object paradigm is no longer adequate for this description of a symbiotic relationship that has drawn the artist to the 'source of need' in which the hermetic and Orphic aspects combine in a 'rhetoric of necessity.'

Rhetoric has, in other words, been rehabilitated and can no longer be identified with the 'rhetoric of failure' and non-being analysed in the discussion of *Texts for Nothing* (indeed the only work to be considered in this chapter which hearkens directly back to rhetoric in this pejorative sense is 'Fizzle 4,' 'I gave up before birth'). Beckett's development of a 'syntax of weakness' in *How It Is*, *Ping*, and *Lessness* results, not surprisingly, in the creation of a new rhetoric, for the repetition and variation of innovations, however radical, inevitably results in a new system, even if it cannot be so neatly classified as classical rhetorical usage. In 'Still' and 'Sounds,' a 'syntax of weakness' has become a 'rhetoric of success,' a rhetoric which is capable of affirming being, of letting being into the work of art. The fundamental distinction between the 'necessity of rhetoric' and the 'rhetoric of necessity' is that whereas the former expresses the being of the author and his legitimate need for form which will authenticate his being, the latter admits both this need and the living reality of the someone or something who is now shown as man in the world. Not a fictive self, not a surrogate, not even a phantom, but an actual human subject. The 'rhetoric of necessity' leads to an engagement with the perennially vexing issues of the meaning and value of the life man leads in the world. The moral significance of the word, always an issue in Beckett (even when his various characters had tried to deny their being), is now in the forefront.

The publication of the short prose texts termed 'fizzles' ('foirades'), most of which were written around 1960,[4] throws important light on the various directions that Beckett followed after the radical breakthrough of *How It Is* with its 'impossible' conclusion. Beckett's disparaging title, 'foirades' or 'farts,' applies more aptly to the texts first published under that title in *Minuit* than to 'For to end yet again' and 'Still' which were included under the same title in the published book form of the collection. The latter two works are major innovations which more properly belong to a consideration of Beckett's works after *Lessness*. The original 'fizzles' (along with 'Afar a bird,' a companion piece to 'I gave up before birth') are, however, important for the critic's view of Beckett's works after *How It Is*. Three main strategies are apparent in these six 'fizzles': 'I gave up before birth' and 'Afar a bird' revert to the 'rhetoric of failure' and non-being characteristic of *Texts for Nothing*; 'Horn came always' and 'Old earth' explore the possibility of an 'I' in the world; 'He is barehead' and 'Closed place' employ a third-person detached narrative point of view in an attempt to pull back from the radical conclusion of *How It Is* which threatened the very authority of the authorial voice.

'I gave up before birth' recounts the 'impossible' situation of a disembodied 'I' who refuses to accept that his 'I' has ever been implicated in the words of the voice or, for that matter, in a bodily existence in time. All characteristics of a living human presence are projected upon (or foisted upon) a 'he' who does not truly possess his own being because of the negations imposed by 'I': 'he'll never say I anymore, he'll never say anything anymore ... because of me' (32). Although the 'I' concludes by stating 'I'll feed it all it needs' (33), it is obvious that all the 'I' will offer is the means for the 'he' to 'end' without truly having been. 'Fizzle 3,' 'Afar a bird,' intensifies this rhetoric of self-denial and also complicates the 'I-he' opposition of its predecessor by the addition of a third party, thus creating a complicated narrative structure which resembles that of 'Text 4': 'it was he had a life, I didn't have a life, a life not worth having, because of me, it's impossible I should have a mind and I have one, someone divines me, divines us ...' (26). This 'someone' is a type of vulture-artist who attempts to reconcile or unite the 'I' and the 'he.' But the act of integration meets with as little success here as it did in 'Text 4': 'I wait for me *afar* for my story to begin, to end, and again this voice cannot be mine' (94, italics mine). There is nevertheless a fragmented narrative in 'Afar a bird,' and this accounts for its differences from 'I gave up before birth,' which it otherwise virtually repeats. The 'story' (which most resembles that of *From an Abandoned Work*) fails miserably because it does not explore the role of the 'someone' who 'divines us,' but concentrates instead on the 'I-he' opposition. Once again there is a killing relationship: 'he'll do himself to death, because of me, I'll live it with him, I'll live his death ...' (26).

'Fizzle 2,' 'Horn came always,' and 'Fizzle 6,' 'Old earth,' use an 'I' narrator that is more or less recognizably human and involved in representative actions which are not denied by a detached narrator behind the action, as in the two 'fizzles' just discussed. The narrator in the first of these two 'I' narrations recounts the effects of the nocturnal visits of a person named Horn (a go-between, ostensibly involved in some type of detective work). Previously, the narrator had tried to avoid all self-perception and all motion by staring at the ceiling of his room. But the visits of Horn coincide with his desire to be seen again: 'I'll let myself be seen before I'm done. I'll call out, if there is a knock, Come in!' (20).[5] Horn's presence further necessitates a recognition of a reality that belies this 'I''s attempts at a solipsistic existence. There is indeed 'something' out there: 'It is in outer space, not to be confused with the other, that such images develop. I need only interpose my hand, or close my eyes, to banish them, or take off my eyeglasses for them to fade. This is a help, but not a real protection, as we shall see' (21). But the story concerning Horn only contains allusions to a period 'of five or six years ago' (20). We have no confirmation of the present position of the 'I'. If anything, it seems likely that he has again succumbed to the dream of

From an Abandoned Work, of 'a long unbroken time without before or after' (echoed in the descriptions of only 'feeling' that he is in time and the description of the 'unbroken plane of the ceiling').

'Old earth' makes a much more positive (albeit perplexing) declaration of being in the world and in continuous time. The various tenses employed in the first few sentences establish a being who admits his complicity in an organic cycle of birth and death: 'I've seen you' (i.e. 'old earth'), 'it will be me,' 'it was never us,' 'It won't be long now' (43). Outside and inside are united here in a way totally distinct from that found in 'Horn came always,' where the narrator only manages a few steps within his room or at best a greeting of Horn at the threshold. This 'I' returns home at night, grasps a bough of his 'little oaktree,' pulls himself up, and goes in. The final image of this beautiful little work is emotionally resonant of a loss, of a 'too late' apprehension of a reality which the narrator acknowledges, but still cannot make meaningful. 'Still, standing before the window,' he appears detached from the spectacle of the cockchafers' 'nightflight.'[6] His 'now' is not allowed to stand as a point fixed in a moving time. As he watches the sky, he (like the insects) makes a 'nightflight' and is transferred to another time, 'other skies, another body' (44). With 'my other's ravening eyes,' the 'I' has seen and been involved with life in the world. But, as an artist (an 'I' that creates other 'I's), the narrator is always 'too late' in creating a life for himself. There are 'moments of life, of mine too, among others, no denying, all said and done' (44). But, while there is 'no denying,' there is, equally, no truly continuous being in time for the narrator since he is so often 'other' to himself. 'Old earth' does, however, make an effective declaration of the complex state of being that the 'I' as artist must learn to live with. It clearly breaks away from the rhetoric of failure and, like *Enough*, manages to convey a sense of being in time, of a life being lived through, however problematic the equation of being may be for the artist.

In 'Fizzle 1,' 'He is barehead,' a third-person narrator describes the journey of a 'he' from a hellish underground towards a world 'above.' This 'he' would appear to be no less a personage than Murphy, toiling his way back towards the land of the living.[7] There is little resemblance between this Murphy and Beckett's earlier hero except that he is bareheaded (Murphy also couldn't bear hats, the memory of the caul was too much for him) and is also admirably suited for walking – 'Murphy had first-rate legs' (9). Ironically enough, the emphasis is now upon the physical and not the mental attributes of the protagonist – 'the great head where he toils is all mockery' (7). Whereas the earlier Murphy had visualized himself in the 'Belacqua fantasy' leisurely dreaming his way through his life before leisurely toiling his way up hill to Paradise, this new version of Murphy shows him toiling painfully through a labyrinth which may at best lead back to the world. And the third-person narrator of this 'fizzle' is decidedly much less sympathetic towards Murphy than was the narrator of *Murphy*. This Murphy is a 'puppet' and does in fact 'whinge,' like all the other patent fabrications or dupes of the authorial voice.

The narrator is actually quite indifferent to, and even ignorant of, the goal of the journey: 'Where is it then that life awaits him, in relation to his starting-point, to the point rather at which he suddenly realized he was started, above or below? Or will they cancel out in the end, the long gentle climbs and headlong steeps? It matters little in any case, so long as he is on the right road, and that he is, for there are no others, unless he has let them slip by unnoticed, one after another' (10—11). The implication that Murphy has a freedom of choice in pursuing his way through the labyrinth is disingenuous, for it is obvious that he is only an allegorical cipher at the disposal of the author (a possibility masked in *Murphy* by the use of techniques of conventional realism and the narrator's apparent recognition of Murphy's independence). The narration ends with the status of Murphy's quest unresolved. But from the author's point of view it still supplies materials for future manipulation, 'fresh elements and motifs, such as these bones ...' (15).

This 'fizzle' could indeed be regarded as Beckett's own wry admission that at this point in his writing he was still not able to escape allegory, even though he had theoretically cast it out in 'Dante ... Bruno . Vico .. Joyce.' For here we have Dantean echoes, Bruno's 'maxima and minima' (14), and Vico's 'providential' view of history ironically recast in an allegorical fashion – 'as destitute of history as on that first day, on this same path, which is his beginning' (12). But Murphy is not even a 'living symbol'; he is doomed never to breathe the air up 'above,' 'the true life-giving' (13). 'Not life/necessarily': if not, one of the theoretical consequences is likely to be allegory.

In 'Fizzle 8,' 'For to end yet again,' the 'something there' is definitely 'not life' and becomes an 'object' in order that the creating consciousness may lay claim to his own need to write a fiction. This is by no means to agree with the often expressed view that Beckett is now concerned only with 'stasis' or 'fixed absolutes': the vital interest in this 'fizzle' is the being of the author, his very human need to create something that will testify to his continued existence, even if it does involve a denial of life for the 'expelled.' The very short prose fragment *Abandonné* (1972), an early version of the prologue section of 'For to end yet again,' emphasizes the priority of the 'skull' or creative consciousness over the 'other' discovered in the glimmering 'remains' of the imagination:

> Lieu du crâne noir clos seul le crâne front posé sur une planche vide alentour. Seul le crâne sans plus ni tronc ni traits fixe dans le noir. Crâne lieu dernier lieu des restes où luit de loin en loin dans le noir un reste. Dernier restes des jours du jour jamais lumière aussi faible que la leur aussi blanche. Exemple une main ouverte poignet ceint du fil d'argent doigts recourbés comme pour fondre. Seule la main avec poignet sans plus lent éclair dans le noir. Ainsi à la fin il commence le crâne à se faire pour finir s'éteindre recommence au lieu d'abandonner,[8]

Beckett jettisons *Abandonné* at the very point when (to quote from the translation of the last sentence of *Abandonné* in 'For to end yet again') 'the skull makes to glimmer again in lieu of going out.' But *Abandonné* does 'go out' at the very point when the resurrection of the flickering ashes of the imagination is imminent. The most probable reason for this abandonment is a reluctance on the part of this skull to involve himself with an other and the question of authority that would subsequently be raised.

Abandonné could only be continued if a story of some sort fed the glimmers of the imagination. In 'For to end yet again,' the indispensable narrative elements are the little body of the 'expelled' among 'his ruins' and the two white dwarfs who come to collect him. The 'white bodies marble still' (60) of the dwarfs are the 'unshakable pillars' of this world in which the little body is toppled – 'the expelled falls headlong down and lies back to sky full little stretch amidst his ruins' (59). The primary problem in coming to terms with the work is to determine the relationship between the 'skull alone in the dark,' the 'cyclopean dome' of the dwarfs, and the skull of the little body.

We saw in *Lessness* how Beckett employed a 'syntax of weakness' in order to corroborate a vision in which author and other coexisted in a 'ruins' coterminous with the world. 'For to end yet again' is written partly as a reaction against this vision and shows a loss of belief in the ability of art to accommodate the life of a little body who is distinct from the authorial consciousness. Nevertheless, the skull of 'For to end yet again' has to admit the need for an other, if the creative act is to continue beyond a few sentences. But in this instance the little body is not the coequal of the detached 'I,' merely a dupe at the disposal of a creating self who is only concerned with validating his own being. The abolition of the distinctions between within and without in *Lessness* which served as a clearing ground for being has become in 'For to end yet again,' 'Skull last place of all black void within without till all at once or by degrees at last this leaden dawn checked no sooner dawned' (56).

He has not been able to 'stir,' 'to make it,' to take 'the space of a step.' The promise of a new beginning in *Lessness* has become only a prop to allow the author to begin (and end again) in this sequel piece. The 'endless grey' is no longer relieved by a promise of a return of the blessed days of 'blue the passing cloud.' The 'old love new love' of *Lessness* that intimated a return to the passions of life as experienced in time has become identified in 'For to end yet again' with the old dream of 'Alba' in which art is employed as a vehicle for transcendence: 'Atop the cyclopean dome rising sheer from jut of brow yearns white to the grey sky the bump of habitativity or love of home' (59). But in 'For to end yet again' the whiteness 'neither on earth nor above' is identified with the 'monstrous' dwarfs, not with the ministrations of a beautiful woman who 'stoop[s] with fingers of compassion / to endorse the dust' ('Alba'). Nature's course has been abortively forestalled in order to establish the primacy of art over life. The skull of this 'fizzle' admits, in other words, the necessity of rhetoric, the need for an artificial structure to sustain its glimmering remains. What this skull does not, however, believe in is the compatibility of this construct with a little body who is able to 'take up [its] life and walk.' This is not the 'my skull shell of sky and earth' of 'The Vulture': 'Sepulchral skull is this then its last state all set for always litter and dwarfs ruins and little body grey cloudless sky glutted dust verge upon verge hell air not a breath' (60). There is no vulture-artist here; the story explicitly takes place beneath 'a sky forsaken of its scavengers' (59).

Rather than 'stoop to the prone' (a task which this artist leaves for his minions, the white dwarfs), the skull of 'For to end yet again' assists in toppling the little body so that he will never again take up his life: 'fallen unbending all his little length as though pushed from behind by some helping hand' (60). The enigmatic fifth sentence of *Abandonné* which Beckett omitted from 'For to end yet again' described an open hand that in its need was turned back upon itself – 'doigts recourbés comme pour fondre.' In 'For to end yet again,' this 'deeper need' is 'screened' by manipulating the little body so that it serves the author's interests. We don't need to trouble ourselves with the mythology of modern

astronomy with its 'white dwarfs' and so on in order to see the significance of the dwarfs in this work. These grotesque assistants of the
author, 'so alike the eye cannot tell them apart' (54), are an even more
bizarre version of the twins Art and Con of *Watt* fame. They seem to
have 'sprung from nowhere' (59), just as Malone's hunchbacks did when
he wanted to play in his dark. The author is in league with the grotesque
creations of art in order to dispose of the troublesome presence of the
little body. Except for the revealing phrase about the 'helping hand,' the
authorial presence pretends to have a detached, even indifferent, view
of the whole proceedings. He does, however, have a sharp eye for what
transpires in his domain; the 'expelled' is 'invisible to any other eye' (56)
except his own privileged one. His 'bird's-eye view' (58) suggests a
majestic solitude very different from that of the vulture-artist 'dragging
his hunger': 'Eagle the eye that shall discern him now mingled with the
ruins mingling with the dust beneath a sky forsaken of its scavengers.'
The inhuman nature of this authorial point of view is most clearly
brought out in the description of his 'monstrous' servants, the dwarfs.
Their 'lidded eyes' suggest the reptilian and this image links up with
the earlier comment on the sated dust which can engulf no more – 'Or
mere digestive torpor as once the boas which past with one last gulp
clean sweep at last' (58–9). Their 'monstrous arms' enable them to pick
up the litter 'without having to stoop' (57). This exact phrase was applied
to the old man in *Enough* who with his arms 'like a tired old ape' (155)
was able to scoop up handfuls of petals. But however grotesque the old
man's appearance, he was still human, not only a mere contrivance of
art; his eyes expressed emotion – 'blue bloodshot apparently affected.'
'Without having to stoop' implied in *Enough* an affirmative revision of
'The Vulture.' The 'eagle eye' of the author and the 'lidded' ones of the
dwarfs deny the living reality of the little body's blue eyes: 'Eyes in their
orbits blue still unlike the doll's the fall has not shut nor yet the dust
stopped up' (60). No wonder the little body cannot 'believe' his eyes
when faced with the unreal whiteness of the dwarfs. There can be no
communication between these servants of art and a little body with
claims to being. The little body is never allowed to speak: 'Breath has
not left him though soundless still and exhaling scarcely ruffles the dust'
(59–60).
'Fizzle 7,' 'Still,' is one of Beckett's most successful resolutions of
the central problems posed by the 'impasse.' These problems, whether
viewed as a series of oppositions between creator and created, being
and fiction, word and world, the artist's dream of a book independent of

the world, and his unavoidable commitment to this world, are ultimately aspects of one all important issue: the relationship between art and life. In 'Still' a remarkable reconciliation of ostensible contraries such as motion and stillness, sounds and silence, light and darkness is effected by means of a language that combines a rhetoric of necessity and a syntax of weakness. Viewed within the context of the post-trilogy writings, the achievement of 'Still' can perhaps be most easily appreciated by stressing the obvious: it is the most recognizably human of Beckett's works since *Enough*. There is no longer the complex and vexed questioning of the reality and being of the 'something' located in the room, box, rotunda, et al. which has been the hallmark of Beckett's writing since the trilogy. The matter of fact statement that there is an identifiable human protagonist in 'Still' can easily be underestimated. For Beckett to present an 'other' that is admitted not only as real but as a human reality is, in the context of the residual works, an act of revolutionary significance. 'Still' testifies to Beckett's belief in the compatibility of art and life, and his recognition of a number of Orphic connections between artist, man, and world.

By dispensing with the conventions of both first-person and third-person narration in 'Still,' Beckett is able to achieve a more complete détente between the claims of the author and other than was achieved even in *Lessness*. The *modus vivendi* is more satisfying in 'Still' because the authorial voice is less concerned with presenting his own views of a timeless, soundless world that 'never was.' The 'passing light' is not therefore a 'figment' in 'Still,' but rather an essential reality of the text. Unlike Murphy, the protagonist of 'Still' does not sit out of the sun 'as though he were free.' The nothingness associated with the closing of his eyes must not be identified with a Murphean quest for the so-called true void of the self. More properly, the act of closure in 'Still' involves apperception, the mind's perception of itself as a part of the world 'outside' against which it can never be hermetically sealed. No matter where the man directs his sight, total absence of light, total absence of perceiving or being perceived is not possible: 'Or anywhere any ope staring out of nothing just failing light quite still till quite dark though of course no such thing just less light still when less did not seem possible' (49). Even the climactic meeting of head and hand in which their 'needs' are brought into a tremulous equilibrium is not merely self-reflexive, but recognizes a need for being which requires a relation of both inside and outside worlds: 'As if even in the dark eyes closed not enough and perhaps even more than ever necessary against that no such thing the further shelter of the hand' (50–1). However much the protagonist tries to cut himself off from the external world, his futile actions serve only to underline the impossibility of such escapism. The self must come face to face with its bodily reality and with the world of nature outside the 'open window' of 'Still.' There is no refuge from 'suffering – that opens a window on the real and is the main condition of the artistic experience,' as Beckett affirmed in *Proust*.[9] Self-perception cannot be avoided and, as Beckett told John Gruen, when man comes face to face with himself he experiences the abyss. But this 'nihilation' is also a creative experience that confronts us not only with our 'stupidities' and 'obscenities' (as Beckett told Gruen), but with the responsibility to make sense of the 'mess.'[10]

The little body of 'Still' is not cast into an inhospitable world of endless shifting sands, a world of ruins. Instead he finds himself in a world with which a number of vital identifications are possible. Foremost among these connections is that between the rising and setting of the sun and the opening and closing of the man's eyes. The protagonist of 'Still' is a human being, not a statue as in 'For to end yet again' whose only life is in 'the eyes last bright of all.' The skies have opened before him and his own animation allows him to duplicate within his room the path traced by the sun in its rhythmic rise and fall. Both ends of this cycle are life-giving, as the allusion to the 'old statue' of Memnon in 'Still' emphasizes: 'Legs side by side broken right angles at the knees as in that old statue some old god twanged at sunrise and again at sunset' (48).

The sun in 'Still' is not, like that in the opening of *Murphy*, restricted to a set course, 'having no alternative.' Neither is the human figure of 'Still' completely predetermined in his actions. The 'old gods' are alive in 'Still' and point to the possibility of a meaningful relationship between man and nature, a connection forged from the 'as-if's and 'figments' of the imagination. The protagonist of 'Still' is, like the Belacqua of 'Dream of Fair to Middling Women,' a 'trine man: centripetal, centrifugal and ... not. Phoebus chasing Daphne, Narcissus flying from Echo and ... neither ... The third being was the dark gulf.'[11] The only details from the outside world mentioned in the text are the 'tree or bush' and 'that beech in whose shade once.'[12] Like the narrator of *From an Abandoned Work*, this 'subject' is fascinated by 'all things still and rooted.' But in 'Still' there is a suggestion that a human relationship is possible with such objects, especially the tree, a 'column of quiet,' in the words of 'Dream of Fair to Middling Women.'[13] This identification becomes explicit in 'Sounds,' the sequel to 'Still,' where the man embraces the tree 'as if a human.' Phoebus is still chasing Daphne. The 'reversed metamorphosis. The Laurel into Daphne. The old thing where it always was, back again' (*Watt*, 44) is viewed here in an affirmative way as the protagonist tries to repopulate his little kingdom. The change of vision evident in 'Still' is further emphasized by the fact that Narcissus is no longer flying from Echo. The last sentence shows him 'listening for a sound.' There is still a 'centripetal' and 'centrifugal' movement in 'Still' – eyes open and close 'in what if not quite a single movement almost' (48). But the 'third being,' the 'dark gulf,' does not represent here a 'dark zone' such as was typified by the third zone of Murphy's mind. 'Still' makes it clear that a zone which could be termed the void of the true self does not exist; the phrase 'no such thing' is used twice to indicate that complete darkness, the obliteration of the awareness of the self as an entity in the world, is finally impossible. This is not to deny the importance of the inner world, simply to recognize what Beckett's narrators have so often tried to deny: being cannot have meaning unless it acknowledges an integration of both inner and outer, sense and non-sense, art and nature.

'Sounds' carries on directly from the last sentence of 'Still.' In this sequel, the protagonist, 'head on hand listening for a sound,' has transferred his attention from the problematic status of his own stillness to the stillness of the world around him. The second sentence of 'Sounds' echoes distantly but distinctly its counterpart in 'Assumption' ('The buffoon in the loft swung steadily on his stick and the organist sat dreaming with his hands in his pockets'): 'Or if none [sounds] hour after hour no sound of any kind then he having been dreamt away let himself be dreamt away to where none at any time away from here where none come none pass to where no sound at any time no sound to listen for none of any kind.'[14] The wish to be 'dreamt away' in order that the obligations of the creative act may be abrogated is a central assumption in both works. But there are a number of important differences between the two works which must also be acknowledged. First of all, 'Sounds' is not anchored upon the impasse of 'He could have shouted and could not.' The protagonist of 'Sounds' is not struggling against a 'wild rebellious surge that aspired violently towards realization in sound.' This attempt at quelling the voice of the 'other' within is no longer relevant for the unnamed narrator of 'Sounds,' since he is presented as a self whose being is not challenged by an alien force. Secondly, he is not troubled, as Beckett's first artist-hero was, by the problem of the relationship between creating and created self. Fictive selves have been abandoned in 'Sounds.' The 'buffoon in the loft' is no longer swinging 'steadily on his stick': 'Room too quite still some time past and loft where such sounds once all night.'

Without a fictive self (the buffoon), the 'organist' of 'Sounds' is no longer able to indulge in a carefree dreaming, 'hands in his pockets.' 'Head in hand,' his 'prestidigitation' is now much more pensive and anxiety-ridden. If there are no longer any sounds in his room (or head), he must seek them outside his 'building.' The opening sentence is primarily concerned with the possibility of visits from others which would break the silence of this 'stillest night' and definitely substantiate the claims of the world upon this 'he.' His ambiguous attitude towards any such visitation is conveyed in a series of negatives: 'none come some time past mostly no want no not no want but never none of any kind.' The 'he' is not sure whether visitors are desired or not: 'no want' is itself negated then reaffirmed; the 'he' seems to be making a virtue of necessity since 'never none' come anymore. The nostalgic ending of the last sentence implies a suppressed desire for company (even if not of the human kind) and resonates with an emotional remembrance of things past, 'the nightbirds some time past in such numbers once such numbers.'

The 'he' listens 'not for nothing' (an implicit rejection of the aesthetic that governed most of the *Texts for Nothing*), even though the air is 'too still for even the lightest leaf to sound.' The vigil is not in vain for the 'he' knows that there are sounds, but that they are unable 'to carry the brief way here.' Since the sounds 'die away' before they arrive, the 'he' must go to where they originate. The remarkable middle section of 'Sounds' shows that, if the temptation to be 'dreamt away' is to be constrained, the man must admit his deeper need for a connection with the world, an interchange of 'giving and receiving' that is by no means 'farcical,' as 'Three Dialogues' would have it. The strangest and most moving scene describes how he embraces the tree as if it were a loved one: 'and stand beneath or with his arms round it certain moods and head against the bark as if a human.' This most recent 'he' listens to and embraces the tree; he wants to become one with his Echo and Daphne. An important parallel to the man's situation in 'Sounds' occurs in the third partition of Burton's *Anatomy of Melancholy* ('Love – Melancholy'). Beckett's solitary embraces the tree as (in Burton's words) 'Apollo did the baytree for his Daphne.'[15] There are a number of striking parallels between 'Sounds' and a section of Burton's 'Cure of Love – Melancholy' which describes marriage as a means of overcoming the solitude which fosters melancholy. In the course of evaluating the pros and cons of marriage, Burton cites the case of a famous scholar who had formerly heaped 'dicteries against women' but now recants and supports his learned praise of women by reference to a number of authorities:

Read what Solomon hath said in their praises, Prov. xiii and Syracides, cap. 26 et 30, 'Blessed is the man that hath a virtuous wife, for the number of his days shall be doubled. A virtuous woman rejoiceth her husband, and he shall fulfill the years of his life, in peace. A good wife is a good portion (*et xxxvi*, 24), an help, a pillar of rest', *columna quietus*; *Qui capit uxorem, fratrem capit atque sororem* (who takes a wife takes a brother and sister). Et v.25 'He that hath no wife wandereth to and fro mourning.'[16]

The to-and-fro visits to the tree in 'Sounds' suggest, however, that the man has changed his attitude towards women and would, like Burton's recanter, 'Ask the world and all women forgiveness.' Whereas in 'Dream of Fair to Middling Women' Beckett railed at the frailties of women and vainly sought an ideal 'column of quiet,' the man in 'Sounds' is one of those unfortunate creatures of fable who are burdened by their wish come true and who vainly seek to reverse the metamorphosis.

The concluding sentences of 'Sounds' hold out the possibility of an affirmative reading which does not, however, turn a blind eye to the harsh realities of Beckett's world. Breathing, however faint, is still an affirmation of life: 'Breath itself sigh it all out through the mouth that sound then fill again hold out again so often once sigh upon sigh no question now some time past but quiet as when even the mother can't hear stooped over the crib but has to feel pulse or heart.' All violent expressions of breath now seem to belong irrevocably to the past. Although there is now almost no movement of air ('as though no more air to move no more than in a void'), a balanced reading of 'Sounds' has to point out that this negative 'as though' is just as much a wishful speculation as that applied to the tree ('as if a human'). There remains a muted assertion that life still persists. The 'sighs' do periodically punctuate the stillness. Hence the final sentence, 'Leave it so ... no such thing as a sound' is more reflective of the narrator's own wishes than of the reality presented by the text. To be 'dreamt away' makes nonsense of the long struggle of the Beckett 'someone' to validate his claims for being in the world. Now that the world has been regained, an effort must be made to make sense of it, that is, to combine sense and nonsense, sounds and soundlessness. If 'Sounds' is a 'fizzle' that 'makes air,' it is still a 'fart fraught with meaning' (*How It Is*, 45).

'Dreamt away' in the last half of the concluding sentence of 'Sounds,' the protagonist of 'Still 3' has returned to his position in the chair: 'Whence when back no knowing where no telling where been how long how it was.' The opening phrases remind one of *The Unnamable*'s opening flurry of queries and clearly sets the 'Still' sequence in opposition with Beckett's more famous trilogy. 'Still 3' is distinguished from *The Unnamable* in a number of vital ways: this 'subject' does not question his identity (the 'who now' of *The Unnamable*'s opening sentence is significantly absent). This subject is unnamed, but he is not shut in as was the Unnamable. He is 'before a window,' even if the 'open' window of 'Still' and the open door of 'Sounds' are now conspicuously absent. The last phrases of the opening sentence, 'how long it was,' emphasize that it is impossible for art and language to deal with the 'place' attained through a dream that carries the self out of the world. The real subject remains 'how it is' with its investigation of being in time.

'Still 3,' composed of thirteen 'sentences,' divides into two equal parts. The first six sentences recount the 'return' from the 'dream.' The seventh and pivotal sentence evaluates this return and prepares the way for the intervention of the imagination: 'Back then and nothing to tell but some soundless place and in the head in the hand where such questions once names like ghosts where what how long weirdest of all.' Time is now the 'weirdest' question 'of all,' not only with reference to the period of 'dreamt away,' but also with regard to time in the world. The 'dim question' of time has faded because 'eyes closed as shown always the same dark now from now all hours day and night.' Hence there is 'no nightbird to mean night at least or day at least.' He imagines, however fanciful it might be, that 'with the right valley wind' he can just make out the 'incarnation bell' or Mother Calvet. 'Still 3' is not a text for nothing, but a text for being, for, although this implied 'I' cannot make his fictions come to life, he does not deny his own existence. Closing one's eyes on reality can never completely eradicate the knowledge of the 'miserable light.' The 'incarnation bell' testifies to his bodily reality. But this 'I' will remain a spectral presence until he again directs himself to questions of time in the world and moves away from the 'soundless place' of 'dreamt away.'

The man is terrified by the unexpected appearance of visions of dead faces and desperately tries to return to the 'soundless place' of his 'dreamt away' state, a refuge from these expressionless and soundless creatures whose presence is so disturbing. He tries desperately to escape from them, with the plea, 'try dreamt away saying dreamt away where.' The protagonist's horrified reaction to these figures may be due to the fact that, even though he keeps them 'at arm's length,' he has realized that their 'expressionless' stare is similar to his own – eyes closed, in the chair. He too is now one of the vanquished, a 'lost one' whose being is expressionless as long as he cannot integrate the various aspects of self represented by dream, chair, and visions of the imagination. The final 'out' leaves the final status of self highly problematical: has he been dreamt away, will the imagination flicker into being again, is he still in the chair with eyes closed? 'Still 3' shows that even a 'syntax of weakness' can become a rhetoric of failure unless it is sustained by an acknowledgment of the necessity of art.

'As the Story Was Told' ('In Memoriam Günther Eich') was written a few months after the completion of the 'Still' trilogy. This very short story is a moral fable that shows that simply to be in the world is by itself not enough to validate being. To live in the world involves a number of very difficult ethical questions which the self can only decipher or make meaningful (if only for itself) by admitting its responsibility for the decisions which determine the value to be attributed to being. Before these judgments can be made, the self must integrate various aspects of its being: he who suffers, he who observes the suffering, he who acts and he who keeps his distance, and – for the artist – he who experiences and he who records.

The 'I' of 'As the Story Was Told' seems to be only a passive recipient of the story about the 'sessions.'[17] All knowledge of the events that transpire there are based on the hearsay of an unidentified informant who could more properly be regarded as the real narrator of the story of the 'sessions.' While events of a 'harrowing nature' take place in the tent, this 'I' does not even know where he was supposed to be at the time (perhaps he too has been 'dreamt away'). He is told that he was in 'a small hut in a grove, ' at a distance where 'even the loudest cry still could not carry, but must die on the way' (a dramatic contrast to the whispering fall of a leaf that 'dies away' in 'Sounds'). The 'I' has no direct contact therefore with the old man who is being subjected to 'ill treatment' at the sessions. But his aesthetic and moral detachment is punctuated by the appearance of the messenger who gives the 'I' a paper recounting the verdict and the consequences of the session's inquiries. This paper is torn in four and handed back. Later the narrator says he learnt that the old man had 'succumbed ... though quite old enough at the time to die naturally of old age.' This knowledge of the man's fate finally stirs the passive narrator into action, if only of a verbal kind (perhaps a verbal complement to his earlier objection – 'I trust I was not more sensitive than the next man, but finally I had to raise my hand'): 'But finally I asked if I knew what the man – I would like to give his name but cannot – what exactly that he would or could not say. No, was the answer, after some hesitation, no, I did not know what the poor man was required to say, in order to be pardoned, but would have recognized it at once, yes, at a glance, if I had seen it.' The strange phrasing of 'I asked if I knew' implies that we may be dealing with various aspects of one self which have been splintered apart and not yet fully reintegrated. The handing of the paper to the 'I' implies that he is a person of authority. What needs to be investigated is the use this 'I' makes of his authority and this in turn involves a consideration of why this 'I' does not bridge the gulf with his other selves – the messenger who brings the news, and the 'poor man' who expires.

The 'I' of 'As the Story Was Told' has not found out what the old man had to say in order to be pardoned, that is to say, he has not yet imagined it. (The text makes it clear that to see – with the eyes open or closed – is equivalent to imagine.) So far his imagination has only been exercised in a pseudo-naturalistic recapturing of the childhood memory of the 'summerhouse.' Unless he can establish an identification with the 'poor man,' his own writing will tend towards allegory or 'other speaking' with a false objectivity masquerading as an 'aesthetic distance.' An imaginative and moral empathy between creative consciousness and the 'someone' is possible, and indeed necessary. The 'condemned' is real whether he is referred to as a someone, a poor man, McCabe, Günther Eich, or, for that matter, Samuel Beckett. If the 'I' could only 'see' that his own being supplies the answer that would have pardoned the old man, he would tell the story, not simply be its passive recipient. 'As the Story Was Told' does not present, in the manner of 'Text 5,' a version of an 'obscure assize, where to be is to be guilty.' The self must accept its guilt and complicity, but at the same time it must also accept its innocence for, if the self does not act on its beliefs, it can only perpetuate the incompatibility of mercy and justice 'down here,' a problem which cannot all too conveniently be foisted on God, as Beckett's Belacqua in 'Dante and the Lobster' did.

'La Falaise' (1975) is a shortened version – only twenty very short sentences – of a longer work, 'Pour Bram.'[18] The highly elliptical nature of 'La Falaise' makes it more difficult than in the 'Still' trilogy or 'As the Story Was Told' to delineate a recognizably human context. John Pilling points out that Beckett has omitted in the final redaction the statements that the cliff has 'a man-made look' ('Elle a l'air faite par l'homme').[19] The human presence is, however, synecdochically presented in the opening sentences, 'Fenêtre entre ciel et terre on ne sait où.' The window is clearly identified with the 'eye' that searches vainly for the verification of another living presence ('Enfin quelle preuve d'une face?'). The first part of the text (the first ten sentences) presents a scene which is remarkable for its barrenness: the cliff is colourless ('une falaise incolore'), neither the crest nor the foot of the cliff is visible to the searching eye, there are no sea birds, the only permanent fixtures are two patches of white sky which border the cliff. The 'eye' is already considering the possibility of an escape to a transcendental beyond: 'le ciel laisse-t-il deviner une fin de terre?' But the feverish beating of the eye after another self or the 'unself' is completely unsuccessful in this opening section. An abandonment of the search would, however, be even more disastrous: 'Il [l'oeil] se désiste et la folle s'y met.' This eye is, nevertheless, a 'poet's eye' that 'in a fine frenzy rolling, / Doth glance from heaven to earth, from earth to heaven.' 'The lunatic ['la folle s'y met'], the lover [the search after a living face] and the poet are,' as Shakespeare said, 'of imagination all compact.'[20]

The power of the imagination finally comes to the rescue and gives life to the debris sighted on a ledge of a cliff: 'Patience elle s'animera de restes mortels.' The imagination in 'La Falaise' is finally able to penetrate the hermetic surface of the cliff: a human skull emerges from the rock.[21] While this startling and bizarre appearance supplies a focus and hence a measure of solace for the 'poet's eye,' the skull tries to resist this call to being: 'Du coronal il tent encore de rentrer dans la roche.' The metamorphosis is incomplete and only momentarily substantive: 'Par instants la falaise disparaît. Alors l'oeil de voler vers les blancs lointains. Ou de se détourner de devant.' The 'blancs lointains' are inaccessible: turning away will only lead to further self-negation or the onset of madness. In the last words of 'La Falaise,' the eye is waiting for another 'seizure' by the imagination so that yet another attempt at integrating his various aspects of self can take place. This is not to foist a comfortable consolatory 'sop to mind' gloss on Beckett's bleak vision, simply to recognize that as long as it is the eye of the poet that is searching there will necessarily be another beginning, and that it will concern 'something,' if 'not life / necessarily.' As long as there is the 'suffering of being' that 'opens a window on the real,' there will be the possibility of a self-creation that includes both poet and man.

10

Shakespeare and *Company*: Beckett's *As You Like It*

'Be not solitary. Be not idle.'[1] Beckett has in his own ways taken to heart these last words of Burton's *Anatomy of Melancholy* as he gets on with the business of writing in his most recent trilogy of prose texts, *Company* (1980), *Ill Seen Ill Said* (1981), and *Worstward Ho* (1983). Central in all these works is the problem of incorporating the various aspects of self or voice which the act of creation has always brought into play in Beckett's fictions. For over half a century, Beckett has been exploring fundamental perplexities raised by the pursuit of a life in writing. In this simple yet profound sense, all his writings might be deemed an ongoing attempt to legitimate autobiographies, to try to establish 'the self's life in writing.' In *Company* the stark opening, 'A voice comes to one in the dark,' is immeasurably complicated by the injunction which immediately follows: 'Imagine.' And what is imagined is a number of persons who compete for authorial control of the text: 'Use of the second person marks the voice. That of the third that cankerous other. Could he speak to and of whom the voice speaks there would be a first. But he cannot. He shall not. You shall not.'[2] The emphatic denunciation of the first person is made in order to forestall the incredible difficulties which have surrounded the status of the 'I' in Beckett's prose, most obviously in *The Unnamable* with its impasse.

Over three decades later, Beckett shows in *Company* that he can exercise a certain control over the confusion of identities and the ontological dilemmas which are thereby engendered. *Company* shows Beckett magisterially orchestrating the 'intractable' materials of *The Unnamable* so that the business of writing can indeed 'go on.' But *Company* does not attempt to formulate new solutions to the problematic status of being within the world of a text; it is a great summary work in which Beckett marks out the essential problems which the act of writing raises for him. The basic problem goes back to those crucial points in *Mercier and Camier* and 'The Calmative,' where there occurs what was earlier referred to as 'the fall into fiction.' This fall leads to a bifurcation of self which in *Company* becomes the 'you' that once resided in the world above, and the 'he' that now resides in the dark below. In *Company* many of the fifteen 'memories' of our world supplied by 'you' are a mocking incorporation of elements from Beckett's own life, some of which are easily identifiable from Deirdre Bair's biography of Beckett.[3] But the true biography of the writer in Beckettian terms must also involve that 'he' or 'one in the dark' and his relationship to the antecedent self or 'you.'

And enveloping this already complex ontology is the question of the ultimate authorial responsibility or, as *Company* phrases it, a 'Devised deviser devising it all for company' (46). Even the commonsensical interpretation that the 'one in the dark' is only self-reflexively creating the stories of 'you' and 'he' – but will not admit his originating 'I' – cannot circumvent the reality that this first person would still only be a 'devised deviser.' There must be another source of being that is ultimately responsible for the narration, one which represents a radical alterity to that posited within the text itself.[4] *Company* does not attempt to work out any new solutions to these questions; indeed, the fifty-eighth and final paragraph is followed by the one word, 'Alone,' which closes the work. At the point of closure, the 'you' can be 'solitary' and, of course, 'idle.' But, as we will see, in the text itself Beckett has effected his own variation on the Burtonian dicta for fending off a debilitating melancholy. In *Company* – as in virtually all of his prose works – the Beckettian creator is 'with himself on behalf of himself, with his selves on behalf of his selves.'[5] This aesthetic tenet involves much more than merely self-reflexivity: it involves a sense of moral obligation. To incorporate these 'halves' or selves so that the fragments might form new wholes is the essential quest that motivates Beckett's radical experiments in his prose.

After the summary of these issues in *Company*, Beckett in *Ill Seen Ill Said* and *Worstward Ho* does make significant breakthroughs in his exploration of the types of being possible for both the 'deviser' and the 'devised.' Each needs to substantiate his own being, and this cannot be done without acknowledging and then exploring the nature of their interrelationships. The Beckettian literary contract is therefore ultimately a social contract which, if its mediations are carefully traced, can be related to our world. In *Ill Seen Ill Said* and *Worstward Ho*, it is the very nature of this literary and social contract that is at the heart of the matter. These strange, difficult, yet beautiful pieces have moved very far from the solipsistic 'self-love' of Chapter 6 of *Murphy*.[6] In fact, a much more appropriate frame of reference – however strange it might at first seem – is Chapter 6, Book 1, of Rousseau's *The Social Contract*: 'If, then, we eliminate from the social pact everything that is not essential to it, we find it comes down to this: "Each one of us puts into the community his person and all his powers under the supreme direction of the general will; and as a body we incorporate every member as an indivisible part of the whole." '[7] Rousseau later adds an important clarification of the responsibilities which go with this 'pact': 'It should nevertheless be clear from what I have so far said that the general will derives its generality less from the number of voices than from the common interest which unites them – for the general will is an institution in which each necessarily submits himself to the same conditions which he imposes on others.'[8] *Ill Seen Ill Said* and *Worstward Ho* are two of Beckett's most radically innovative pieces, technically speaking; but this *Avant-Garde* experimentation with language and form is directed towards finding new means of incorporating the competing voices into a 'common interest.' In these companion pieces, Beckett has managed to work out some new non-authoritarian relationships between his author and others; in Beckett's new literary contract, the 'literary' is, finally, subsidiary to the contractual obligations of a more fundamental and democratically conceived 'general will' in which pity, compassion, and, above all, love are, in the last analysis, the most important terms for defining the nature of 'company.'

It is indeed fitting that Beckett, at the height of his powers, should develop in *Company* a series of extended parallels with the work of Shakespeare, that master 'deviser' who characteristically arranged a contrapuntal harmony from a host of competing voices. It is also appropriate that Beckett, whose first work, 'Dante ... Bruno . Vico .. Joyce,' was published by Shakespeare and Company, should, fifty years later, choose Shakespeare for *Company*.[9] The cluster of Shakespearean echoes with which Beckett's text concludes is an acknowledgment of some profound and deeply embedded correspondences: 'And how better in the end labour lost and silence. And you as you always were' (63). In 'labour lost,' it is, of course, love which is lost in Beckett's rewriting. This amended allusion to Shakespeare's second comedy is conjoined with an abbreviated echo of Hamlet's last words, 'the rest is silence.' The sentence which follows contains the most significant Shakespearean reference of all for an illumination of Beckett's *Company*: 'And you as you always were,' with the added implication that this is 'as you like it' – 'Alone.' Ostensibly 'all's well that ends ill' in this tale in which, at the final reckoning, there is an admission that there has been 'much ado' about 'naught anew.' For although the 'you' has sought to wring a confession from the 'listener' to the effect that it is truly his 'I' at the centre of the discourse, this has, apparently, turned out to be only a 'labour lost.'

But this is, by no means, the whole story; all is not lost, especially love. *Company* is about the romance of the writer with words, with those words which seek companionship. To be 'Alone' may be 'as "you" likes it'; it is, however, definitely not the way 'he' or the other aspect of the 'one in the dark' likes it. It is the dramatic interplay between 'you' and 'he' and the words alone and company that is at the heart of *Company*. And these are also key words in Shakespeare's lexicon, from his earliest comedies to the complex byplay between them in a work of his maturity, such as *As You Like It*, a comedy of mistaken identity that is pierced through with tragic undertones. Shakespeare 'stripped Thomas Lodge's plot down to the bare bones'[10] in his redaction for *As You Like It*, and then added the voices of Touchstone and Melancholy Jaques. Beckett strips still further, retaining only the voices of Touchstone, Jaques, and that of the 'deviser' (the Oberon, Rosalind, Prospero types) in his skeletal *mise-en-scène* for his own version of *As You Like It*. The comic and melancholic counterpoints are particularly focused in the second half of *Company* where the Shakespearean echoes and allusions are most prevalent and help to clarify the 'he' and 'you' roles which function (as did Shakespeare's Melancholy Jaques and Touchstone figures) to put in a critical perspective the central themes of love and the 'simple life,' and the real versus the fictional.

In *Company*, Beckett works a very strange metamorphosis. The 'he' or 'cankerous other' who 'reasons ill' with what judgment remains would, at first, seem identifiable with a type of Melancholy Jaques. As the Duke said of his morose jester: 'He is too disputable for my company'; and, consequently, 'your poor friends must woo your company.'[11] Beckett's 'he' does, initially, appear to embody typically Jaquesian sentiments such as, 'I thank you for company, but good faith, I had as lief been myself alone.'[12] Beckett's 'he' would also seem to 'rail against our mistress the world and all our misery'[13] (and misery does *not* in this instance love company, as proverbial wisdom counsels us). 'He' even manages a variation of Jaques' famous definition of 'a melancholy of mine own'[14]. 'What kind of imagination is this so reason-ridden? A kind of its own'

(33). Such a reading would, however, constitute a case of mistaken identity. For it is the 'he' who, in a transformation worthy of comparison with those in Shakespeare's comedies, is really the Touchstone figure. On the other hand, it is the 'you,' ostensibly drawing the 'hearer' towards the world via the fifteen memories of a former life above, who ends up 'Alone,' like Jaques scorning all company. 'He'/'you' are obviously in some ways two aspects of an unvoiced 'I,' but it is 'he,' that 'cankerous other,' who finally acknowledges the need, the 'craving' for company, as did his prototype in so many ways, that sophisticated clown Touchstone.

'In order to be company he must display a certain mental activity. But it need not be of a high order' (12). This is patently untrue, especially in the second half of *Company*, where 'he' exhibits all the improvisational ingenuity (in short, wit) that the clown employs to ensure his survival. The 'he' displays (as did Touchstone) a 'swift' and indeed often 'sententious'[15] wit in striving to supply company for himself 'in the dark.' Beginning with paragraph thirty-one, there is a new emphasis upon devising diversions for entertainment (this impulse is marked by the refrain, 'Let there be ...'). The touchstone phrase 'the test is company' is invariably invoked to decide which course to adopt, as in 'which of the two darks is the better company.' The 'he' even wonders at one point if the hearer might not be 'made more companionable if not downright human' (27). Always the 'he''s stress is on being 'more companionable' / 'more entertaining' (43). A veritable theatrical company[16] emerges in the dramatic use of the first person plural possessive: 'where our old hearer lies' (33). In the third paragraph, there had been an emphatic disclaimer that there would not/cannot be a 'first person'; contrary to that injunction, 'he' has contrived to 'speak to and of whom the voice speaks.' This movement away from an isolated 'he' and towards a society of others 'in the dark' is underscored by the growing identification between 'he' and the deviser, whether 'devising it all himself included for company,' or 'devised deviser devising it all for company.'

'Deviser,' 'company,' and 'incorporate' are vital terms in Shakespeare's comic repertoire. Devise is very prominent at both the beginning and ending of *As You Like It*: the play's resolution is initiated by Rosalind's 'I shall devise something.'[17] She is Shakespeare's stage manager or dramatist *within* the play; but there is, of course, another centre of authority *beyond* the confines of the play itself, as acknowledged by Rosalind in the epilogue where the artificiality of the play itself is directly commented on, 'to like as much of this play as please you.'[18] In other words, she too is a 'devised deviser.' Beckett has 'incorporated' a striking number of echoes from Shakespeare's language as he explores the vexed issue of how his 'he' and 'you' are somehow incorporated in the text, and this, in turn, raises perplexing questions about their relationships to the world outside the text.

The frequent echoing of Shakespearean language reinforces the development of parallels with themes from *As You Like It*, for example, the iambics of paragraph fifty-one, 'And wonders to himself what in the world such sounds might signify' (50), and, in the same section, the Shakespearean feeling of 'Whence in the world those wafts of villainous smell' (52). In this paragraph, there is perhaps even a mocking reference to Touchstone's name: 'Touch? The thrust of the ground against his bones.' The enumeration of the various postures which the 'crawling creator' may adopt, of which the 'repent amble' is the 'least common,' hence 'possibly of all the most diverting' (44), could even be seen as a crude pun literalizing Touchstone's last words in which he catalogues the seven types of lie, beginning with the 'Retort Courteous.'[19] Beckett's 'crawling creator' in *Company* is (in perfect iambic pentameter) deemed to have failed: 'With bootless crawl and figments comfortless' (51). But the 'he' as creator (or deviser) has not crawled in vain; his words and figments have not been 'bootless.' For his 'craving' or hunger for company does indeed 'revive,' and this in turn generates other words and other figments. In the last 'he' paragraph, the 'hearer' is described with 'hands invisibly manacled' (57); this does not, however, signal an impasse in the creative process. This is not Malvolio in his 'dark room'; this is Touchstone, ready to escape, Houdini-like, with his wit and imagination when he needs to: 'Other details as need felt. Leave him at that for the moment' (57). There will be 'some other carrion. Yet to be imagined' (51). The identification of 'he' with the aesthetic of 'The Vulture' is the surest indication that there will be other incarnations of this 'he' as Beckett further explores the art-life nexus.

On the other hand, it is the voice of 'you,' who started off by trying to draw the 'listener' to the world and an admission of a life above, that ends up admitting failure. 'You' ends up in the position of the Melancholy Jaques who prefers himself just as he is, 'Alone.' The 'you' and 'he' need each other – without their 'incorporation' the creative act cannot continue. And that is why *Company* ends when it does. They must be 'Alone,' yet together: this is the company upon which Beckett's work depends for its very existence.

The trajectory towards the final 'Alone' experienced by the 'you' can be plotted by seeing how in the fifteen 'memories' of life above in our world the hunger for communication and for love is continually frustrated, driving this self inwards to the light of his own imagination, in the dark of his own mind. Company means 'to break bread with,' to partake of a ritual sharing (the 'feast' at the end of a Shakespearean comedy is the fullest symbolic development of the word company which is so crucial in those plays). In Beckett's *Company*, there is no such sharing or communion. In paragraph nine the father of 'you' 'left the house soon after his breakfast with a flask and a package of his favourite egg sandwiches for a tramp in the mountains' (13), so that he could avoid being in the house when his child was born (like the Melancholy Jaques, 'you' is 'out of love' with his 'nativity'[20]); in paragraph twenty-four, 'you' is 'alone in the garden' while the mother makes the water-thin bread and butter' (21–2) of which the 'very naughty boy' is not allowed to partake; in paragraph twenty-nine, the boy is 'back home at nightfall supperless to bed' (his only recourse now is to feed his own visions of 'the faint shape of high mountain,' a sighting which was openly mocked by his parents); in paragraph thirty-three, the boy takes pity on a poor creature, a hedgehog in search of food, 'glows' at his 'good deed,' then discovers that his charity has resulted in a cruel death by starvation: 'You are on your back in the dark and have never forgotten what you found then. The mush. The stench' (31). Like the Melancholy Jaques upon the death of his 'velvet friend', you 'moralize[s] the spectacle' (if somewhat less mawkishly), and comes to a conclusion very similar to Jaques': ' "Tis right," quoth he, "thus misery doth part / The flux of company." '[21] Throughout these episodes the unifying theme is of a transubstantiation that fails to materialize.

There is one major exception to this pattern of negation in paragraph forty which deals with 'Bloom of adulthood.' In this Joycean paean of accommodation, two 'memories' are incorporated, that of the young boy in the summerhouse chuckling along with his father who retreats there 'on summer Sundays after his midday meal' (39), and that of the adult meeting his lover in the summerhouse: 'you sit in the bloom of adulthood bathed in rainbow light' (39). A strangely poetic 'trinitarian' unity survives even the obsessive fascination with mathematical calculations. There is a bizarre communion of creator/created and deviser/devised in the grotesque yet compelling coupling of 'Dissolve to your father's straining against the unbuttoned waistband. Can it be she is with your child without your having asked for as much as her hand?' (42). The juxtaposition of male and female pregnancy[22] suggests that they are both metaphors for literary creation and that the whole scene – so very different from all the other memories – is intended to highlight art as the privileged means of mediating the irreconcilable dualities of life in the world. There is, however, one last glimpse of an ideal 'natural' unity between lover and loved one in paragraph forty-eight, the final memory of adulthood. Under the aspen tree, the lovers silently commune, 'eyes in each other's eyes' (48). Time inexorably engulfs such beatific visions, and the last three memories deal with the exigencies of old age.

But the 'last scene[s]' of 'this strange eventful history' do not end, as Jaques' seven ages of man did, with 'second childishness, and mere oblivion, / Sans teeth, sans eyes, sans taste, sans everything.'[23] On the contrary, the last scenes of Beckett's *Company* explore a much more positive development, the necessary convergence of 'you' and 'he' in the fabling of the artist-man who can creatively combine the world above and the dark below. While *Company* may be regarded as Beckett's critical autobiography in which he acknowledges his failure in many instances to effect just such a synthesis, it is important to recognize that such failures are not the fundamental goal of Beckett's literary works; they aim at much more traditional affirmations, even if, as in *Company*, they cannot be fully substantiated. These points are present in the next 'memory,' paragraph fifty-three, which might be called 'the Prospero scene':

A strand. Evening. Light dying. Soon none left to die. No. No such thing then as no light. Died on to dawn and never died. You stand with your back to the wash. No sound but its. Ever fainter as it slowly ebbs. Till it slowly flows again. You lean on a long staff. Your hands rest on the knob and on them your head. Were your eyes to open they would first see far below in the last rays the skirt of your greatcoat and the uppers of your boots emerging from the sand. Then and it alone till it vanishes the shadow of the staff on the sand. Vanishes from your sight. Moonless starless night. Were your eyes to open dark would lighten. (54)

The echoes of Prospero, the most famous of Shakespeare's 'devised devisers,' are not intended merely in an ironic way. Beckett's 'revision' acknowledges a literary debt while at the same time 'transforming' the original Prospero to fit Beckett's own 'as he likes it.' The similarities, albeit transformed, between Prospero in his 'magic robes' who boasts of his 'potent art' over 'ebbing Neptune,' and a Beckett tramp in his greatcoat who watches powerlessly as the 'wash' ebbs and flows, are in fact greater than the obvious differences. Prospero goes to the shore to 'break my staff" and the Beckett 'you' watches the shadows of his staff vanish, but neither abjures the power of 'heavenly music,'[24] which, in the case of the Beckett 'you,' is identified with the power of words to create beauty and meaning, not with divine forces.

Both still strive for the attainment of certain ideals; the 'starless night' of Beckett's Prospero scene echoes the last words of his 'Whoroscope': 'and grant me my second / starless inscrutable hour.' Despite the apparent litany of negatives, Beckett's language really celebrates an ebbing that can never end in an absolute 'sans everything': 'Died on to the dawn and never died.' And, most telling of all, Beckett omits reference to Prospero's last words, 'I'll drown my book. As we have many times seen, one of the most remarkable and original aspects of Beckett's aesthetic is that it is founded on the startling equation, art = death. But this death is itself a rebirth into a new state of being 'in the dark' in which the artist-creator's responsibilities entail making sense of the connections between light and darkness, above and below, art and life and, in the case of *Company*, the 'he' and 'you' figures. It is, in fact, this death that leads to the creation of the book, not its 'drowning.'[25]

The final two memories further enforce the concentration upon the writer / deviser wrestling with the question of time. In paragraph fifty-six, we are presented with the scene of the writer in his box watching the endless waxing and waning of the shadows of his watch cast by the 'lamp lit above you.' Even Prospero's staff couldn't defeat the ravages of time with its 'whoroscope.' The very last memory makes even more explicit the progress of the 'you' towards the role of an artist-writer who must, whether he likes it or not, somehow search for ways to reconcile the quest for an ideal wholeness with the realities of life in fragmented time: 'Somehow at any price to make an end when you could go out no more you sat huddled in the dark' (60). The very odd syntax of this sentence, two distinct statements juxtaposed without any coordination, summarizes in miniature the situation Beckett had to face in the post-trilogy prose and leads us back again to the opening of *The Unnamable*, where the 'I' 'simply stayed in ... instead of going out in the old way.' The 'you' of *Company* would, like the Unnamable, avoid the full responsibilities of artistic creation, opting for any type of formal closure to escape from the perplexities of his own being and its relationship to various 'fables' – 'somehow at any price to make and end.' And it is at this very point in *Company* that the old rhetoric of denial and negation suddenly reappears: 'the process continues none the less lapped as it were in its meaninglessness' (61); 'Till finally you hear how words are coming to an end. With every inane word a little nearer to the last' (62). *Company* is another of Beckett's critiques of his creators' reluctance to accept the obligations of creating a fable or 'true story' to make sense of their apparently impossible, unreal, and meaningless situations.

One is never truly in the Beckettian act of creation 'Alone.' What Beckett said a long time ago is still true: the artist is 'with his selves on behalf of his selves.' 'You' and 'he' are 'company'; they are two of these selves who must quite literally be half of a whole, namely, of that mute listener who obdurately refuses to voice his own 'I.' Why doesn't the 'I' speak in *Company*? Why does the 'you' reject 'the fable of one fabling of one with you in the dark'? (63). Why 'in the end' is 'labour lost' and 'silence' the only good? Silence is 'better' because it at least circumvents the ontological conundrums of a devised deviser, that is, of an other who is the originating authority behind any fable one might contrive and who, furthermore, might properly belong to a different dark than that occupied by his figments and hence be forever inaccessible. What distinguishes *Company* from the rest of the *oeuvre* is that, while it recapitulates the process whereby Beckett's prose fiction broached these vexing issues, it does not, however, offer any new speculations on how they might be worked out. The fundamental problem which *Company* does not tackle, one which Beckett will take up once again in *Ill Seen Ill Said* and *Worstward Ho*, is that of creating a life in time for the 'figments' in the dark.

In *Company*, we are told that there is 'no tense in the dark' (34) and 'you are no older than you always were' (26). Hence to say that things are 'changing' and that 'words are coming to an end' is simply expressive of a need for formal, as distinct from ontological, closure; the latter is only possible when being has been somehow affirmed, and this necessarily involves an engagement with words within the temporal domain. Art and life need to be somehow connected; fables need to be made real. This may not be as the 'you' in *Company* likes it, this may not be how most Beckett critics would like it to be; nevertheless, this is how it is in Beckett's fiction, and this has been the driving force behind his writing career. Before Hamlet utters his final words, 'the rest is silence,' he implores Horatio 'to tell my story.'[26] The 'you' and 'he' in *Company*, in the dark, dead to the world, need to find a way of telling their story. The artist is never 'alone.' The 'he' who was earlier abandoned with 'hands invisibly manacled' is still somewhere present. The last words of this text could be read 'Alone & c.'

11

Companion Pieces: *Ill Seen Ill Said* as a 'Serena' / *Worstward Ho* as a 'Sanies'

If in *Company* the word love is conspicuous by its absence from the 'labour lost,' it is vitally present in the companion pieces *Ill Seen Ill Said* and *Worstward Ho*, with their essentially contra indicatory titles. In these two pieces, Beckett has returned to the central theme of his prose which was suspended in *Company*: the relationship between the hungering authorial eye and that 'other' whose own needs and claims to being must somehow be accommodated within the creative act. It is the 'labouring' of the authorial eye as it seeks for a 'sighting' and comprehension of the other that overcomes 'solitude' and that draws these texts towards an authentic sense of 'company.' And in *Ill Seen Ill Said* and *Worstward Ho*, strange as it may initially sound, it is love that is the central theme whereby Beckett seeks to salvage the 'labour' of *Company*. This is particularly evident in *Ill Seen Ill Said* where the controlling pattern of a 'sighting' is depicted by means of a courting, a marriage, a divorce (or widowhood), and, finally, in the old woman's fable, homage to a lost one. The theme of love works on two very different, yet necessarily interrelated levels: the old woman, that other 'sighted' (or 'conjured') by the hungering authorial eye at the beginning of the text – an ironic variant of 'love at first sight' – is described in her widow's 'weeds,'[1] and the perceiving eye is termed a 'widowed eye' (22) when he loses sight of her. They are in it together, until death do them part.

The relationship between author and other as a type of marriage is obvious enough in a text which opens under the sign of Venus. It is, however, equally important, if not so obvious, in *Worstward Ho* with its closing speculations about a radically different cosmology: 'What were skull to go. As good as go. Into what then black hole.'[2] But what is 'left of skull not go.' Hence the memory which precedes this passage lingers, and it is of an old woman 'stooped as loving memory some old grave-stones stoop' (46). For 'better or for worse', the authorial eye needs the other, and in these companion texts the image Beckett compulsively returns to is that of an old woman kneeling on the stones, vainly invoking lost loves.

The opening of *Ill Seen Ill Said* shows, yet again, that the vulturine eye of the 'imaginary stranger' (12) has 'stoop[ed] to the prone who must / soon take up their life and walk'; in this instance, the old woman 'who from where she lies she sees Venus rise' (7) is one of 'the prone.' Conjured into being by the hungry eye, she nevertheless pursues an existence within this 'skull shell of sky and earth' that is independent of the searching eye, which is, variously, 'glutted,' or left to 'digest its pittance.' *Ill Seen Ill Said* is the story of the relationship between this 'relentless eye' and the other it seeks to fathom in an act of creation, which is, paradoxically enough, based on the death of a 'figment' who no longer has 'the misfortune to be still of this world' (8): 'What is it defends her? Even from her own. Averts the intent gaze. Incriminates the dearly won. Forbids divining her. What but life ending. Hers. The other's. But so otherwise. She needs nothing. Nothing utterable. Whereas the other. How need in the end? But how? How need in the end?' (16). Why can't he who has devised her 'divine' her? Why is the 'intent gaze' finally 'avert[ed]'? Why doesn't she need to speak – 'Nothing utterable' – whereas he must see and speak, however 'ill'? These are the ontological issues which Beckett will explore in dramatically new ways.

Ill Seen Ill Said as a new poetic entity turns out to be nothing other than a radical rewriting of that very old literary form the 'serena' (three of which appear in the *Echo's Bones and Other Precipitates* collection), the troubadour lament of the lover waiting for evening and union with his loved one. It is 'always evening' in this text in which an old woman who 'rails at the source of life' also strangely endorses the permanency and value of love in her pilgrimage with her flowers to the tomb of stones.[3] Her story or 'fable' does count, and Beckett's words cannot be reduced in our reading to a series of philosophical axioms and comments on the purely formal properties of his writing. The intensely personal nature of love lost and 'life ending' comes out in her story, which is more than a devised ploy in an author/other relationship. Whatever Beckett's intentions might be to erase these personal dimensions, they ineluctably work their way back into his writing.[4]

This is made clear by some striking connections between *Ill Seen Ill Said* and the last section of 'Serena II' in which the young poet recognizes, as Lawrence Harvey points out, 'the coming death of his mother and his oneness with her'[5]:

> This clonic earth
> all these phantoms shuddering out of focus
>
> ...
>
> the fairy tales of Meath ended
> so say your prayers now and go to bed
>
> ...
>
> here at these knees of stone
> then to bye-bye on the bones[6]

Here we have the 'railings at life' ('this clonic earth'), the calm or tomb image, and the religious overtones which pervade her story (and his). Most suggestive of all is the reference in 'Serena II' to 'in the claws of the Pins in the stress of her hour' (referring to the poet's description of his bitch imagining that she is dying as she gives birth). The twelve 'guardians' who so mysteriously ring the old woman's horizon in *Ill Seen Ill Said* may also have their source in this allusion to 'The Twelve Bens (or Pins), a series of mountain peaks six miles in diameter in the Connemara district of Galway in western Ireland.'[7] But in this late work the twelve do not threaten her, but instead offer her a type of protection: 'Always afar. Still or receding. She never once saw one come toward. Or she forgets' (10). Even the vulturine eye cannot truly 'seize' her in 'his claws.'

The image of the old woman as a widow 'immaculately black' also echoes the poem 'Malacoda' which follows the three 'Serena' poems in *Echo's Bones*. There the young poet tries to shield his mother at the time of her husband's death. But this he cannot finally do: 'hear she must see she must.'[8] In *Ill Seen Ill Said*, it is the observer who must now see and speak, however 'ill.' The old woman does not need to converse with anyone (not even herself, we are told). Whereas in the 'Serena' poems there is a growing sense of self-division, it is merely self-reflexive (for example, 'I surprise me,' in 'Serena I'). In this late work, the questioning is much more profound for it acknowledges the old woman as other, a separate identity who, even though the creative sighting evidently conjures her up, still pursues a being separate from the devouring gaze of the searching eye. Unlike the early 'Serena' poems which are often narcissistically esoteric in their concern with a self in conflict with a world (rather than with the troubadours' traditional theme of love in conflict with the world), *Ill Seen Ill Said* focuses on 'phantoms shuddering out of focus,' thus raising the larger issues of self and world / love and world. All is, however, set within a 'skull,' thereby also raising the problematical questioning of their ontological status as fictions. Yet the very fact that all of this patently transpires within the head, the 'mad house of the skull' (20), allows for the woman's story with its evocative imagery to make claims for a reality of its own just as significant as that of the 'imaginary stranger'; in fact, the latter cannot exist without the former.

The strange beauty that is born in *Ill Seen Ill Said* is, ironically enough, far more faithful to the ethos of the troubadour originals than were Beckett's efforts in *Echo's Bones*. The spell of Venus[9] weaves a magic that 'dispels' the 'railing': she appears, like the star, 'as though by enchantment' (13) in the 'zone of stones.' Her 'presence' is what gives resonance to 'poetic' images[10] which would otherwise be little else than a romantic *mise-en-scène*. As we will see, it is her 'changing' or 'disappearance' which initiates the closing movement of the text and brings to the fore a crisis in the relationship of author and other that shifts the text away from the 'serena' and towards a dramatic rewriting of 'The Vulture' in order to effect closure.

Before this wished-for apocalyptic closure is examined, it is important to appreciate what has been accomplished in the emotional reality of the old woman's 'winter's tale.' A particularly Beckettian 'terrible beauty is born' when, in a complex rewriting of Yeats' line from 'Easter 1916,' the narrator, in a vain attempt to forestall her 'vanishing,' insists that her appearance is 'unchanged. Utterly' (50). But a change is undeniably taking place, and with her imminent disappearance all will, for the vulturine eye, indeed be 'changed, changed utterly.'[11] Yet the smile that lingers on the old woman's lips as her eyes close for the last time insulates the beauty of the 'serena' against the desperate struggle of the narrator/observer in the closing spasms of the work. The smile tells of a joy quite different than that sought for by the vulture-artist who finally seeks to 'devour all.' The old woman's compulsive journeying to the tomb gives new meaning to Yeats' lines about how a political event has transformed his countrymen:

Hearts with one purpose alone
Through summer and winter seem
Enchanted to a stone
To trouble the living stream

In *Ill Seen Ill Said*, as in 'Easter 1916,' the 'stone's in the midst of all.' The woman is truly 'enchanted to a stone,' the tomb to which she carries her 'wreath or cross.' Although she strikes at times the Memnon pose, her simple human devotion (figment or not) does not lead, as it does in Yeats' gloss, to 'Too long a sacrifice / Can make a stone of the heart.' Her smile testifies that she is 'in short alive as she alone knows how neither more nor less. Less! Compared to true stone' (50). To adapt another line from 'Easter 1916', 'love / bewildered [her] till [she] died.'[12] Beckett's beautiful 'serena' is born through the process of dying and the 'terrible beauty' is oddly and disturbingly human. *Ill Seen Ill Said* is in many ways the most personal of Beckett's post-trilogy texts and it is important to remember this when considering the more impersonal nature of the marriage of convenience (or rather necessity) between author and his other.

The ontological drama of *Ill Seen Ill Said* turns upon the conflicting points of view embodied by the narrator (or perceiver), and the narrated (or perceived), the old woman who is variously sighted in her cabin and en route to and from the tomb or cromlech. The old woman is acknowledged as other to her author who 'conjures' her into being, even if he cannot 'divine' her, and whose devouring vulture gaze seeks her, often vainly, in order to corroborate his own being. Indeed, the old woman is surrounded by an aura of paradisial imagery ('halo,' 'radiance,' 'haze,' et al.), since she exists for herself, whereas the observing eye's very claim to possess a being of his own is contingent upon a relationship with her. And this is so tentative and intermittent that he, in dramatic contrast, is plunged at times into a hellish state of non-being in which all is 'confusion'; as he cannot determine what status to attribute to the old woman, he cannot, logically enough, decide what being he might himself claim to have. We are told early in the work that 'she has one. And who has her' (13), thus implying a privileged relationship of sorts, a marriage, as it were, between the observer and the sighted one. But if he 'has' her, he certainly does not 'have her to hold'; from the very beginning something prevents the 'eye' from truly 'seizing' her, let alone 'divining' her. This false equation of having or possessing with being is particularly acute in the final movement of *Ill Seen Ill Said* when the old woman is vanishing once and for all.

The physical objects that constitute the would-be verisimilitude of her world are also disappearing. In her absence, the eye needs the details of pseudo-realism to make any claims to being, however fraudulent or fictionally contrived they may be: he needs these props of conventional realism to give himself the illusion he exists. But if she is no longer there, then these pseudo-objects are not even 'cold comfort,' their would-be substantiality nothing more than literary sleight-of-hand. Hence the need 'One other still far to seek,' and why 'Far behind the eye the quest begins' (55).

The Beckettian equation has indeed changed: the other is no longer discovered 'pre-existent' (as Beckett said it was in *Proust*), but 'post-existent.' She is dead in a way no other Beckett fictional sighting has been. Therefore, the act of 'taking up her life and walking' is even more problematical than it has been in previous works. No wonder the 'observer' proclaims in the first of a handful of paragraphs which self-consciously comment on this ontological 'impossibility':

Already all confusion. Things and imaginings. As of always. Confusion amounting to nothing. Despite precautions. If only she could be pure figment. Unalloyed. This old so dying woman. So dead. In the madhouse of the skull and nowhere else. Where no more precautions to be taken. No precautions possible. Cooped up there with the rest. Hovel and stones. The lot. And the eye. How simple all then. If only all could be pure figment. Neither be nor been nor by any shift to be. Gently gently. On. Careful. (20)

But the images of the old dead woman are not 'pure figments.' All would indeed be very simple if this were the case: she could then be manipulated for the narrator's convenience, as was the case in 'authoritarian' texts such as *The Lost Ones* or 'For to end yet again.' The narrator in fact has recourse to this very idea in the next paragraph which is fully devoted to commentary on this bizarre act of re-creation with a 'dead' figment which, nevertheless, persistently asserts claims to being: 'Not possible any longer except as figment' (30). There is, however, a 'shift to be': once the figure is sighted, even though acknowledged as dead, it comes to life in the eye's recounting of her in the present tense. Such are the needs of the imagination to have something to satiate its own hunger that it is able to bring into being an other, however evanescent the glimpses of her are. In the final paragraph of the text, this 'haze' of ambiguity about her status (fictional and real, dying, dead, yet alive, and so on) seems the only certainty to acknowledge as the 'curtain' closes on this ontological parable of 'the hardly there and wholly gone': 'like the last wisps of day when the curtain closes. Of itself by slow millimetres or drawn by a phantom hand' (59).

No wonder then that the ravenous eye seems 'mocked by a tissue that may not serve': 'No matter. No matter now. Such the confusion now between real and – how say its contrary? No matter. That old tandem. Such now the confusion between them once so twain. And such the farrago from eye to mind. For it to make what sad sense of it may. No matter now. Such equal liars both. Real and – how ill say its contrary? The counter-poison' (40). A 'literalist of the imagination,' confronted by an image of an old woman who is already dead, does indeed seem to have 'no matter' to work with. Yet she nevertheless takes on being in one of the strangest and most compelling paradoxes in the Beckett *oeuvre*. In the end, the eye must make do, however 'ill seen' and 'ill said.' One must make do with whatever one finds when desperately seeking to find a way of 'how to need in the end.' The real, the concrete physical details of her world, are so patently fabrications or fictional contrivances (the trap door which is 'so cunningly contrived of the ebony floorboards, for example) that it is impossible to distinguish between the real and its contrary, that is, the imaginary or fictional, where the real itself is already fictional. Still, when forced to turn away from the old woman who periodically disappears, this eye will have to make do with the ersatz matter of her cabin and surrounding landscape/mindscape. After the 'panic' of paragraph fifteen where the 'confusion' is only deemed comprehensible if she could be 'pure figment,' 'two small skylights come to the rescue'; later, 'white walls' will appear on cue when needed.

In the midst of all this confusion, ostensibly amounting to 'nothing,' there still remains, bizarre as it undoubtedly is, a 'something.' It is a something, however ill-defined, for in the midst of the pseudo-realism there is one verity to substantiate the old woman's resurrection in the imagination: 'Time truth to tell still current' (13–14). There still remains a 'trace of her face,' which is much more specific than the 'Haze sole certitude' which follows the sweeping dismissal, 'The mind betrays the treacherous eyes and the treacherous word their treacheries' (48). The mind (reason) cannot accept the old woman's being, which is logically impossible; the eye, on the other hand, needs an image to appease its hunger for being and an outside reality. Language, however, can double-cross both of them: it can bring about (as we have seen elsewhere in Beckett) a *modus vivendi* that encompasses logic and perception, negation and affirmation. 'A gleam of hope' thus remains for the eye soon to be 'widowed,' namely, that language can find a way of incorporating being, even at the point of extinction.

The narrator, however, abandons this option in the last few paragraphs and is instead increasingly attracted to more extreme and more simplistic solutions to his ontological dilemma. He thirsts for the 'joy at journey's end' where there will be 'No trace of all the ado' (56). There is, however, a major qualification which is vital for not only a reading of *Ill Seen Ill Said*, but for all of Beckett's fiction: 'Absence supreme good and yet' (58). The eye cannot 'tear itself away from the remains of trace. Of what was never.' To do so would naturally involve his own obliteration.

Earlier this eye, anticipating the disappearance for good of the old woman, a radical divorce that would leave the eye in an impossible situation – alone – had attempted to deny his dependency on her. He 'fled'; when he returns ('Back after many winters') she is in the throes of vanishing. He cannot escape the obligation of following this creature to the end and confronting the implications for himself of her problematic status. Only vainly can the 'I' claim 'Alone the eye has changed. Alone can cause to change' (53). Inexplicably, she changes on her own and possesses a being 'other' to that of the vulturine eye. To try and regain control of the change or 'vanishing' so that it does not necessitate another 'shift to be' the eye invokes a wished-for apocalyptic closure: 'Grant only enough remain to devour all. Moment by glutton moment. Sky earth the whole kit and boodle. Not another crumb of carrion left. Lick chops and basta. No. One moment more. One last. Grace to breathe that void. Know happiness' (59). This is Beckett's most explicit rewriting of 'The Vulture' since the first of the *Texts for Nothing*, and his most burlesque.[13] In *Ill Seen Ill Said*, the importunate eye is depicted 'dragging his hunger through the sky / of my skull shell of sky and earth,' and he does, in the first sighting, show himself 'stooping to the prone': 'From where she lies she sees Venus rise.' But the major revision of 'The Vulture' in *Ill Seen Ill Said* occurs at precisely this point: how can she, who is already dead, not 'still of this world,' be said to be one of those 'who must / soon take up their life and walk'? The last two lines of 'The Vulture' ('mocked by a tissue that may not serve / till hunger earth and sky be offal') are those which are recalled in the concluding sentences of *Ill Seen Ill Said*. The vulture-artist would no longer seem to be in a position where he has to be frustrated and 'mocked'; the old woman's death would apparently signify that the 'tissue' can indeed 'serve,' her disappearance rendering 'hunger earth and sky,' 'the whole kit and boodle,' 'offal.' However, this is clearly not the case: his final 'prayer' involves crude self-mockery: 'Grant only enough remain to devour all. Moment by glutton moment. Sky earth the whole kit and boodle. Not another crumb of carrion left. Lick chops and basta.'

The last two lines of 'The Vulture' are especially difficult and elusive. Lawrence Harvey has commented: 'Perhaps the most enigmatic aspect of the poem comes in the last line,' and 'what is more difficult to understand is the end of the hunger itself.'[14] Certainly within the context of *Ill Seen Ill Said*, Harvey's speculation that 'possibly the poet is saying' that 'inspiration ... must yield to the indispensable calm that is a kind of death of self'[15] is definitely inadequate. If the real originality of Beckett's poetic theory is, as Harvey argues, that poetic death 'is for him very closely and it may be necessarily associated with real death'[16] (and I have argued this in a much more complex way), it is easy to see why the rewriting of the last two lines of 'The Vulture' in the last paragraph of *Ill Seen Ill Said* is necessarily such a burlesque. In this text, written almost fifty years after 'The Vulture,' the question of being and poetic creativity, the whole question of real – and how say its contrary' is incredibly complicated. What was 'once so twain' (as say in 'The Vulture') is now 'confused.' If her death is only a poetic one, if being is itself only a fictional entity, then where is the real death that must coincide with it truly to render 'hunger earth and sky' 'offal'? The narrator with his vulturine eye would invoke an absolute closure, that is, bring about his own demise so that even hunger for poetic creation would be annihilated. Yet this too is illusory and leads only to self-mockery; the vulturine eye is itself a fictional being and dependent for its survival on a sighting of an other. Hence this eye cannot Chronos-style 'devour all,' swallowing his own hunger, as it were. 'Grant only enough remain' (meaning 'time'), he begs; this will not, and cannot, be vouchsafed. Without his other, there can be no 'shift to be' for the creative self; without her, he is deprived of time and, consequently, of a claim to being. He cannot 'know happiness.' He can quite literally in fact know nothing until his hunger is again directed to the 'prone who must / soon take up their life and walk.' And when this does happen, and happen it must unless the skull goes 'blank' for good, the creative eye will find itself confronted again with the vexed relationship of his identity vis-à-vis the other. Unless a *modus vivendi* can be worked out, he will find himself taking up his own life in the 'place of the skull' (57), a veritable Golgotha of pain and mockery, and it will be a useless 'passion.' There is no 'joy at journey's end' for the eye/narrator of *Ill Seen Ill Said*, only the formal closure of 'deposition done,' and a desperately ironic plea for an absolute ending. Yet this hope for a final ending is itself ironically mocked in the final paragraph of *Ill Seen Ill Said*: the 'Pour en finir enfin une dernière fois' is translated in the English version as 'For the last time at last for to end yet again.'[17] There will be other endings if there are other beginnings. We must read critically the narrator's final efforts at closure in *Ill Seen Ill Said* if we are to be able to see what has actually been created and what can truly withstand the final dose of irony and self-mockery: there is the very beautiful and haunting 'serena' of the old woman's 'winter's tale.' In the reversal of the Shakespearean theme, she is herself turned into a stone or 'statue,' yet still manages to leave behind a redemptive series of images of a lost love kept alive within the midst of an inevitable movement towards death. Most suggestive of all is that 'ghost of an ancient smile' (49), a Gioconda smile of an inexplicable nature that the crass artistic manipulations of the eye of the narrator striving for an imposition of artistic form cannot violate: it gives an 'imperceptible tremor unworthy of true plaster' to the 'cast' of her death mask. This is, to adapt Pater's words on da Vinci's masterpiece, the 'germinal principle, the unfathomable smile.'[18] Venus and 'The Vulture' are not only 'in opposition' in *Ill Seen Ill Said*: they are also, finally, 'in conjunction.'

The opening 'On' of *Worstward Ho* is clearly reminiscent of the last words of *The Unnamable*, 'I can't go on, I'll go on.' This dialectical see-saw of yes and no is now reduced to the simple injunction, 'Say on. Be said on.' The passive voice circumvents the problem of an 'I' and the related problem of a 'Deviser' to whom the words belong. Although the question of the ultimate authority for the words invoked is hereby avoided, the vexatious nature of the problem is still duly and flatly acknowledged: 'Say for be said. Missaid.' Even if 'missaid' the text must 'somehow on.' This is truly the ultimate priority: the text must go on, until the last words are reached, 'Till nohow on. Said nohow on.' The telegraphese of the opening paragraph summarizes in a miminalist syntax of weakness the strategy of Beckett's companion piece to *Ill Seen Ill Said*. Rather than the expansive questioning implicit in *Ill Seen Ill Said*'s 'how need in the end,' we are now confronted with an 'anyhow on.' Whatever remains in this spectral X-ray of the skull – the dim light, the skeletal portrait of the old woman, the old man and the child – will be 'preyed upon,' and this 'gnawing to be gone' testifies to a concomitant hunger for being. Now that the 'only good to be gone' (the void and silence of *The Unnamable*, and the closure of *Ill Seen Ill Said*, for example) is recognized as a 'vain longing' the recourse is, logically enough, towards 'worstward' (and word), that is, the words that acknowledge and affirm (however 'treacherously,' however tentatively) the reciprocal relationship involved in the act of creating, of 'going on.' In Beckett's 'poetic logic' two negatives do make a positive: the Unnamable's romantic striving for absolutes is 'ununsaid' in *Worstward Ho*. The 'know happiness' of *Ill Seen Ill Said* has not led to any final solution either: the prayer was in vain, and the 'preying' on these bones, these spectral remains, must still go on.[19]

The text quite literally discharges its responsibilities: it is a 'sanies' or 'discharge from ulcers or infected wounds' (as Beckett used the term in 'Sanies I and II' of *Echo's Bones*).[20] The 'drivelling scribe' and 'few drops mishaphazard. The strangury' at the end of *Ill Seen Ill Said* initiate the movement from 'serena' to 'sanies.' In *Worstward Ho*, the skull 'secretes': words 'ooze' from its 'soft' as the 'preying on the remains' (the 'shade-ridden void'), the 'gnawing on these bones' continues and confirms the need to be. There is even a 'pox on void' (43), implying that as long as the 'clenched staring eyes' of this skull are active they will have to create something, even if it is out of nothing, for they are 'Germ of all' (10). Even the striving for an absolute self-cancellation can only be legitimately sought within the coordinates established by the skull and its sightings of the old woman, man, and young boy, all of whom are repeatedly termed 'vasts of void apart.'

Miraculously, there is 'enough still' to carry on with. This text is anything but 'soft headed,' even if two of the crudest puns depict an 'ooze' from 'soft,' and a hole in the head, a 'black hole' (46) no less, which would swallow skull and all. But this attempt at final closure, an echo of the closing of *Ill Seen Ill Said*, is rejected: 'What left of skull not go. Into it still the hole. Into what left of soft. From out what little left' (46-7). This is the 'worst why of all of all' because it is Beckett's most explicit disavowal of the great dream of his 'people' that the void offers release or transcendence. Choosing his most comic title for a work of fiction since the early texts 'Dream of Fair to Middling Women' and *More Pricks than Kicks* may be one way in which Beckett is indicating a summing up of his *oeuvre*.[21] The crude joking shows that in the end is also the pun, neatly counterpointing the 'bons mots' of *Murphy*, and also showing that in the end, however minimally, we are still confronted by words echoing each other. These are the bones, the skeletal remains of Beckett's corpus, and they still validate that being and language – not the art of failure, with its 'nothing to express and nothing to express with' – have always been central to his vision. Beckett's so-called inane words are not empty-headed, destitute of sense in *Worstward Ho*: they do not lead to 'inanition,' but supply that 'leastness' of words necessary to sustain the hunger for being, and even make an art out of it. Beckett's cosmology of the creative consciousness or 'skull' is still an 'intense inane,'[22] to borrow Shelley's phrase to describe a dim point in the extreme of space. Shelley used the phrase to summarize a transcendent vision of man, freed from all 'clogs,' becoming 'what even the stars are not – a pure ideal.'[23] Beckett is setting in ironic and realistic perspective his own vision (as well as that of the Romantic literary tradition of which he is heir): it is the 'clogs,' the 'ooze' and 'secretion,' the biological and earthly impedimenta of bodies, places, and appetites that must again be faced: 'Sick of it back sick of the either. So on. Somehow on. Till sick of both. Throw up and go' (8). The 'inane' is surely not conceivable as a formless void since there are inescapable and undeniable contingencies.

The baffling simplicity of Beckett's juggling of negatives and affirmatives in *Worstward Ho*, specifically the central theme of 'Fail better worse now' (10), can be made sense of once a basic point of reference is established. Beckett is actually trying to calibrate as finely as words will allow him that 'leastness' which constitutes the essential affirmation of language and being in his work. The basic point of reference, as indicated by the title of the piece itself, is that for the Beckettian voice the perverse quest which would abrogate the obligation to express has more often than not chosen 'to be gone' as the only 'good.' Hence, to 'go for good' (8), meaning finally and completely, becomes the basis for any positive 'value': therefore, 'worstward' is defined as that which leads away from 'void' and 'all gone' and affirms, however minimally, presence, being, language. This fundamental recognition of a change in Beckett's poetic logic was acknowledged in the poem 'dread nay' (1974). Here a head that seems 'as dead' is suddenly and inexplicably disturbed: there is a 'stir' that gives 'dread / nay to naught,' that is, it testifies that some consciousness of being still intermittently flickers in. In other words, this 'dread nay,' given the proclivities of the Beckettian persona for an ultimate negative, is paradoxically that which refutes, no matter how marginally, the desire for total self-cancellation:

at ray
in latibule
long dark
stir of dread
till breach

long sealed
dark again
still again[24]

The poetic archaic 'latibule,' a den or lurking place where one might retreat, is, like the word 'grot' in *Worstward Ho*, a lexical indicator of something which is obsolete, but which can suddenly reappear: 'Then in that grot or gulf such dimmest light as never' (16). The Beckettian 'author' can try to minimalize these first signs of life, but he cannot in good faith deny that they are 'simply there.' For example: 'dimmest dim' is declared 'Best bad worse of all' (35), but this is still a sign of light and life, and it is deemed preferable to 'somehow undimmed' which is 'worser still.' The 'best bad worse' minimizes the signs of being to 'meremost minimum' (9), without however allowing for, or even desiring, total extinction.

While the speaker, or more accurately 'the spoken,' of *Worstward Ho* refuses to add ('Add? Never' [22]), he cannot, on the other hand, subtract so as to wipe the slate clean. He can literally subtract from the portrait of 'the first one' (who is first standing, then kneeling, and then, towards the end of the text, suddenly termed 'a woman'): 'Head in hat gone. More back gone. Greatcoat cut off higher. Nothing from pelvis down. Nothing but bowed back. Topless baseless hindtrunk' (22). But this ridiculously fragmented leftover is still enough to confirm that there is a presence which still has potential claims to a human status. Minima and maxima do coincide in this instance, and their reality has to do with the nature of both art and life. Beckett's 'better worse' in *Worstward Ho* is heading towards a 'leastness,' which is irrefutably still a something, and not towards a 'worstward' that can be glibly identified with a 'Nohow on,' which, realistically, any text ineluctably closes with.

One of the most important paragraphs emphasizes that an absolute denial of 'On' is not possible:

Worse less. By no stretch more. Worse for want of better less. Less best. No. Naught best. Best worse. No. Not best worse. Naught not best worse. Less best worse. No. Least. Least best worse. Least never to be naught. Never to naught be brought. Never by naught be nulled. Unnullable least. Say that best worse. With leastening words say least best worse. For want of worser worst. Unlessenable least best worse. (32)

'Naught not best worse' for, if it truly were, it would terminate once and for all any viability of the premise 'On.' An 'unnullable least,' on the other hand, allows for the continuance of the text upon which the speaker/spoken himself depends for his own being. Beckett's 'On' is more than the simple reversal of 'No'; it is a complex affirmation of being.

The 'oozing' sanious words of *Worstward Ho* are also confirmations of a 'worsening' that is led towards a 'leastness,' a central concern in the latter parts of the text. The words, what remains of them, are no longer concerned with the question of a deviser, or Ultimate Authority: 'Whose words? Ask in vain. Or not in vain if say no knowing. No saying. No words for him whose words. Him? One. No words for one whose words. One? It. No words for it whose words. Better worse so' (20). This issue in abeyance, the text can occupy itself with the more fundamental and authentic issue of 'say,' even if this is understood to stand for 'be missaid.' Throughout *Worstward Ho*, 'say' clearly takes priority over 'see,' thereby also circumventing the dilemma of the 'real' and its unsayable 'counter-poison' in *Ill Seen Ill Said*. Although one of the most powerful images present here is that of 'Clenched eyes. Staring eyes' (11), the vision vouchsafed by this text is ultimately determined by the nature of 'mis-said,' not 'misseen.' 'Clenched staring eyes' is highly ambiguous for it suggests an opening which is also a closing: it is the 'Germ of all,' but the actual expression (or 'oozing,' in this instance) takes place in the verbal discharges of 'the skull.' Words become the ultimate determina-tors of reality. In preying on the 'remains,' the skull is really hungering after words, for example, 'They then the words' (30) and, an even more striking example, 'Oozed from softening soft the word woman's' (35).

The issue of say/see is tackled in some of the most difficult paragraphs in the last twenty sections of the text. The skull records that 'Less seen and seeing when with words than when not' (40), all is 'undimmed' which 'words had dimmed' (39). But the sighting cannot, of course, be communicated, and the fact that words must recount what is seen makes clear which finally takes precedence, by necessity. There are only 'Blanks for when words gone' (41); there is 'No ooze from seen undimmed.' Blanks, gaps, lacunae punctuate the text and no one would want to gloss over this reality of Beckett's vision. Nor should one deny that voids and blanks are contained within an affirmation of language and its tropism towards being: 'Try better worse another stare when with words than when not' (39).

For Beckett the question of language and being, the true 'twain' in his fiction, has always involved, from 'Assumption' to *Worstward Ho*, the question of alterity: the ontological issues raised here concern the author ('skull,' 'one pinhole') and other ('shades,' 'three pins') relationship. The crucial statements all concern an alterity that is somehow only understandable by means of a series of interrelationships. The key paragraph occurs roughly in the middle of *Worstward Ho* and is definitely at the centre of Beckett's speculations here:

First back on to three. Not yet to try worsen. Simply be there again. There in that head in that head. Be it again. That head in that head. Clenched eyes clamped to it alone. Alone? No. Too. To it too. The sunken skull. The crippled hands. Clenched staring eyes. Clenched eyes clamped to clenched staring eyes. Be that shade again. In that shade again. With the other shades. Worsening shades. In the dim void. (22–3)

The 'syntax of weakness' in this passage lets 'being into literature' by overcoming the subject-object dualism that characterizes conventional sentence structure. 'First back on to three,' with its suggestion of an author imposing his will on others, is quickly altered to 'Simply be there again,' which takes the so-called authorial self into the common dark and 'ooze' occupied by his others (the old woman, and the couple). He is also a shade, 'with the other shades'; they exist separately from him, but they share the same zone of fictive being. His existence depends upon theirs. 'All' of them are 'back in the skull together' (26). Hence the startling 'doubleness' of 'clenched eyes clamped to clenched staring eyes': to project himself as existing, possessing being in a fictional realm (the text of *Worstward Ho*), the skull itself must assume a fictive status. Yet there still remains that sense of another who is at once inside and outside the text, one who ultimately authorized the text itself, in other words, an alterity that leads us towards the name of the author, Samuel Beckett, even though he cannot literally be found there. The images of a skull within a skull and of 'stare clamped to stare' are perhaps the most arresting ones in this strange world, and they dramatize the question of a deviser ('Whose words'), without however leading to an impasse. This image must be clearly distinguished from apparently similar ones in *The Unnamable* and other texts where the image of another eye closing behind the eye of the skull creating *within* the text leads to a rejection of all claims for being. Here a mutuality of needs is acknowledged.

In *Worstward Ho*, where the images of the three spectral human remains reach us the way rays might from some long dead cosmos, there is one passage which stands out, for it is an emotive poetic cluster that could, if further developed, flesh out the X-ray print of this minimalist text. It is the sixth last paragraph and, for once, builds up an image instead of 'leastening,' or 'worsening,' or simply repeating it: 'Nothing and yet a woman. Old and yet old. On unseen knees. Stooped as loving memory some old gravestones *stoop*. In that old graveyard. Names gone and when to when. *Stoop* mute over the graves of none' (46, italics mine). Several key junctures in the *Echo's Bones* collection are drawn together here. The 'stoop' image brings to mind 'The Vulture' ('stooping to the prone who must / soon take up their life and walk'), and this is , of course, particularly ironic, for the old woman is herself stooping as if ready to join the 'graves of none,' and the skull stoops to this image in his 'gnawing to be gone.' Echo's bones have turned to stones and all that is left is the faint reverberation of a voice. Two other echoes still linger, however: the very beautiful image of 'Alba' –

who though you stoop with fingers of
compassion
to endorse the dust
shall not add to your beauty

– and the central image of the title poem (and last in the collection) 'Echo's Bones' with its graveyard setting ('asylum under my tread'). *Echo's Bones* is obviously still vital to Beckett's vision at this point: 'First the bones. On back to them. Preying since first said on foresaid remains' (17–18). The vulture preying, the old woman praying: both images, so very different yet so closely identified in *Ill Seen Ill Said* and *Worstward Ho*, must be kept in mind to appreciate Beckett's art which is still so resonantly suggestive of literary and humanistic possibilities.

The literary quest of 'On. Say on' has not been 'bootless.' *Worstward Ho* is, strange as it may seem, a Beckettian 'Defence of Poetry.' Stripped of their rhetoric, several of Shelley's famous statements on the essence of poetry could, for example, still find corroboration in Beckett's *Worstward Ho*:

[Poetry] is universal, and contains within itself the germ of a relation to whatever motives or actions have place in the possible varieties of human nature.

and:

Poetry enlarges the circumference of the imagination by replenishing it with thoughts of ever new delight, which have the part of attracting and assimilating to their own nature all other thoughts, and which form new intervals and interstices whose void forever craves fresh food.[25]

The 'ooze' of 'leastening words' may appear to be the antithesis of these romantic effusions about the value of the imagination. But to notice only the grotesque contrast would not be enough: underneath the surface dissimilarities lies a common ground. Beckett's 'Germ of all' is still, however 'leastened,' the eye of a visionary poet who places the human within universal and cosmological frameworks. The 'circumference of the imagination,' that nowhere where the poet must find a way on, is enlarged until it approaches 'bounds of boundless void' (47). But these voids are finally only comprehensible by seeing them within the context of human nature, of the 'poetry of life.'[26] The most important identification of all between these 'Defences of Poetry' is their assertion, one explicitly, the other implicitly, that 'The great instrument of moral good is the imagination.'[27] The development of Beckett's art has, in a most complex way, explored the relationship of self and other, and Beckett has developed his own form of 'sympathetic imagination'[28] whereby the authorial self can identify and feel for others as he feels for himself. The cluster of references to *Echo's Bones* just before the text's ending shows Beckett's 'skull' 'put[ting] himself in the place of another and of many others'[29]: 'Same stoop for all' (46). Beckett endorsed a similar 'germ of a relation' in the manifesto 'Poetry is Vertical' (1932), an *Avant-Garde* aesthetic more naturally akin to the Romantic tradition than to the formalist biases of postmodernism: 'Poetry builds a nexus between the "I" and the "you" by leading the emotions of the sunken, telluric depths upwards toward the illumination of a collective reality and a totalistic universe.'[30] Over fifty years later, in *Worstward Ho*, Beckett echoes poetically the same nexus: 'Another. Say another. Head sunk on crippled hands. Vertex vertical. Eyes clenched. Seat of all. Germ of all' (10). In the act of 'going on' the head is 'unsunk' and there is an 'I'/'you', self/other relationship which could lead us towards a new understanding of a 'collective reality,' but only after we have very carefully worked our way through the mediations of Beckett's literary world.

12

Beckett Incorporated: Fragments and Wholes

It should be clear from my previous analyses that Beckett is much more concerned with an affirmative relationship of language and being than most of his critics have suggested or assumed. It seems to me that only a recognition of the possible compatibility of language and being can revitalize the tradition of Beckett criticism which has needlessly cut itself off from a dimension of Beckett's writing that is of the utmost importance in the current *crise de langage*. Beckett is a great writer because he is a great moralist who is concerned with how one is to live. Beckett's writings are not therefore by any means *sui generis*: his originality lies in his appropriation and reworking of the tradition so that his own beginning was possible. This is the truly reactionary aspect of his revolutionary experiments with language. An acknowledgment of this neglected aspect of his art is the 'reactionary' dimension of my efforts to come to terms with his formal and ontological investigations. It is this remarkable ability to go 'back' in order to go 'on' that is central to the definition of the *Avant-Garde* which I proposed at the beginning of this study as a more suitable frame within which to approach Beckett than the tenets of postmodernist critical theory.

The truly radical nature of Beckett's work is intimately aligned with a reactionary need to reconstruct the traditional role of the author with its commitment to the relationship of man and world, word and world. Beckett's concept of authority investigates the radical possibility of co-existence with the 'other' that leads the writer into a new zone of ontological exploration, arguably the most important development in contemporary fiction. In the post-trilogy texts, an affirmative answer is finally, if tentatively, offered to the Unnamable's pitiful rhetorical plea, 'oh misery, will I never stop wanting a life for myself?' The new sense of community which startlingly emerges in the post-trilogy texts could be characterized as an 'art of living.' The text has not totally displaced either the authorial or the human presence. It is perhaps Beckett's greatest achievement to have rendered the world of the text a realm in which man is not simply characterizable as a dehumanized transit area for words of anonymous significance.

My emphasis upon the Orphic qualities of the language in many of his later texts runs counter to a great deal of contemporary literary theorizing which is primarily concerned with the disjunction between word and referent. Roland Barthes, for example, contends that the 'Hunger of the Word, common to the whole of modern poetry, makes poetic speech terrible and inhuman. It initiates a discourse full of gaps and full of lights, filled with absences and over-nourishing signs.' Gerald L. Bruns glosses this commentary in terms of the incongruity between word and voice which he declares 'is, of course, the central theme of Samuel Beckett's fiction, which dramatizes the terrible movement of the human voice, as it is propelled by words not its own toward empty space, there finally to disappear.'[1] I have tried to show that the 'hunger of the word' always involves in Beckett a reciprocal hunger for the word that tries to fill the absences with the presence of a human point of reference. The human voice is not 'propelled' towards an 'empty space' where it 'disappears'; on the contrary, the human voice is drawn towards the 'source of need,' which is now seen to be in the world and in language. When Beckett maintained in the early sixties that the most important and exciting development in modern literature was the attempt to let being into a discourse from which in his view it had been excluded, he was not sure whether he would succeed with his own efforts (though he thought that others after him would).[2] Considering Beckett's own very demanding standards, the highest praise which could be accorded him – one which he would certainly not claim for himself – is to affirm that he has in some of his later texts revealed some of the ways in which being can be made compatible with literature.

What we must not do, of course, is to misconstrue the nature of Beckett's 'art of living.' Deirdre Bair makes a fundamental mistake in the concluding remarks of the first Beckett biography:

In all of this century, it would be difficult to come upon another writer who has so lived through his art that it has become the substance of his life. Beckett himself insists that his life is 'dull and without interest. The professors know more about it than I do.' He abhors the interest in his person and insists with intense sincerity that 'nothing matters but the writing. There has been nothing else worthwhile.'

Over and over again, he has said, 'I couldn't have done it otherwise. Gone on I mean. I could not have gone through the awful wretched mess of life without having left a stain upon the silence.'[3]

Bair's work is basically unsatisfying because of its unauthorized status: Beckett 'would not help ... would not hinder.'[4] The crucial point is not that Beckett has 'lived through his art' (after all, we all have to live through something), but that he has succeeded in making his art a living embodiment of a human presence in language, an achievement which entails much more than merely leaving 'a stain upon the silence' – any second-rate writer could do that. In his later texts, Beckett has managed more than he perhaps ever thought he could: he has established his own 'authority' and yet also allowed the 'other' to be, without help or hindrance. That this other is shown in some texts to be human being is the most radical and reactionary insight Beckett has to offer us. It holds out the possibility of a new conception of humanism that might allow for the creation of the fictions required to release us from many of the useless and crippling fictions of family and state, self and other, language and literature that we have trapped ourselves within. Seeing the 'mess' makes it much less 'wretched' and, as Beckett said, offers us our only chance of 'renovation.'

For us there exists then at least these consolations; but what then is the situation for the artist who has fragmented himself and then tried to satisfy his hunger for being by the creation of new wholes which would incorporate his various selves? Beckett has supplied a very moving portrait of the anticipated end of this seemingly endless process, a 'self-portrait' or 'postscript' which also acknowledges the otherness of these different selves, in the prose piece 'Fragment,' dated July 1986.[5] 'Fragment' is about one thousand words long and consists of only seven 'paragraphs' and eighty-nine 'sentences.' In this work, Beckett offers, as it were, a post-mortem appraisal of his career and the position in which he finds himself after over a half-century of writing: 'Lift his past head a moment to see his past hands. Then lay it back on them to rest it too. After all it did.'

In the opening paragraph, a 'he,' seated at his table, 'saw himself rise and go.' Throughout the rest of the piece, the focus is upon the 'appearance' and 'disappearance' of this other self who is also – somehow – regarded as 'himself.' This other could be seen as a harbinger of an ultimate disappearance in death, as a kind of beckoning 'doppelganger,' and this is an intensely compelling portrait for anyone who cares about Samuel Beckett the man; or, and just as moving in a different way, it could be seen as yet another embodiment of the death which has preceded artistic creation for Beckett and which I have emphasized in my readings. What makes 'Fragment' so emotionally charged in its very restraint is that these two readings are now virtually convergent: the imminent reality of death is impinging upon that 'metaphorical' death which Beckett as a realist has tried to authenticate in an amazing series of explorations which he has classed as 'ontospeleological.'

In a room suspended high above the earth, this 'he' no longer gazes through his window at the earth, but instead chooses to 'see through the clouded pane the cloudless sky.' The phrase 'cloudless sky' (which was first used in 'Assumption' to indicate a striving for transcendence) is, however, quickly drawn back, as is always the case in Beckett, to the realities of life in time. The table at which 'he' sits, head in hands, is the same writing desk to which he had clung for survival 'as when Darly for example died and left him.' The reference is to Arthur Darling, Beckett's close friend, about whom he had written in the poem 'Mort de A.D.'[6] The last part of 'Fragment' is dominated by the image of time forever hammering out the seconds, minutes, hours ... 'Nothing but the strokes. The cries. The same as ever.' 'Fragment' concludes with one of the most striking sentences in the whole Beckett canon, a 'sentence' which, while it formally lacks either subject or verb, is a beautifully cadenced rhetorical closure of the 'life sentence' which Beckett the artist-man has almost finished serving: 'And patience till the one true end to time and grief and self and second self his own.'[7] 'Fragment' is a delicately crafted literary whole; ontologically, there is, of course, 'something wrong' here: this last sentence could only stand as Beckett's epitaph if he did in fact cease to write.

And, naturally, this he has not done, as the two even shorter pieces appended to 'Fragment' to form *Stirrings Still* testify. A 'he' is once again shown going 'out' to seek a self in an outer world that is still somehow felt and thought to be connected with the antecedent selves in the room suspended above the world, even though the final instalment of this latest trilogy makes clear only that there is no new solution to this perplex. Hence *Stirrings Still* must renounce the rhetorical flourish of the final sentence of 'Fragment' and can only vainly echo fragments of that work's ideal of a conclusive coincidence of selves in death: 'Such and much more such the hubbub in his mind so-called till nothing left from deep within but only ever fainter oh to end. No matter how no matter where. Time and grief and self so-called. Oh all to end.' Conspicuously absent in this revised 'ending' are any references to 'patience' or 'true end': once out the self is inextricably caught up in the throes of creation with its ontological displacements of time ('patience'), being, and language. The 'missing word' which 'he' 'could not catch' from 'deep within' must, in all likelihood, be life (or a facsimile thereof, such as 'true end'), an essential word which would encompass the fundamentals of any existential reality.

These vital signs are, however, shrouded in such confusion that Beckett trots out the jaded joke that this incarnation of 'he' might not even be 'in his right mind.' The 'remains of reason' are, in a futile effort, duly brought 'to bear on this perplexity.' Reason will, as we know, not be able to resolve the maddening questions of being which are raised by the language of a fictional world which is somehow still regarded as connected to ours. Somehow the 'confinement' of the 'he' in the sense of incarceration must be reconciled with the sense of confinement as a labouring for the birth of another being. And this is precisely what is missing from the text – the 'stirrings' are stillborn. Once out in the so-called world this 'he' seems, ironically enough, even further removed from any identifiable social reality: for example, the phantasmagoric image of 'he' in some sort of geriatric Terrestial Paradise in which 'hoar grass' is 'long and light grey in colour verging here and there on white.'

Beckett 'press[ed] on' to the very end seeking new ways of making sense of the places to which his other selves have taken him; the exploration continued until there was, literally, a 'stir no more.' The whorls of gnarled syntax in *Stirrings Still* testify to Beckett's efforts to search for the telling combination of words that would give shape and significance to the 'hubbub in his mind.' 'Hubbub' is itself a *mot juste* for characterizing the situation of the writer Samuel Beckett: its roots lead back to a Gaelic interjection of contempt and to an Irish war-cry; its use in *Stirrings Still* underlines Beckett's final efforts to make some sense of that perplex which for him was, in the last analysis, always a source of creative confusion. Samuel Beckett's death on 22 December 1989 relieved him of these duties; our efforts to understand more fully his fundamental questioning of the nature of art and its relationship to us and to our world must press on.

Notes

Fuller details of works cited in the text and in the notes are given in the bibliography.

FOREWORD / MANIFESTO

1 Frederick C. Crews, *The Pooh Perplex: A Freshman Casebook*, 69
2 The views of Esslin are described later in my 'Foreword.' Hugh Kenner's
  approach is the most explicitly formalist: in *Samuel Beckett: A Critical
  Study*, he avoids central issues of the 'Beckett perplex' simply by terming
  Beckett's art one of 'pure connoisseurship' (97). For Kenner, Beckett's
  'works do not undo the world' (or even really challenge it); hence Kenner
  is 'obscurely appeased' by his cherishing of the symmetries that locate his
  'unassimilable' Beckett, 'aloof' (207) from a world outside the confines of
  his art. Unlike Kenner, Ruby Cohn in *The Comic Gamut* is passionately
  committed to trying to explain the 'unique suffering artist-human' in
  Beckett. Cohn does not, however, show in this study (or in her later analyses
  of the prose) just *how* Beckett works out the art-life nexus. Whereas Kenner
  absolves himself of this perplex by essentially saying that there is no
  problem to be resolved, Cohn asserts that there is in Beckett a questioning
  of the 'boundary between art and life' (298), and, by asserting such, proceeds
  as if the problem were thereby adequately resolved.
3 Martin Esslin, Introduction to *Samuel Beckett: A Collection of Critical Essays*, 9.
  It is interesting and revealing in regard to the influence of 'Three Dialogues' to note that a recent collection of critical essays reprints it as an
  appendix: *Critical Essays on Samuel Beckett*, ed. Patrick A. Murray.
4 Martin Esslin, 'Samuel Beckett,' *Encyclopaedia Britannica Macropaedia*
5 Frank Lentricchia, *After the New Criticism*, particularly chapter 5, 'History
  or the Abyss: Poststructuralism'

6 In the English section of the forthcoming chapter on 'Beckett Criticism' for *Anglo Irish Studies: A Guide to Research*, I document the development of the formalist bias in Beckett scholarship in much greater detail.

7 Cohn, *The Comic Gamut*, 294

8 Susan D. Brienza, *Samuel Beckett's New Worlds: Style in Metafiction*, 21

9 Edouard Morot-Sir brilliantly lays out and then lays to rest the mock debate over Beckett's 'Cartesian' allegiances, an issue which had been touted as a central concern in Anglo-American Beckett scholarship. See his 'Samuel Beckett and Cartesian Emblems,' in *Samuel Beckett: The Art of Rhetoric*, ed. E. Morot-Sir et al., 25–104. In the Frankfurt school, a genuine methodological controversy over the crucial question of 'realism' had begun to take shape around the works of Beckett who was becoming a focal point in debates between Lukács, Brecht, and Adorno. See *Aesthetics and Politics: Debates Between Bloch, Lukács, Brecht, Benjamin, Adorno*, trans. and ed. R. Taylor, Afterword by Fredric Jameson.

10 An interesting exception to this pattern is Michael J. Shapiro's 'Literary Production as a Politicizing Practice,' in *Language and Politics*, ed. Michael J. Shapiro: Beckett's works are cited throughout as 'touchstones'; Shapiro also argues that Beckett's writing 'is part of his resistance to power' (238).

11 Peter Bürger, *Theory of the Avant-Garde*; see particularly chapter 3, 'On the Problem of the Autonomy of Art in Bourgeois Society.'

12 Beckett's statement to Lawrence E. Harvey 'during conversations in 1961 and 1962.' See Harvey's *Samuel Beckett: Poet and Critic*, 247–9.

13 Iain Wright, ' "What Matter Who's Speaking?": Beckett, the Authorial Subject and Contemporary Critical Theory,' 71

14 Bürger, *Theory of the Avant-Garde*, 49

15 Ibid., 49

16 The phrase is Rubin Rabinovitz's in *The Development of Samuel Beckett's Fiction*, 'Conclusion.'

17 Bürger, *Theory of the Avant-Garde*, 50

18 Beckett's comment to Harvey; see *Samuel Beckett: Poet and Critic*, 247–9.

19 This phrase, originally used by W.B. Yeats in *Ideas of Good and Evil* to describe Blake, and 'foregrounded' in Marianne Moore's 'Poetry,' is a particularly fitting description of Beckett's 'narrators,' and raises the question of the realistic bases of Beckett's fiction.

20 Beckett's comment to Harvey; see *Samuel Beckett: Poet and Critic*, 247–9.

CHAPTER ONE: The Art of Hunger

1 *Worstward Ho*, 37

2 This distinction, which Beckett made with reference to Proust's aesthetic, is one which applies equally to his own work. See Beckett's *Proust*, 67.

3 'The Vulture,' in *Collected Poems in English and French*, 9. 'The Vulture' is quoted *in toto* later in this first chapter.

4 The words appear on the dust-jacket of the Grove Press paperback edition.

5 'Assumption' (1929), 271. It is interesting to note that 'Assumption' was republished at the time when Beckett had just completed *The Unnamable*: see *Transition Workshop* (1949), 41–3.

6 Cited in John Pilling, *Samuel Beckett*, 89

7 See Beckett's letter to Sighle Kennedy, published as 'Appendix A' in her *Murphy's Bed*, 300.

8 Beginning with Richard N. Coe's *Samuel Beckett*, study after study begins with 'The Art of Failure,' or variations thereof.

9 Samuel Beckett, 'Dante and the Lobster,' in *More Pricks than Kicks*, 9

10 Ibid.

11 John Gruen, 'Samuel Beckett Talks about Beckett,' 108

12 'Denis Devlin,' 289

13 Gerald L. Bruns, *Modern Poetry and the Idea of Language: A Critical and Historical Study*, 1. While I am indebted to Bruns' distinction between the Orphic and hermetic poles of language, my readings of Beckett are very different from his. His chapter on Beckett is one of the weakest in the whole book and essentially repeats the entrenched rhetoric of the corpus of Beckett criticism: 'Narrative without narration: *langue* without *parole* – it is towards this radical formula that the whole of Beckett's fiction tends' (183).

14 Ibid., 2

15 'Poetry is Vertical,' which appeared originally in *transition*, is reprinted in Sighle Kennedy's *Murphy's Bed*, 303–4. Dougald McMillan in *transition 1927–38: The History of a Literary Era* states: 'For number 21, Jolas devised a statement declaring "Poetry is Vertical." The manifesto is largely Jolas's own, but it is possible that Carl Einstein and Hans Arp also made suggestions and contributions. The names of the other signers were solicited individually' (65). Deirdre Bair's suggestion that Beckett signed the manifesto simply to ingratiate himself with the *transition* group is most unlikely considering the great care he has taken in putting his name to anything, his 'biography' included. See Bair, *Samuel Beckett: A Biography*, 141.

16 'Dante ... Bruno . Vico .. Joyce,' in *Our Exagmination Round His Factification for Incamination of Work in Progress*, 3

17 Ibid., 3, 10, 4

18 Elizabeth Sewell, *The Orphic Voice: Poetry and Natural History*, 182. 'Poetic logic' is a key term in 'Book Two: Poetic Wisdom' of Vico's *The New Science*. The impact of this section on Beckett was made clear in 'Dante ... Bruno . Vico .. Joyce.' 'But it is in Book 2, described by himself as "tutto il corpo ... la chiave maestra ... dell'opera," that appears the unqualified originality of his mind' (5). In this introductory section, my aim is to reconstruct Beckett's own poetic logic.

19 Edgar Wind, *Pagan Mysteries in the Renaissance*, 162. The only critic who has seriously tried to delineate a critical vocabulary appropriate for a discussion of Beckett's works is Edouard Morot-Sir in his remarkable seventy-nine-page essay, 'Samuel Beckett and Cartesian Emblems,' in *Samuel Beckett: The Art of Rhetoric*. I argue that the Orphic dimensions of Beckett's works are a more fruitful way of broaching these key issues than the Manichaean ones which Morot-Sir introduces.

20 Ibid., 206–9

21 Sighle Kennedy referred to the question of mythological allusions in *Proust*: 'Beckett's study provides a further range of doubleness. Proust's contraries are matched with contraries from Greek myth' (*Murphy's Bed*, 50).

22 *Proust*, 47

23 For an extended discussion of this synthesis of the 'ideal' and the 'real' in *Proust* see 55–6.

24 'Dream of Fair to Middling Women,' University of Reading Beckett Collection, 8

25 Ibid., 64

26 At his last meeting with Eugene Jolas, editor of *transition: An International Workshop for Orphic Creation*, Beckett read with him Goethe's 'Harzreise im Winter' ('Winter Journey to the Harz Mountains'), the first stanza of which served as the 'source' of Beckett's poem 'The Vulture.' See *Samuel Beckett: An Exhibition*, ed. James Knowlson, 42

27 *Proust*, 59

28 W.K.C. Guthrie, *Orpheus and Greek Religion*, 285

29 John Fletcher, *The Novels of Samuel Beckett*, 239

30 Guthrie, *Orpheus and Greek Religion*, ix

31 'Denis Devlin,' 289

32 Beckett's words used in the letter to Axel Kaun (1937), cited in Lawrence E. Harvey, *Samuel Beckett: Poet and Critic*, 434

33 'Echo's Bones,' *Collected Poems in English and French* (1977), 28

34 In 'Denis Devlin,' Beckett refers to himself as a 'miserable functionary'

(290) in his role as critic, which is, at best, 'semi-artistic,' since it is a role which, although it recognizes certain fundamental needs, cannot deal with them.

35 Friedrich Nietzsche, *The Birth of Tragedy and the Genealogy of Morals*, 50

36 *Murphy*, 189

37 Sighle Kennedy's argument in *Murphy's Bed* that Beckett has embodied a 'mantic' language in his first novel is unconvincing and 'Procustean.' See chapter 7, '*Murphy*'s Mantic Language.'

38 *Watt*, 52

39 These three references are from Raymond Federman's *Journey to Chaos: A Study of Samuel Beckett's Early Fiction*, 108; 111; 98.

40 An echo of the last mocking entry in the 'Addenda' to *Watt*: 'no symbols where none intended'

41 Hans Vaihinger's *The Philosophy of As-If* is an important influence throughout my readings of Beckett's prose. As defined by Vaihinger, a 'true fiction' contains a studied contradiction of formal logic in order to open up otherwise inaccessible areas of knowledge. A tension is thus inherent in all systems of thought based upon a 'fictional' deviation from chaotic actuality. The 'as-if' form of the fiction suggests an unreality, a sense of impossibility in the initial assumption since it depicts a situation, *as* it would be *if* ... : ' "As-if" is "not a mere trope, and yet it is not a real analogy," it is between "a rhetorical comparison and actual equivalence" ' (92).

42 *Mercier and Camier*, 7

43 This is the phrase used by the Unnamable to describe his ill-fated predecessors (197).

44 'The Calmative,' in *Stories and Texts for Nothing*, 27

45 This new 'movement' anticipates Beckett's description of the writing of *Molloy* which he made to John Pilling: 'writing *Molloy* was like taking a walk.' See *Samuel Beckett*, 53.

46 Another possible allusion is to a similar scene involving a 'homicidal maniac' in Fritz Lang's *M*, a film which Beckett very much admired. See Deirdre Bair, *Samuel Beckett: A Biography*, 242.

47 *Three Novels: Molloy, Malone Dies, The Unnamable*, 18

48 It is important to note Beckett's double emphasis on both the 'real' *and* the 'ideal' in this revision of the Terrestial Paradise. However 'pure' the air may be, it is still part of a 'terrestial atmosphere' (280); the landscape and gardens are wild and overgrown, 'In a word, a little Paradise for those who like their nature sloven' (277).

49 *Proust*, 14, 55

50 'Three Dialogues,' 17. Beckett's critical theories are often adjusted or even subverted when it comes to their actual testing in particular texts. Failure to see this leads to reductionist readings via the intentional fallacy.

51 I have echoed Beckett's phrasing from *Proust* here in order to emphasize the point made in the preceding note.

52 Letter to Axel Kaun (1937), cited in Harvey, *Samuel Beckett: Poet and Critic*, 434

53 Samuel Beckett, 'La peinture des van Velde,' 352 (my translation)

54 'Denis Devlin,' 289

55 Beckett's distinction as made to Tom F. Driver, 'Beckett by the Madeleine,' 22

56 'For Avigdor Arikha' (1966), reprinted as preface to *Samuel Beckett by Avigdor Arikha: A Tribute to Samuel Beckett on His 70th Birthday*

57 This idea of an archaeology of poetic knowledge is pervasive in *Proust*. The specific references cited are from 48.

58 Walter A. Struss, *Descent and Return: The Orphic Theme in Modern Literature*, 269

59 Ibid.

60 Ibid., 271

CHAPTER TWO: The Rhetoric of Failure in *Texts for Nothing*

1 Israel Shenker, 'Moody Man of Letters,' 1, 3

2 For example, Ruby Cohn's judgment that the fact only one piece had then (1962) been translated into English was due to Beckett's assessment they had 'failed,' *The Comic Gamut*, 170. If this had indeed been Beckett's criterion for justifying a translation, he would probably not have bothered to translate any of his works since he has repeatedly stated that there is 'something wrong' with all of them.

3 *Stories and Texts for Nothing*, 130–1. A commonly accepted date for *Texts for Nothing* is 1950. But John Fletcher and Raymond Federman suggest that the writing may have lasted as late as 1952 (*Samuel Beckett: His Work and His Critics*). Beckett's letter to Jérôme Lindon on 10 April 1951 tells of his work in progress that appeared as *Textes pour rien* (1958): *Beckett at Sixty*, 19.

4 Martin Heidegger, *Being and Time*, 232

5 *Proust*, 54

6 Dante Alighieri, *The Divine Comedy*, trans. Geoffrey L. Bickersteth, 'Hell,' Canto xv, 46–54

7 A comparison with the original French reveals that Beckett's translation

stressed the connection between 'Text 1' and its counterpart 'The Vulture,' the first of the thirteen poems of the *Echo's Bones* collection; the original reads: 'oeil patient et fixe, à fleur de cette tête hagarde de charognard, oeil fidèle, c'est son heure, c'est peut-être son heure' (*Nouvelles et textes pour rien*, 131.) The addition of 'vulture' in the English version makes the echo much more explicit.

8 Dante's first reference to 'my Comedy' is followed by a cluster of imagery that calls to mind Joe Breem's heroic deed, 'did what was to be done and came back' (79): 'as comes back he who, whiles, goes diving through the sea, to work an anchor loose, when it is fouled by a rock or other snag, and who strains himself upward and draws in his feet' ('Hell,' Canto XVI, 133–6).

9 The reference to Mr Joly in 'Text 2' hearkens back to Verger Joly of *Molloy* part two and looks forward to 'Still 3' (1973) (printed as an 'Appendix' to John Pilling's 'The Significance of Beckett's *Still*,' 156–7). In the latter work a man sits before a window listening for a sound that will prove that life still persists. With the proper conditions, it might be possible to hear the incarnation bell. Note that in 'Text 2' 'Mr Joly is in the belfry, he has wound up the clock, now he's ringing the bells' (83). Mother Calvet is also mentioned again in 'Still 3': 'Or Mother Calvet with the dawn pushing the old go-cart for whatever she might find and back at dusk' (156).

10 The glass imagery in subsequent 'Texts' emphasizes the breakdown of the ideal synthesis of 'Text 1' which was achieved 'under that ancient lamp' (a reading lamp that is identified with the 'lighthouse' in the Joe Breem story); in 'Text 6' the 'lightships at night' (104) are only a memory of an irrecoverable past. 'Text 6' elaborates an image in which a child gazes into a mirror while the true self hides behind the 'bluey veils' of the eyes, 'staring back sightlessly' (103); even the realistic reference to Glasshouse Street (where Neary had dined in *Murphy*) suggests that in this 'Text' the self is lost in a labyrinth of mirrors. Glass imagery is employed in the description of life 'above' in order to outline the difficulty of apprehending the true image behind the mirror reflection: the glass door is 'black with the dust of ruin' (110) in 'Text 7'; the existence of the narrator's fictional creation is only 'confirmed by the vast show windows' (115) in 'Text 8.' The last reference to glass imagery comments on the failure of the previous attempts: the 'I' of 'Text 9' pictures himself as an idiot 'who stares at himself in a glass' (117).

11 Compare this statement with the Unnamable's, 'Not to have been a dupe, that will have been my best possession, my best deed, to have been a dupe, wishing I wasn't, thinking I wasn't, knowing I was, not being a dupe of not being a dupe' (314).

12 'Accusative' does not appear in the original French version which simply reads, 'le seul pour qui j'existe.' Beckett told Shenker that after *The Unnamable* there was 'no accusative.' By adding the word in *Texts for Nothing*, Beckett is clearly signalling a departure from the impasse of the trilogy. Beckett had earlier used the word in 'Sanies 1' of *Echo's Bones and Other Precipitates* – 'her whom alone in the accusative / I have dismounted to love.' But the 'voice' of 'Text 4' is unable to surmount the logic of language, the syntactical division of subject and object, in order to effect such an ideal union. Nevertheless, the mention of the 'accusative' does allow for the continuation of the *Texts for Nothing*: the central image of 'Text 5' is the trial of 'the accused' (97).

13 Franz Kafka, 'A Hunger Artist,' in *Selected Short Stories of Franz Kafka*, 200

14 Tom F. Driver, 'Beckett by the Madeleine,' 23. Beckett told Driver that he had read Kafka's short stories in the German.

15 Franz Kafka, 'A Hunger Artist,' 189

16 'Denis Devlin,' 292. See also 'Crisscross to Infinity,' a short prose text which Beckett sent to Joseph Browne for a special Beckett edition of *College Literature* 8, no. 3 (1981), 310, in which the figure eight appears in both vertical and horizontal positions. The title chosen for the work was made by Browne and it is a rather unfortunate one since it makes the text sound like some sort of metaphysical Grand Prix. Carlton Lake in *'No Symbols Where None Intended'*: *A Catalogue of Books, Manuscripts and Other Materials Relating to Samuel Beckett in the Collection of the Humanities Research Center*, 174, details the variants of this work, all of which appear under Beckett's provisional title 'The Way.' This work could be regarded as a highly formalized revision of the circuitous rhetoric of 'Text 8,' but in both instances the formal aspects of the work are in telling contrast with unresolved ontological perplexities.

17 'Whoroscope,' in *Collected Poems in English and French*, 4

18 'Three Dialogues,' 18

19 Ibid., 21

20 Ibid

21 Cited in Richard Alan Lanham, *A Handlist of Rhetorical Terms*, 78, 92

22 Roman Jakobson, 'Two Aspects of Language and Two Types of Aphasic Disturbances,' in *Fundamentals of Language*, with Morris Halle, 78. It must be emphasized that throughout this study my use of Jakobson's 'two aspects' is indicative only of the adaptation of a convenient model that will help me to approach the question of language for being. A basic weakness of Jakobson's structuralist argument is that it does not show how the poles

of similarity and metonymy come to constitute language as a whole. The terms 'similarity' and 'contiguity' were crucial in the associationist psychologies of the empiricist philosophers. Jakobson appears to have adapted them to his formalist-structuralist model without making a concerted effort at a further clarification. There is, in fact, a further confusion of the meaning of 'contiguity' in Jakobson's transportation of it to the linguistic model. For Jakobson, 'contiguity' is identified with the contexture of physical detail (metonymy) as well as with the syntactical order of the sentence itself. Underlying Jakobson's basic binary opposition is the crucial question of the subject-object structure of the sentence. This question leads to a consideration of the compatibility of language and being which is my central topic.

23 Ibid

CHAPTER THREE: Rhetoric and the Sublime in *From an Abandoned Work*

1 Beckett's statement to John Pilling, cited in John Pilling, 'The Conduct of the Narrative in Samuel Beckett's Prose Fiction,' 495. Beckett told Barry Smith that the published version is all that exists of the work ('*Texts for Nothing*: A Thesis,' Questionnaire Appendix).
2 Beckett uses this phrase, which anticipates *Murphy*, chapter 6, in 'Dream of Fair to Middling Women,' 106.
3 'Alba,' in *Collected Poems in English and French*, 15
4 *From an Abandoned Work*, in *No's Knife: Collected Shorter Prose 1945–1966*, 140
5 It is interesting to note that in 'Dream' and *More Pricks than Kicks* Alba acts as a kind of mother-figure for that 'very young man,' the helpless 'ephebe,' Belacqua. Her surname, 'Perdue' (shades of Proust's Albertine), also conveys her role as an embodiment of Belacqua's lost vision of 'whiteness.'
6 Compare with Beckett's criticism of Rilke: 'He changes his ground without ceasing ... because he cannot stay still. He has the fidgets ... But why call the fidgets God, Ego, Orpheus and the rest?' (*The Criterion* 13 [1934], 705).
7 In the 1956 version published in *Trinity News*, there was a description of his mother's death: 'Her death, I don't remember much about her death, all I remember is the frying-pan coming down on her head and the bacon and eggs leaping out like pancakes and going to waste.' The deletion is important for thematic as well as stylistic considerations. The omission leaves in doubt the question of whether the narrator has in fact killed

anyone. At any rate, he replaces his would-be victim: 'Day after unremembered day until my mother's death, then in a new place soon old until my own' (20).

8 Balfe was also the name of a popular Irish song-writer. *From an Abandoned Work* is Beckett's first prose work written originally in English since *Watt* (finished 1944–5). The 'awful English' seems in part to be a result of Beckett's Anglo-Irish ancestry. Compare the section 'Ah my mother and father to think they are probably in paradise ...' with Martin Doul's great 'cursing scene' in J. M. Synge's *The Well of the Saints* – 'Yet if I've no strength in me I've a voice left for my prayers, and may God blight them this day ...' (89).

9 Barbara Hardy, 'The Dubious Consolations in Beckett's Fiction: Art, Love, and Nature,' in *Beckett the Shape Changer*, 130

10 Ibid., 136

11 The phrase 'little book' is first used in 'Dream of Fair to Middling Women' (25) to indicate the narrator's ill-fated attempt to create a well-ordered story.

12 'Dante ... Bruno . Vico .. Joyce,' 22. All unidentified quotations in this section are from this same page.

13 This narrator would certainly have reason to concur with T.E. Hulme's remark in 'A Lecture on Modern Poetry' (1914): 'I don't want to be killed with a bludgeon, and references to Dante and Milton' (reprinted as an appendix in Michael Roberts, *T. E. Hulme*, 259).

14 Thomas Weiskel in *The Romantic Sublime* argues that the sublime is now a moribund aesthetic, 'to please us, the sublime must now be abridged, reduced, parodied, grotesque' (6). He states, 'a humanistic sublime would constitute an oxymoron' (12). Yet a 'humanistic sublime' is perhaps Beckett's greatest achievement as he moves towards language and being in the works after *The Unnamable*.

15 The last chapter of Longinus' *On the Sublime* is entitled 'The Decay of Eloquence.'

16 Jean Onimus, *Beckett* 51

CHAPTER FOUR: Rituals of Syntax in *How It Is*

1 Beckett uses the phrase 'narrator/narrated' with reference to *How It Is* in a letter addressed to Hugh Kenner. See the latter's *A Reader's Guide to Samuel Beckett*, 94. In my reading, narrator refers to the underground 'man'; author to the 'external' source of the 'voice.'

2 *How It Is*, 7

3 The 'ill ...' triad of *How It Is* completes a rhetorical pattern first used in

Watt: 'to belong to the same story heard long before, an instant in the life of another, ill told, ill heard, and more than half forgotten' (74).

4 Tom F. Driver, 'Beckett by the Madeleine,' 23. See, for example, H. Porter Abbott's influential article 'Farewell to Incompetence: Beckett's *How It Is* and *Imagination Dead Imagine*,' 36–47.

5 Driver, 'Beckett by the Madeleine,' 23

6 A term used by Beckett in the *How It Is* notes in the ETE 56 notebook (Reading University Beckett Archive). Cited in John Pilling, *Samuel Beckett*, 184

7 Morse Peckham, *Man's Rage for Chaos: Biology, Behaviour and the Arts*, ix

8 'Dream of Fair to Middling Women,' 8

9 The 'mute language' theme of *How It Is* may be indebted to Vico's theory of the evolution of languages: 'the language of the gods was almost entirely mute,' that of the heroes 'an equal mixture of articulate and mute,' 'the language of men, almost entirely articulate and only very slightly mute' (446, 'Book II, Poetic Wisdom'), in *The New Science of Giambattista Vico*. For Vico all three categories 'were, after all, men,' but for Beckett in *How It Is* this is by no means an inevitable conclusion; after all, how human is a fiction?

10 The 'coal-sack' of *How It Is* is a 'literalization' of the metaphor of the galactic void referred to throughout Beckett's writing: the 'coal-sack' and 'dark arena' of 'Dream of Fair to Middling Women' (14), the black starless sky of the end of 'Dream' and 'A Wet Night,' the 'dismal patch of night sky' Murphy's sky-light commands, 'the galactic coal-sack, which would naturally look like a dirty night to any observer in Murphy's condition' (188), Watt's vision when he leaves Knott's of 'the mirrored sky, its coal-sacks, its setting constellations' (224). Malone's star-gazing reminds him of London, 'And what have stars to do with that city?' (184), and the reference to the skylight in 'Text 7' is preceded by the description of a 'deadly calm at the heart of my frenzies' (107), which suggests that the void of the 'galactic coal-sack' is a permanent feature of Beckett's cosmology. If, as Beckett said in 'Denis Devlin,' art is the 'sun, moon and stars of the whole mind,' that whole must include the void.

11 This phrase is directly adapted from Dante: 'that sack / wherein the whole world's evil is contain'd' ('Hell,' Canto II, 17). Beckett significantly substitutes 'suffering' for 'evil,' and Dante's subsequent phrase 'Justice of God' is replaced by 'I don't give a curse for it' (38). Other easily identifiable Dantean allusions in *How It Is* are: 'if I were above the stars' (43), 'both parts and whole as when he sets out to seek out all of him sets out to seek out the true home' (103), and 'more than ever by the earth undone'

(108). The last echo of Dante – 'this new formulation this new life' (142) – tries to vindicate the authorial voice's Justice and Authority. The true declaration of the 'vita nuova' occurs in the last few pages as the 'I' asserts his own authority.

12 'Recent Irish Poetry' (1934), reprinted in *The Lace Curtain* 4 (Summer 1971), 60

13 'Dante ... Bruno . Vico .. Joyce,' 17. A complex pattern of cloth imagery is woven through *How It Is*. The jute sack and the mud that wipes are set in opposition to 'useful things a cloth to wipe me that family or beautiful to the feel' (12) Note especially the dramatic disclosures of the scenes of life 'above': 'the hangings part heavy swing of the black velvet' (85). These revelations are balanced by images of erasures: 'veils most clear from left to right they wipe us away' (89), and an image of concealment: 'face to the ground macfarlane on top of all turn the head in the cover of the cloak make a chink' (78). The cloth imagery traces the progress of the 'I' from cradle ('swaddle and lace' [12]) to grave ('shears of the black old hag whose click clack two threads a second' [106] and contrasts dramatically with the first image of the mother sewing (10). There is hence a 'macabre transubstantiation' in *How It Is* whereby 'the grave-sheets serve as swaddling-clothes' (*Proust*, 8).

14 See, for example, William Hutchings' excellent analysis of the reverberations of Beckett's excremental imagery in ' "Shat into Grace" or, A Tale of a Turd: Why It Is in Beckett's *How It Is*,' 64–87.

15 Beckett is here exploiting Vico's theory of the three ages of man: 'part one before Pim the golden age' (47), with Pim 'training early days or heroic prior to the script' (61); with 'script' comes the 'democratic' period which in turn leads to the 'dynasties' of the 'scribes.' But, in accordance with Vico's 'Providential' cycle, there is necessarily a return to the 'sacred' writing of the hieroglyph and the 'barbarism' of man as he creates again his destiny.

16 Robert Champigny, *The Ontology of the Narrative: An Analysis*, 70

17 *More Pricks than Kicks*, 175; *Murphy*, 49

18 'The End,' in *Stories and Texts for Nothing*, 72

19 The 'deterioration of the sense of humour' can be traced back to the first image of 'windows at night': the author figure improves daily at the expense of the 'I' 'below' who goes from 'bad to worse bad to worse steadily' (9). The status of the 'I' as a fiction renders the whole issue of 'the sense of humour' problematical, for laughter is a uniquely human characteristic. Clinging to the species, the 'I' is one of 'those who laugh too soon' (26). The question of time and being is also part of the humour

theme. Since the 'I' is not in living time, his humour does not possess any real vitality: 'the joke dies too old' (38), 'enough to make you laugh soon and late if you could come to think of it' (16). The 'wish to laugh' (110) results more often than not only in a 'mute laugh' (33). The three kinds of laugh described in *Watt* have been superseded by a laugh that does not so much pass judgments on life as deny the very existence of life (compare with the 'guffaw of the knowing non-exister' in *Murphy*: 'three laughs four laughs brought off the kind that convulse an instant resurrect an instant and then leave for deader than before' [110]). Although *How It Is* contains some wildly funny bits ('you can shit on a Bom sir you can't humiliate him a Bom sir the Boms sir' [60]), the humour has 'deteriorated' because the reader is never quite sure whether he is laughing with or at the 'I,' whose status is problematical. The 'WORSE AND WORSE' of the concluding section is the final deterioration which precedes what I argue is an affirmation of being, an act which is, perhaps, beyond humour.

20 The attempts of the 'I' to 'cling to species' emphasize the confusion as to whether he is real or imaginary, man or fiction (Watt was the first 'to fall from species' [85]). The evolutionary theme is related to the efforts of the 'I' to establish his being in time – 'the primeval mud,' 'the fragility of euphoria among the different orders of the animal kingdom beginning with the sponges' (38), 'mad or worse transformed à la Haeckel' (42).

21 Roman Jakobson, 'Two Aspects of Language and Two Types of Aphasic Disturbances,' 71

22 Ibid., 72

23 Ibid., 71–2

24 Ibid., 72

25 *Longinus on the Sublime*, 73

26 Ibid., 79

27 Ibid., 84

28 Ibid., 13

CHAPTER FIVE: The Nature and Art of Love in *Enough*

1 Representative critical statements of this 'dismissive' approach to *Enough* are: 'it seems stupid or indecent to over-analyse this story' (Barbara Hardy, 'The Dubious Consolations in Beckett's Fiction: Art, Love and Nature,' 119); 'It is compact and requires careful reading but presents no particular difficulties' (John J. Mood, ' "Silence Within": A Study of the *Residua* of Samuel Beckett,' 389).

2 John Fletcher, *The Novels of Samuel Beckett*, 235

3 Raymond Federman in *Journey to Chaos: A Study of Samuel Beckett's Early Fiction* ostensibly invokes in a positive manner the Orpheus myth in Beckett's prose. With reference to the later works (from *Stories* onwards), he makes the point that: 'The Beckettian creator-hero is no longer playing the inferior role of Eurydice; he now appears as an Orphean figure given the power to create and destroy not only his own inventions, but also his own illusory self' (183).

4 *Enough* in *No's Knife: Collected Short Prose 1945–1966*, 154. *Enough* was composed in 1966, a year after *Imagination Dead Imagine*, which follows it in the *Residua*; the same order is followed in *Têtes-Mortes* except that *D'un ouvrage abandonné* is the first work.

5 These are the words Beckett employs in the concluding sentence of the first paragraph of *Proust* to describe time. Whereas Proust saw men in time as 'monstrous beings,' Beckett sees time itself as that 'double-headed monster of damnation and salvation.' This is a distinctively Orphic description: W.K.C. Guthrie in *Orpheus and Greek Religion* points out that 'time was never thought of as a god by the Greeks except in the Orphic tradition' in which time is ambiguously regarded as Chronos 'the monstrous serpent' and as a 'great power for good and evil' (85, 87).

6 The work contains one other exclamation mark: 'What mental calculations bent double hand in hand!' (155), and two question marks: 'Could it be the bed of some vast evaporated lake or drained of its waters from below?' (157) and 'What do I know of man's destiny?' (159). The question marks are set in opposition to the two preceding exclamation marks; the questions emphasize an impossible 'calculation' while the exclamations emphasize the pleasure of mathematical operations. The lack of any other punctuation in the text is perhaps clarified by this reference to 'Dream of Fair to Middling Women': 'The inviolable criterion of poetry and music, the non-principle of their punctuation, is figured in the demented perforations of the night colander' (123). In *Enough* there is the harmony of Lyre and Cygnus, 'the principle of their non-punctuation.'

7 'Three Dialogues,' 21

8 Compare with Beckett's description of the 'miracle of involuntary memory' in *Proust* (54): 'the central impression of a past sensation recurs as an immediate stimulus which can be instinctively identified by the subject with the model of duplication (*whose integral purity has been retained because it has been forgotten*).' The narrator of *Enough* would in this instance appear to be salvaging a sense of her ownself via the 'miracle of *voluntary* memory.'

9 Beckett's 'I see the flowers at my feet' is explicitly a rewrite of the first line

of the fifth stanza of John Keats' 'Ode to a Nightingale': 'I cannot see what flowers are at my feet.' The fifth stanza is the key transitional one in which the 'I' enters a death-like state in his unsuccessful attempt to become one with the 'immortal Bird.' Beckett's variant in *Enough* is thus in a quite literal grammatical sense more affirmative than Keats' original. Beckett's text does make the man and woman one, while at the same time recognizing their separateness.

10 That she must accept responsibility for her words is evident in a paragraph omitted from the English version: 'Toutes ces notions sont de lui. Je ne fais que les combiner à ma façon. Donné quatre ou cinq vies comme celle-là j'aurais pu laisser une trace' (*Assez*, in *Têtes-Mortes*, 43).

11 See C.G. Jung, 'Freud and Jung: Contrasts,' in *Freud and Psychoanalysis*, vol. 4, *The Collected Works of C.G. Jung*, especially the following section: 'For thousands of years, rites of initiation have been teaching rebirth from the spirit; yet, strangely enough, man forgets again and again the mean-ing of divine procreation ... Fortunately, we have proof that the spirit always renews its strength in the fact that the essential teaching of the initiations is handed on from generation to generation. Ever and again there are human beings who understand what it means that God is their father. The equal balance of the flesh and the spirit is not lost to the world' (340).

12 Harold Bloom, *The Anxiety of Influence: A Theory of Poetry*, 107. Bloom's views could be applied to Beckett as long as the major qualification is made that Beckett does not oppose say a Joyce or Proust, but has internal-ized the psychic drama to focus on the ontology of his fictions.

13 Ibid., 79

14 Richard Cody, *The Landscape of the Mind*, 12

15 Paul Lawley characterized my approach as 'pro-art' in his article 'Samuel Beckett's "Art and Craft": A Reading of "Enough".' While Lawley apparently shares my rejection of the 'art of failure' school of Beckett criticism, his argument is essentially *contra* my discussion in 'The Nature and Art of Love in "Enough,"' *Journal of Beckett Studies* 4 (Spring 1979), 14–34, upon which this chapter is based. The differences between our readings are more than internecine critical skirmishing and focus upon a fundamental dimension of my argument in this study. While my argument does, of course, acknowledge the incredible perplexity contingent upon trying to verify the ontology of the fic-tional creation, I maintain that Beckett does establish a sense of self in *Enough* that is in some ways protected from Lawley's conclusion that 'she can ... use the created world as an agency of reconciliation with

silence and the void of identity; she can, in other words, manipulate her created world so as to prepare for a final renunciation of the act of creation itself' (41), a conclusion which seems to me to be yet another variation of the 'art of failure' school. One of the crucial differences between Lawley's argument and my own is the use we make of several key statements Beckett made to Lawrence E. Harvey in the early sixties. I develop the more positive implications of Beckett's statements that 'Being *has* a form' and that being might be let into literature via 'the proper syntax of weakness;' Lawley develops the implications of Beckett's statements on 'existence by proxy' and a concomitant sense 'of a self that might have been but never got born, as an *être manqué*' (Harvey, *Samuel Beckett: Poet and Critic*, 247–9). These latter aspects of Beckett's thought are clearly evident at points in his work but, as I argue, Beckett in *Enough* and in other major later works is striving to overcome them (and does, at times, succeed). The 'existence by proxy' / '*être manqué*' aspects are, in my view, more appropriately aligned with works such as *The Unnamable* and *Texts for Nothing* in my reading of Beckett's subsequent work, it is the quest for the 'proper syntax of weakness' and the forms of being that is most decisive.

16 *First Love*, 30
17 *Fizzles*, 32–3. This work is a perfect example of 'existence by proxy' and the '*être manqué*'; its fundamental divergence from the vision of *Enough* might even be implied in 'his death alone would not be enough, not enough for me' (31–2).
18 Ibid., 43
19 'Foirade IV' ('Vieille terre'), *Minuit* 4 (May 1973), 71

CHAPTER SIX: 'Tempest of Emblems'

1 Georg Lukács, *The Meaning of Contemporary Realism*, 66
2 *All Strange Away*, in *Rockaby and Other Short Pieces*, 39
3 William Ernest Henley, 'Invictus,' cited in Joseph M. Flora, *William Ernest Henley*, 28–9
4 The image of 'lying side by side' is evoked throughout Beckett as a diagram of the ideal relationship of a man and woman. For example: 'side by side, touching, they recline in the shadow of a great rock, chosen by him for the shadow it gave, on the Silver Strand,' 'Dream of Fair to Middling Women' (166), and 'there is one perhaps somewhere merciful enough to shelter

such frolics where no one ever abandons anyone and no one ever waits for anyone and never two bodies touch' (*How It Is*, 143).

5 Erich Auerbach, cited in Angus Fletcher, *Allegory: The Theory of a Symbolic Mode*, 28

6 A Lise Joly is mentioned in *Mercier and Camier*, 88. The section which deals with the case-histories of a few of Camier's clients is omitted in the English translation.

7 Angus Fletcher, *Allegory*, 52

8 Ibid., 35

9 Samuel Taylor Coleridge, *Biographia Literaria*, cited in Owen Barfield, *What Coleridge Thought* (Oxford University Press 1972), 75

10 Ibid., 86–7

11 Roman Jakobson, 'Two Aspects of Language,' 78

12 This notebook is the 'new material' which Beckett made available to James Knowlson. See his *Light and Darkness in the Theatre of Samuel Beckett*, 13.

13 *Imagination Dead Imagine* is clearly not a drastic reduction of the 'preposterous form' of *How It Is* so that the basic elements 'may be accommodated by a simpler form which will not falsify how it is,' as H. Porter Abbott argues in 'Farewell to Incompetence: Beckett's *How It Is* and *Imagination Dead Imagine*,' 45. The formal achievements of *Imagination Dead Imagine* have tended to be overestimated by critics. Brian Finney views the work as 'at once a powerful and beautiful piece of writing while being, one has to admit, appallingly difficult to understand,' and attributes 'the perplexing obscurity' to the fact that the text 'is a condensation of a much longer work' ('A Reading of Beckett's *Imagination Dead Imagine*,' 65.) The Calder and Boyars first English edition of 1966 described it as derived from a work of fiction 'from which the author has removed all but the essentials.' More recently, Beckett told James Knowlson that *All Strange Away* 'was on the way to *Imagination Dead Imagine*.' Whether based on Beckett's authority or not, it is difficult to accept that 'the author has removed all but the essentials' from *Imagination Dead Imagine*: it is not so much a condensation of *All Strange Away* as a separate work in its own right.

14 *Imagination Dead Imagine*, in *No's Knife*, 161

15 The 'couple' who are lost in the 'storm' are strangely reminiscent of Dante's Paolo and Francesca. In the review 'Papini's Dante' (1934), Beckett rejects Papini's argument in *Dante Vivo* because it would, he believes, reduce Dante to 'lovable proportions ... But who wants to love Dante? We want to READ Dante – for example, his imperishable reference (Paolo-Francesca episode) to the incompatibility of the two operations' (14). In

Imagination Dead Imagine, the two operations of writing and loving are shown to be incompatible – this 'couple' do not even touch and the 'observer' is not even visited by Dante's fleeting moment of compassion and understanding.

16 Brian Finney, 'A Reading of Beckett's *Imagination Dead Imagine*,' 67

17 Brian Finney, *Since 'How It Is': A Study of Samuel Beckett's Later Fiction*, 26; Ruby Cohn, *Back to Beckett*, 249–50; J.E. Dearlove, ' "Last Images": Samuel Beckett's Residual Fiction,' 109–10

18 *Proust*, 57

19 Ibid., 56

CHAPTER SEVEN: The Nature of Allegory in *The Lost Ones*, or the Quincunx Realistically Considered / *Ping* as a 'Hieroglyph' of 'Inspired Perception'

1 *The Lost Ones*, 18

2 *Proust*, 49

3 Susan Brienza, '*The Lost Ones*: The Reader as Searcher,' 148

4 Ibid., 157

5 'Dante ... Bruno . Vico .. Joyce,' 15

6 Ibid., 4

7 The quincuncial figure has long fascinated Beckett: one thinks of the quincunxes of the Square Saint Ruth in *Mercier and Camier*, Molloy's 'strange instrument' composed of 'four rigorously identical v's' (63), and the more 'irregular quincunx' of *How It Is* – 'now his arms Saint Andrew's cross top v reduced aperture' (52). But the most detailed example is found in the abandoned 'J.M. Mime' (1963) where the stage is actually walked off as a 'quink,' and the character's task is to carry stones through all the possible paths created by the maze. There is, however, no key to these paths (as there are for Browne) and Beckett's character gives up his task. The diagram of the 'quink' and a sample of Beckett's mathematical calculations for 'J.M. Mime' are printed in Sighle Kennedy's *Murphy's Bed*, 64–5.

8 Sir Thomas Browne, 'The Garden of Cyrus,' in *Religio Medici and Other Works*, 166; 171

9 Ibid., 136

10 This human 'decussation' could also refer to the goddess of Sleep. Neary in *Murphy* likens the position of his feet to that depicted on 'Greek urns, where Sleep was figured with crossed feet, and frequently also Sleep's young brother, to cross his whenever he felt wakeful' (207). Sir Thomas

Browne also makes this point in 'The Garden of Cyrus': 'Why the Godesses sit commonly cross-legged in ancient draughts ...' (173).

11 Browne, 154

12 Robert Burton, *The Anatomy of Melancholy*, Part I, Sec. 1, Mem. 2, Subs. 10, 'Of the Understanding.' The words which follows this statement emphasize just how ironic Beckett's variant is: 'Regulus, thou wouldst not another man should falsify this oath, or break promise with thee: conscience concludes, therefore, Regulus, thou dost well to perform thy promise and oughtest to keep thine oath' (106). Beckett's narrator in *The Lost Ones* does, however, 'break promise': he concludes by treating others as he himself would not be treated, i.e. as a mere pawn in a literary game.

13 Browne, 167

14 Ibid., 165

15 Ibid., 174

16 Ibid., 176

17 *Murphy*, 144

18 The members of the queues in *The Lost Ones* would not abandon their position for the sake of any merely material gain which might fortuitously present itself. Their rigidly disciplined passion contrasts dramatically with that of the 'girl, debauched in appearance' in 'Ding-Dong' in *More Pricks than Kicks* who 'fell out near the sting of the queue and secured the loaf ... When she got back to the queue her place had been taken of course. But her sally had not cost her more than a couple of yards' (41). Even these few yards would be too precious to the 'searchers' of *The Lost Ones* for them even to consider a temporary abandonment.

19 *Proust*, 7

20 In 'Dante and the Lobster,' there is, as in *The Lost Ones*, an extensive series of metaphorical identifications between reading a 'face' or the face of things and the act of reading a book: for example, 'The Divine Comedy face upward on the lectern of his palms' (9); and 'Belacqua looked at the old parchment of her face, grey in the dim kitchen' (22).

21 Angus Fletcher, *Allegory*, 36

22 'Closed place,' in *Fizzles*, 37. Dantean echoes are particularly strong in this text. The phrase 'Sum the bright lots. The dark outnumbered the former by far' (38) is a formalist adaptation of Dante's 'Flat on the ground face-upward did I see / some, and some sitting all hunched up: again / others were on the move continually. / The latter far outnumbered, it was plain' (*Hell*, Canto XIV, 22–5). But, whereas Dante's plain 'from its bed / rejects all vegetation whatsoe'er' (8–9) and is composed only of 'dry, deep sand' (13), Beckett's 'arena' (etymologically cognate with 'sand') does still possess traces

of a once flourishing nature: The 'track ... is made of dead leaves' (38). This extremely formalized text thus points back to the opening lines of Canto XIV of *Hell* where Dante reflects on his encounter with the speaking man/ tree of the preceding Canto: 'Constrained by affection for my native place, / I picked up and restored the scattered leaves / to him whose strength of voice had now grown less.'

23 The full statement of Beckett's description of the connection between *The Lost Ones* and *Ping* is given in note 28 below.

24 'Closed place,' 38

25 See *Pour finir encore et autres foirades*.

26 'Closed place,' 37

27 Ibid., 38

28 The quotation is from manuscripts in the *John Doe Papers*, Washington University, St Louis. Photocopies of these manuscripts are also found in the University of Reading Samuel Beckett Collection. The first six drafts of 'Bing' are found in these manuscripts. Some critics have mistakenly assumed that the drafts printed in Federman and Fletcher represent the first versions of 'Bing.'

29 Raymond Federman and John Fletcher, 'Appendix II,' in *Samuel Beckett: His Works and His Critics: An Essay in Bibliography*, 325–45

30 *Proust*, 57

31 *Ping*, in *No's Knife*, 165. The incredible repetition with variation in this text precludes documenting each specific reference, as virtually every statement is repeated elsewhere.

32 Beckett's characterization of the Joycean enterprise in the interview with Israel Shenker, 'Moody Man of Letters,' 3

33 Elisabeth Bergman Segrè, 'Style and Structure in Beckett's "Ping": That Something Itself,' 132

34 John J. Mood's summation of *Ping* neatly encapsulates the impasse of critical encounters with this work as long as fundamental aspects of the creative act remain unacknowledged: 'the result is an almost completely self-referring piece of writing, paradigmatic of the entire thrust of Beckett's prose fiction, wherein the descent into an exploration of the self itself becomes a self-referring activity' (' "The Silence Within",' 400).

35 Jakobson, 'Two Aspects of Language,' 68

36 Ibid., 69

37 Mood, ' "The Silence Within",' 397

38 David Lodge, 'Some *Ping* Understood,' 87

39 'Ping' occurs thirty-four times whereas 'bing' appears only twenty times in the French text. In the French original, 'hop' is used before the 'fixed

elsewhere' group instead of 'bing' in order to emphasize physical movements: hence the English text underscores a unity which cannot be divided into the dualism of mental and physical.

CHAPTER EIGHT: Sense and Nonsense in *Lessness*

1 Georg Lukács, *The Meaning of Contemporary Realism*, 32
2 Ruby Cohn, *Back to Beckett*, 265
3 Samuel Beckett, *Lessness*, dust-jacket. A.J. Leventhal in a lecture on *The Lost Ones* at Trinity College Dublin, spring term 1972, stated that the comments on the dust-jacket of *Lessness* were by Beckett.
4 Samuel Beckett, *Lessness*, *New Statesman* 89 (1 May 1970), 635. This publication prints the entire text on one page. The three columns of print are more graphically expressive of the text as a visual hieroglyph than the book-length publication with its oversized type. As with *Ping*, it is virtually impossible to tabulate each reference, since in this instance each 'sentence' is repeated twice.
5 The phrase is from 'For Avigdor Arikha,' cited *in toto* in my first chapter.
6 'Three Dialogues,' 20
7 Beckett's own words describing the 'facts' of *Lessness* appear on the back cover of the Calder and Boyars edition (1973).
8 Beckett's characterization of the 'yes or no' dialectical see-saw in *Murphy*, 41
9 Nietzsche's words, cited in Hans Vaihinger, *The Philosophy of As-if*, 346
10 Beckett's statement to John Pilling (see his dissertation, 'The Conduct of the Narrative in Samuel Beckett's Prose Fiction,' 31)
11 *Proust* 7
12 In 'Dante ... Bruno . Vico .. Joyce,' Beckett describes the 'last stage' in Vico's theory of history as 'a tendency towards interdestruction: the nations are dispersed, and the Phoenix of Society arises out of their ashes' (5). There are some striking similarities between *Lessness* and Beckett's 'war poem,' 'Saint-Lô,' which deals with his own experiences as a 'refugee' in a city that was being rebuilt. Of particular interest is the connection between the 'all gone from mind' of *Lessness* and the last two lines of the poem: 'and the old mind ghost-forsaken / sink into its havoc.' The Phoenix theme is present in the first two lines of 'Saint-Lô': 'Vire will wind in other shadows / unborn through the bright ways tremble.' See also Beckett's account of his work with the Irish Red Cross in Saint-Lô in 'The Capital of Ruins,' published in Eoin O'Brien, *The Beckett Country: Samuel Beckett's Ireland*.

13 Susan Brienza and Enoch Brater in 'Chance and Choice in Beckett's *Lessness*' argue that the life of the 'he' lacks any power of self-perpetuation: 'The "he" of *Lessness* might be one of the unfortunate sinners left issueless after the Flood ...' (252). But this view could be refuted even in terms of their earlier comments which compared the language of *Lessness* with that of Hebrew grammar and syntax (248): for, as Sir Thomas Browne in 'The Garden of Cyrus' points out: 'And under a Quintuple consideration, wanton antiquity considered the Circumstances of generation ... The same number in the Hebrew mysteries and Cabalistical accounts was the character of Generation; declared by the Letter *He*, the fifth in their alphabet; according to that Cabalistical *Dogma*: If *Abram* had not had this Letter added unto his Name, he had remained fruitlesse and without power of generation' (170–1). Since 'Assumption' the 'he' has performed just such a creative role for Beckett

14 Elizabeth Sewell, *The Field of Nonsense*, 2
15 Ibid., 3
16 John Fletcher, *The Novels of Samuel Beckett*, 236
17 Brater and Brienza, 'Chance and Choice in Beckett's *Lessness*,' 248
18 'Echo's Bones,' 28
19 Tom F. Driver, 'Beckett by the Madeleine,' 24
20 'Le Concentrisme,' Reading University Beckett Collection. The same phrases are used in *Proust* (71). Compare with Sewell's comment in *The Field of Nonsense* that nonsense is 'perfectly comprehensible' (23).
21 Elizabeth Sewell, *The Field of Nonsense*, 40
22 Ruby Cohn, *Back to Beckett*, 220
23 Elizabeth Sewell, *The Field of Nonsense*, 41
24 Ibid., 188

CHAPTER NINE: The Rhetoric of Necessity in *Fizzles* and the 'Still' Trilogy

1 *Proust*, 57
2 'Denis Devlin,' 290–1
3 'something there,' in *Collected Poems in English and French*, 63
4 The dating of the 'fizzles' is still a rather confused issue. In the original French publication in *Minuit* the texts were simply designated as 'circa 1950'; the English collection, *For to End Yet Again and Other Fizzles*, gives dates for the title piece, 'Still,' and 'Closed place' – the 'others' are described as 'circa 1960.' Beckett told John Pilling that all the 'fizzles' were written after *How It Is*. Beckett's somewhat sketchy memory of this period lends plausibility to the view that some of the 'other fizzles' could have

been written before *How It Is*. In previous chapters, I have referred to particular 'fizzles' when I thought they were relevant. I discuss them as a whole in this chapter for the simple reason that Beckett clearly associates them with his short prose texts of the 1970s.

5 Richard Ellmann records an incident in which Beckett, taking dictation from Joyce, inadvertently included the words 'come in,' which were only Joyce's retort to a knock at the door of his study, *James Joyce*, 662. Beckett's inclusion of these same words in 'Horn came always' could also indicate the desire of his 'I' to let the external world impinge upon the private world of art.

6 The 'night flight' in 'Old earth' shows that, however indirectly, the 'I' is able to talk about his life as an artist. Compare with Beckett's statement to John Gruen: 'It is impossible [to talk about my writing] because I am continually working in the dark. It would be like an insect leaving his cocoon'; see also the use of the same imagery in *Proust*: 'the disintegrating effect of loss that breaks the chrysalis and hastens metamorphosis' (25); 'his imagination weaves its cocoon about this frail and almost abstract chrysalis' (31).

7 The first paragraph of the unpublished short story 'Echo's Bones' explains the 'logic' behind the return of Belacqua to our world: 'the debt of nature, that scandalous post-obit on one's own estate, can no more be discharged by the mere fact of kicking the bucket than descent can be made into the same stream twice. This is a true saying.' This 'lost' short story is discussed in Rubin Rabinovitz's *The Development of Samuel Beckett's Fiction*.

8 *Abandonné*. I have quoted the text *in toto*.

9 *Proust*, 16

10 John Gruen, 'Samuel Beckett talks about Beckett,' 108

11 'Dream of Fair to Middling Women,' 107

12 The phrase, 'that beech in whose shade once,' nostalgically echoes the first line of Virgil's first eclogue ('The Dispossessed') and as Richard Cody in *The Landscape of the Mind* points out, 'of all the mythic figures in the poetic theology Orpheus is the one most important to pastoralism' (12).

13 'Dream of Fair to Middling Women,' 86

14 'Sounds,' reprinted from the copy in Beckett Archive, University of Reading, in an Appendix to John Pilling's 'The Significance of Beckett's "Still",' *Essays in Criticism* 28.2 (1978). 'Sounds' is reprinted on 155 and 156; 'Still 3' on 156 and 157. All references to these texts are to this 'Appendix' in Pilling's article.

15 Robert Burton, *Anatomy of Melancholy*, 285

16 The full reference is: Part 3, Sec. 2, Mem. 5, Subs. 5, 621. These Latin

phrases, so perfectly in rhetorical balance, also illustrate that Beckett, contrary to many of his own pronouncements, is indeed concerned with the 'content,' not merely with the shape of 'fundamental sounds.'

17 This text, completed in August 1973, appears in *Collected Shorter Prose 1945–80*, 211–12. All references are from this edition. The trial scene in 'As the Story Was Told' strongly recalls this passage from *The Unnamable* that recounts how the 'I' has been 'shut up somewhere else': 'When all goes silent, and comes to an end, it will be because the words have been said, those it behoved to say, no need to know which ... they [i.e. 'the words'] have to be ratified by the proper authority, that takes time, he's far from here, they bring him the verbatim report of the proceedings, once in a way, he knows the words that count, it's he who chose them, in the meantime the voice continues, while the messenger goes towards the master, and while the master examines the report, and while the messenger comes back with the verdict, the words continue ... (303).

18 John Pilling in 'Beckett after "Still"' gives details of the writing and the first appearance of 'Pour Bram,' which was revised and published under the title 'La Falaise' (see 283, n. 2). My references are to the text in *Celui qui ne peut se servir de mots*.

19 Ibid., 284

20 A *Midsummer Night's Dream*, Act V, Scene 2, Theseus' first speech

21 The images of rock and skull in 'La Falaise' bring to life this petrified image of *The Unnamable*: 'Yes, a head, but solid, solid bone, and you embedded in it, like a fossil in the rock' (393).

CHAPTER TEN: Shakespeare and *Company*: Beckett's *As You Like It*

1 The influence of Robert Burton's *Anatomy of Melancholy* on Beckett has gone virtually unnoticed. Echoes of Burton's work are common in Beckett, especially in his earliest writings and in his work of the seventies: 'a little wearish old man, / Democritus,' of 'Enueg 1' is taken directly from Burton's first page of the satirical preface, 'Democritus Junior to the Reader'; the diametrically opposed ways of dealing with a hostile or mad world, that of Democritus laughing or that of Heraclitus weeping, are important throughout Burton and are commented directly upon in Beckett's short story 'Yellow' in *More Pricks than Kicks*; 'Dream of Fair to Middling Women,' among other unacknowledged borrowings, owes to Burton the name of a central character, Nemo, and the formulation of a central theme – how to make will and nill coincide. As we have seen, there are specific references to Burton in *The Lost Ones* and the *Still* trilogy. Burton's influ-

ence has clearly been a lasting and significant factor within Beckett's developing vision of man's attempts to live a fulfilling, or at least a sane existence, in a mad world. As the narrator of *Enough* says of her companion, 'one day he halted and fumbling for his words explained to me that anatomy is a whole.' Beckett's own 'Anatomy of Hunger' is guided by the same impulse which led Dante to write: 'to find a way really to live' ('Hell,' Canto III, 65).

2 *Company*, 8.

3 Linda Ben-Zvi in 'Fritz Mauthner for *Company*,' 65–88, details and catalogues these 'memories.'

4 The self-reflexive argument has been influential throughout the history of Beckett studies. With reference to *Company*, Eric P. Levy's comments are representative of this trend to oversimplify the problems which Beckett faces in his prose: 'By emphasizing the act of imagination, Beckettian narration becomes self-referential, a closed system where experience can be presented that relates only to the special purposes of the "reason-ridden" imagination which conceives it and not to the movement of a self through time called life.' See Levy, '*Company*: The Mirror of Beckettian Mimesis,' 97.

5 'Denis Devlin,' 289

6 Murphy's 'Spinozan' 'self-love' is highlighted in the epigraph for chapter 6: '*Amor intellectualis quo Murphy se ipsum amat.*'

7 Jean-Jacques Rousseau, *The Social Contract*, 61

8 Ibid., Book II, chapter 4, 76

9 My title for this chapter is, among other things, an implied critique of Ben-Zvi's article cited above. Beckett's views on language – it should be obvious by now – are far too complex to be explained adequately by Mauthner's radical nominalism.

10 Helen Gardner, '*As You Like It*,' 215

11 Shakespeare, *As You Like It*, 80 (II.5), 82 (II.7).

12 Ibid., 97 (III.2)

13 Ibid., 98 (III.2)

14 Ibid., 112 (IV.1)

15 Ibid., 135 (V.4)

16 If he could, Hamlet would get 'a fellowship in a cry of players' (a partnership in a theatrical company), III.2 – which Shakespeare and Beckett, in various ways, were to do.

17 *As You Like It*, 125 (IV.3)

18 Ibid., 141 (V.4)

19 Ibid., 136 (V.4)

20 Ibid., 113 (IV.1)
21 Ibid., 71 (II.1)
22 There is an interesting discussion of male pregnancy in Paul Lawley's
   'Samuel Beckett's "Art and Craft": A Reading of *Enough*,' 33–4. One could
   say that this image of creativity was present from the very beginning of
   Beckett's prose: in 'Assumption' the 'something' is given 'birth' via the
   'maieutic' intervention of the Woman – albeit the price of this is death for
   the central character.
23 *As You Like It*, 87 (II.7)
24 *The Tempest*, 110 (V.1)
25 Compare with 'Assumption': 'By damning the stream of whispers he had
   raised the level of the flood, and he knew the day would come when it
   could no longer be denied. Still he was silent, in silence listening for the
   first murmur of the torrent that must destroy him' (270).
26 Compare with Prospero's final words in which he was to 'deliver all' –
   'the story of my life.' The authentic story or 'autobiography' of the
   'author' and his 'other' is best described by Touchstone's aphorism: 'truest
   poetry is the most feigning' (III.3).

CHAPTER ELEVEN: Companion Pieces: *Ill Seen Ill Said* as a
'Serena' / *Worstward Ho* as a 'Sanies'

1 *Ill Seen Ill Said*, 30
2 For a further discussion of 'cosmological markers' in Beckett's early and
   later works see Sighle Kennedy *Murphy's Bed* and Charles Krance, 'Odd
   Fizzles: Beckett and the Heavenly Sciences,' 96–107.
3 The very short prose text 'One Evening' (1980) seems, in many ways, to
   have been an extract from an earlier version of what became *Ill Seen Ill
   Said*. An old woman in widow's black discovers an old man's dead body
   lying among the 'wild flowers,' a 'tableau vivant if you will,' 7–8.
4 For a detailed examination of this characteristic of Beckett's creative process see S.E. Gontarski, *The Intent of 'Undoing' in Samuel Beckett's Dramatic
   Texts*. Gontarski's emphasis upon formalist achievements as Beckett's primary means of controlling the 'biographical material' is, however, highly
   problematical.
5 Harvey, *Samuel Beckett: Poet and Critic*, 96
6 'Serena II,' in *Collected Poems in English and French* (1977), 23
7 Harvey, *Samuel Beckett: Poet and Critic*, 93
8 'Malacoda,' *Collected Poems in English and French* (1977), 26
9 The 'star of evening' is mentioned in 'Serena III,' *Collected Poems in English
   and French* (1977), 25.

10 Marjorie Perloff in 'Between Verse and Prose: Beckett and the New Poetry' has raised (yet again) the general question of Beckett's 'poetical nature' and its relevance to the canon, especially the later prose. With reference to *Ill Seen Ill Said*, Perloff poses the question, 'How should we interpret this querulous, compulsive, sometimes maddening babble?' (198). Her answer, that 'in charting this thematic development, the question of prosody is central' is, however, open to serious questioning. Surely the 'poetic' nature of the *oeuvre* needs to be investigated by showing how the 'poetic' elements are incorporated into the particular structure of each work. The issues at stake are unique to Beckett's prose, and are not such as are lost somewhere 'between verse and prose.'

11 W.B. Yeats, 'Easter 1916,' 202–5

12 The measurement of this period of suffering and bewilderment cannot be effected solely by the solar and zodiacal patterns so evident in *Ill Seen Ill Said*: as Beckett stated in *Proust*, 'There is a moral climate and a sentimental calendar, where the instrument of commensuration is not solar but cardiac' (43).

13 Angela B. Moorjani (*Abysmal Games in the Novels of Samuel Beckett*) and Susan D. Brienza (*Samuel Beckett's New Worlds*) both recognize the references to 'The Vulture,' but neither develops the parallels beyond a preliminary gloss: 'And, again, as in "The Vulture," this imaginary life/death moment would be preceded by the mind devouring its own tissue of illusions and rejoicing in its emptiness [sic]' (Moorjani, 151); 'with these lines [of 'The Vulture'] as one clue to Beckett's aesthetic philosophy, we can decipher many of the image patterns in *Ill Seen Ill Said*' (Brienza, 241).

14 Harvey, *Samuel Beckett: Poet and Critic*, 114–15

15 Ibid., 115

16 Ibid.

17 See *Mal vu mal dit*

18 Walter Pater, *The Renaissance: Studies in Art and Poetry*, 89

19 The crudely physical dimensions of Beckett's 'organic' aesthetic which are still evident in *Worstward Ho* were even more evident in his typescript version: in the third paragraph the key sentences 'Move in.' and 'On in.' were revisions of 'Rot in.' / 'Rot on in.' Reading University Beckett Collection, Ms. 260Z.

20 For an extended discussion of Beckett's use of the term 'sanies' see Harvey, *Samuel Beckett: Poet and Critic*, 104.

21 The title also ironically echoes an Elizabethan boatman's cry and may refer to a play by Ben Jonson of similar title or to Charles Kingsley's romantic adventure story *Worstward Ho*!

22 Percy Bysshe Shelley, 'Prometheus Unbound,' 725

23 Ibid., 725, n. 10, editor's paraphrase of the last lines of 'Prometheus Unbound,' Act III

24 'dread nay,' *Collected Poems in English and French* (1977), 33

25 Shelley, 'The Defence of Poetry,' 785, 787

26 Ibid., 789

27 Ibid., 787

28 Ibid.

29 Ibid.

30 'Poetry is Vertical' is reprinted in Sighle Kennedy's *Murphy's Bed*, 303–4

CHAPTER TWELVE: Beckett Incorporated: Fragments and Wholes

1 Gerald L Bruns, *Modern Poetry and the Idea of Language*, 198

2 Lawrence E. Harvey, *Samuel Beckett: Poet and Critic*, 219

3 Deirdre Bair, *Samuel Beckett: A Biography*, 640

4 Ibid., xi

5 Dated July 1986, and dedicated to his former publisher at Grove Press, Barney Rossett, 'Fragment' has recently been published as the opening segment of *Stirrings Still* (1989). Mr Beckett referred me to Mr Rossett who, in turn, granted me permission to quote from 'Fragment.'

6 For a full discussion of 'Mort de A.D.' see Harvey, *Samuel Beckett: Poet and Critic*, 230–4.

7 This Beckett 'sentence' – so very different formally from those of Samuel Johnson – is strangely reminiscent of Johnson's poised and calming cadences in a work such as *Rasselas*. Beckett said of Johnson: 'He must have had the vision of *positive* [Beckett's emphasis] annihilation. Of how many can as much be said' (Letter to Joseph Hone, cited in Deirdre Bair's biography, 254). Of Beckett, too, the same could be said.

Select Bibliography

Beckett Texts Used

Abandonné. Paris: Editions de Georges Visat 1972
'All Strange Away,' in *Rockaby and Other Short Pieces*. New York: Grove Press 1981
'As the Story Was Told,' in *Collected Shorter Prose 1945–1980*, 211–12. London: Calder 1984
'Assumption.' *transition* 16–17 (1929): 268–71
Collected Poems in English and French. New York: Grove Press 1977
Company. New York: Grove Press 1980
'Le Concentrisme.' Reading University Beckett Collection.
'Crisscross to Infinity' ('The Way'). In *College Literature* 8, no. 3 (1983), 310
'Dante ... Bruno . Vico .. Joyce.' In *Our Exagmination Round His Factification for Incamination of Work in Progress*. Paris: Shakespeare and Co. 1929
'Denis Devlin.' *transition* 27 (April–May 1938), 289–94
'Dream of Fair to Middling Women.' University of Reading Beckett Collection
'La Falaise.' In *Celui qui le peut se servir de mots*. Montpellier: Fata Morgana 1975
First Love. London: Calder and Boyars 1973
Fizzles. New York: Grove Press 1976
'For Avigdor Arikha.' Reprinted as preface to *Samuel Beckett by Avigdor Arikha: A Tribute to Samuel Beckett on his 70th Birthday*. Victoria and Albert Museum Publications 1976
'Fragment.' Unpublished prose text 1986. Quoted by permission of Mr Barney Rossett. Published as opening section of *Stirring Still, Manchester Guardian*, 19 March 1989
How It Is. New York: Grove Press 1964

Ill Seen Ill Said. New York: Grove Press 1981

Lessness. In *New Statesman* 89 (1 May 1970), 635

The Lost Ones. New York: Grove Press 1972

Mercier and Camier. London: Calder and Boyars 1974

More Pricks than Kicks. New York: Grove Press 1970

Murphy. New York: Grove Press 1970

No's Knife: Collected Shorter Prose 1945–1966. London: Calder and Boyars 1967

'One Evening'. In *Journal of Beckett Studies* 6 (1980), 7–8. Reprinted in *Collected Shorter Prose: 1945–1980* (London: John Calder 1984), 209–10

'Papini's Dante.' *The Bookman* LXXXVII (Christmas 1934), 14

'Peintres de l'empêchement' (1948). Republished in *L'Herne Beckett*, ed. Tom Bishop and Raymond Federman. Paris: Editions de l'Herne 1976

'La peinture des van Velde.' *Les Cahiers d'art* 20–1 (1945), 349–54

'Poetry is Vertical.' Reprinted in Sighle Kennedy's *Murphy's Bed*, 303–4

Proust. New York. Grove Press 1970

'Recent Irish Poetry.' Reprinted in *The Lace Curtain* 4 (Summer 1971), 58–63

'R.M. Rilke.' *The Criterion* 13 (1934), 705–7

'Sounds' and 'Still 3' Printed as 'Appendix' to John Pilling's 'The Significance of Beckett's *Still*.' *Essays in Criticism* 28, no. 2 (April 1978), 156–7

Stirrings Still, Manchester Guardian, 19 March 1989

Stories and Texts for Nothing. New York: Grove Press 1967

'Three Dialogues.' In *Samuel Beckett: A Collection of Critical Essays*, ed. M. Esslin, 16–22

Three Novels: Molloy, Malone Dies, The Unnamable. New York: Grove Press 1959

Watt. New York: Grove Press 1959

Worstward Ho. New York: Grove Press 1983

Selected Works on Beckett and Other References

Abbott, H. Porter. *The Fiction of Samuel Beckett: Form and Effect*. Berkeley: University of California Press 1973

– 'Farewell to Incompetence: Beckett's *How It Is* and *Imagination Dead Imagine*.' *Contemporary Literature* 11 (1970), 36–47

Bair, Deirdre. *Samuel Beckett: A Biography*. New York: Harcourt Brace Jovanovich 1978

Ben-Zvi, Linda. 'Fritz Mauthner for *Company*.' *Journal of Beckett Studies* 9 (1984), 65–88

Bloom, Harold. *The Anxiety of Influence: A Theory of Poetry*. New York: Oxford University Press 1973

Brienza, Susan D. *Samuel Beckett's New Worlds: Style in Metafiction*. Norman and London: University of Oklahoma Press, 1987.
– 'The Lost Ones: The Reader as Searcher.' *Journal of Modern Literature* 6, no. 1 (1977), 148–68
Brienza, Susan D., and Enoch Brater. 'Chance and Choice in Beckett's *Lessness*.' *English Literary History* 43 (1976), 244–58
Browne, Joseph, ed. *College Literature* (Special Beckett Number) 8 no. 3 (1983)
Browne, Sir Thomas. 'The Garden of Cyrus,' in *Religio Medici and Other Works*, ed. L.C. Martin. Oxford: Clarendon Press 1964
Bruns, Gerald L. *Modern Poetry and the Idea of Language: A Critical and Historical Study*. Ithaca, NY: Yale University Press 1974
Bürger, Peter. *Theory of the Avant-Garde*, trans. M. Shaw. Minneapolis: University of Minnesota Press 1984
Burton, Robert. *The Anatomy of Melancholy*. London: William Tegg and Co. 1879
Calder, John, ed. *Beckett at Sixty: A Festschrift*. London: Calder and Boyars 1967
Champigny, Robert. *The Ontology of the Narrative: An Analysis*. The Hague: Mouton 1972
Cody, Richard. *The Language of the Mind*. Oxford: Clarendon Press 1969
Coe, Richard N. *Samuel Beckett*. New York: Grove Press 1964
Cohn, Ruby. *The Comic Gamut*. New Brunswick, NJ: Rutgers University Press, 1962
– *Back to Beckett*. Princeton, NJ: Princeton University Press 1973
Crews, Frederick C. *The Pooh Perplex: A Freshman Casebook*. New York: Dutton 1965
Dante Alighieri. *The Divine Comedy*, trans. Geoffrey L. Bickersteth. Aberdeen: The University Press 1955
Dearlove, J.E. *Accommodating the Chaos: Samuel Beckett's Nonrelational Art*. Durham, NC: Duke University Press, 1982
– ' "Last Images": Samuel Beckett's Residual Fiction.' *Journal of Modern Literature* 6, no. 1 (1977), 104–27
Driver, Tom F. 'Beckett by the Madeleine.' *Columbia University Forum* 4, no. 3 (Summer 1961), 21–5
Ellmann, Richard. *James Joyce*. London: Oxford University Press 1966
Esslin, Martin, ed. *Samuel Beckett: A Collection of Critical Essays*. Englewood Cliffs, NJ: Prentice Hall 1965
– 'Beckett, Samuel.' *Encyclopaedia Britannica: Macropaedia* 1981 ed.
Federman, Raymond. *Journey to Chaos: A Study of Samuel Beckett's Early Fiction*. Berkeley and Los Angeles: University of California Press 1965
Federman, Raymond, and John Fletcher. *Samuel Beckett: His Works and His*

Critics: An Essay in Bibliography. Berkeley: University of California Press
1970

Finney, Brian. 'A Reading of Beckett's *Imagination Dead Imagine.*' *Twentieth Century Literature* 7 (1971), 65–71

– *Since 'How It Is': A Study of Samuel Beckett's Later Fiction.* London: Covent Garden Press 1972

Fletcher, Angus. *Allegory: The Theory of a Symbolic Mode.* New York: Cornell University Press 1964

Fletcher, John. *The Novels of Samuel Beckett.* London: Chatto and Windus 1971

Flora, Joseph M. *William Ernest Henley.* New York: Twayne Publications 1976

Gardner, Helen. 'As You Like It.' Reprinted in Signet Classic *As You Like It.* New York: The New American Library 1963

Gontarski, S.E. *The Intent of 'Undoing' in Samuel Beckett's Dramatic Texts.* Bloomington: Indiana University Press 1985

Gruen, John. 'Samuel Beckett Talks about Beckett.' *Vogue* 127.2031 (Feb 1970), 108

Guthrie, W.K.C. *Orpheus and Greek Religion.* London: Methuen and Co. 1935

Hardy, Barbara. 'The Dubious Consolations in Beckett's Fiction: Art, Love and Nature.' In *Beckett the Shape Changer,* ed. K. Worth. London: Routledge and Kegan Paul 1975

Harvey, Lawrence E. *Samuel Beckett: Poet and Critic.* Princeton, NJ: Princeton University Press, 1970

Heidegger, Martin. *Being and Time,* trans. J. Macquarrie and E. Robinson. New York: Harper and Row 1962

Hutchings, William. ' "Shat into Grace" or, A Tale of a Turd: Why It Is in Beckett's *How It Is.*' *Papers on Language and Literature* 21, no. 1 (1985), 64–87

Jakobson, Roman. 'Two Aspects of Language and Two Types of Aphasic Disturbances.' In *Fundamentals of Language,* with Morris Halle. The Hague: Mouton and Co. 1956

Johnson, Samuel. *The History of Rasselas, Prince of Abissinia.* London: Penguin Books 1976

Jung, C.G. 'Freud and Jung: Contrasts.' In *Freud and Psychoanalysis,* vol. 4. *The Collected Works of C.G. Jung,* trans. A.F.C. Hull. London: Routledge and Kegan Paul 1961

Kafka, Franz. *Selected Short Stories of Franz Kafka,* trans. Willa and Edwin Muir. New York: The Modern Library 1952

Kennedy, Sighle. *Murphy's Bed.* Lewisburg, Pa.: Bucknell University Press, 1971

Kenner, Hugh. *Samuel Beckett: A Critical Study.* Berkeley: University of California Press 1968

– *A Reader's Guide to Samuel Beckett.* New York: Farrar, Straus and Giroux 1973
Knowlson, James, ed. *Samuel Beckett: An Exhibition.* London: Turret Books 1971
– *Light and Darkness in the Theatre of Samuel Beckett.* London: Turret Books 1972
Knowlson, James, and John Pilling. *Frescoes of the Skull: The Later Prose and Drama of Samuel Beckett.* London: Calder 1979
Krance, Charles. 'Odd Fizzles: Beckett and the Heavenly Sciences.' In *Science and Literature,* ed. Harry R. Garvin. Lewisburg, Pa.: Bucknell University Press 1983
Lake, Carlton, ed. *'No Symbols Where None Intended': A Catalogue of Books, Manuscripts and Other Materials Relating to Samuel Beckett in the Collection of the Humanities Research Center.* University of Texas at Austin: *The Library Chronicle* 1984
Lanham, Richard Alan. *A Handlist of Rhetorical Terms.* Berkeley: University of California Press 1969
Lawley, Paul. 'Samuel Beckett's "Art and Craft": A Reading of "Enough".' *Modern Fiction Studies* 29, no. 1 (1983), 25–41
Lentricchia, Frank. *After the New Criticism.* Chicago: University of Chicago Press 1980
Levy, Eric P. *Beckett and the Voice of Species: A Study of the Prose Fiction.* New York: Barnes and Noble 1980
– *'Company*: The Mirror of Beckettian Mimesis.' *Journal of Beckett Studies* 8 (1982), 95–104
Lodge, David. 'Some *Ping* Understood.' *Encounter* 32 (1968), 85–9
Longinus on the Sublime, trans. H.L. Howell. London: Macmillan and Co. 1890
Lukács, Georg. *The Meaning of Contemporary Realism,* trans. John Necke Mander. London: Merlin Press 1963
McMillan, Dougald. *transition 1927–1938: The History of a Literary Era.* New York: George Braziller 1976
Mood, John J. ' "Silence Within": A Study of the *Residua* of Samuel Beckett.' *Studies in Short Fiction* 7 (1969), 385–401
Moorjani, Angela B. *Abysmal Games in the Novels of Samuel Beckett.* Chapel Hill: University of North Carolina Press 1982
Morot-Sir, Edouard et al., eds. *Samuel Beckett: The Art of Rhetoric.* Chapel Hill: University of North Carolina Press 1976
Murray, Patrick A., ed. *Critical Essays on Samuel Beckett.* Boston: G.K. Hall and Co. 1986
Nietzsche, Friedrich. *The Birth of Tragedy and the Genealogy of Morals,* trans. F. Golffing. New York: Doubleday Anchor Books 1956
O'Brien, Eoin. *The Beckett Country: Samuel Beckett's Ireland.* Dublin: Black Cat Press 1986
Onimus, Jean. *Beckett.* Paris-Bruges: Desclée de Brouwer 1968

Pater, Walter. *The Renaissance: Studies in Art and Poetry*. New York: The New American Library 1959

Peckham, Morse. *Man's Rage for Chaos: Biology, Behavior and the Arts*. New York: Schocken Books 1965

Perloff, Marjorie. 'Between Verse and Prose: Beckett and the New Poetry.' Reprinted in *On Beckett: Essays and Criticism*, ed. S.E. Gontarski. New York: Grove Press 1986

Pilling, John. *Samuel Beckett*. London: Routledge and Kegan Paul 1976

– 'The Conduct of the Narrative in Samuel Beckett's Prose Fiction.' Doctoral dissertation, University of London 1971

– 'The Significance of Beckett's *Still*.' *Essays in Criticism* 28, no. 2 (April 1978), 143–57

– 'Beckett after *Still*.' *Romance Notes* 18 no. 2 (1977), 280–7

Rabinovitz, Rubin *The Development of Samuel Beckett's Fiction*. Urbana: University of Illinois Press 1984

Roberts, Michael. *T.E. Hulme*. London: Faber and Faber 1938

Rousseau, Jean-Jacques. *The Social Contract*, trans. M. Cranston. London: Penguin Books, 1968

Segrè, Elisabeth Bergman. 'Style and Structure in Beckett's "Ping": That Something Itself.' *Journal of Modern Literature* 6, no. 1 (1977), 127–47

Sewell, Elizabeth. *The Orphic Voice: Poetry and Natural History*. London: Routledge and Kegan Paul 1960

– *The Field of Nonsense*. London: Chatto and Windus 1952

Shakespeare, William. *As You Like It*. London: Penguin Books 1978

– *The Tempest*. New York: The New American Library 1964

Shapiro, Michael J., ed. *Language and Politics*. New York: New York University Press 1984

Shelley, Percy Bysshe, 'Prometheus Unbound.' In *The Norton Anthology of English Literature*, vol. 2. New York: W.W. Norton 1979

– 'The Defence of Poetry.' In *The Norton Anthology of English Literature*, vol. 2. New York: W.W. Norton 1979

Shenker, Israel. 'Moody Man of Letters,' *New York Times*, 6 May 1956, Sec. 2, x, 1, 3

Smith, Barry. '*Texts for Nothing*: A Thesis.' Doctoral dissertation, University of East Anglia 1978

Strauss, Walter A. *Descent and Return: The Orphic Theme in Modern Literature*. Cambridge: Harvard University Press 1971

Synge, J.M. *The Well of the Saints*. London: J.M. Dent and Sons 1961

Taylor, Roger, ed. *Aesthetics and Politics: Debates Between Bloch, Lukács, Brecht, Benjamin, Adorno*. London: Verso 1980

Vaihinger, Hans. *The Philosophy of As-If,* trans. C.K. Ogden. London: Kegan
   Paul 1935
Vico, Giambattista. *The New Science of Giambattista Vico,* rev. trans. of 3rd ed.
   (1744), ed. T.C. Bergin and M.K. Fisch. New York: Cornell University Press
   1961
Weiskel, Thomas. *The Romantic Sublime.* Baltimore: The Johns Hopkins Univer-
   sity Press 1976
Wind, Edgar. *Pagan Mysteries in the Renaissance.* London: Faber and Faber 1968
Wright, Iain. ' "What Matter Who's Speaking?": Beckett, the Authorial Subject
   and Contemporary Critical Theory.' *Southern Review* 16, no. 1 (1983), 5–30
Yeats, W.B. *The Collected Poems of W.B. Yeats.* London: Macmillan and Co. 1969

Index

UNIVERSITY OF TORONTO ROMANCE SERIES